Criminal
Justice
& The
Burger Court

Criminal Justice & The Burger Court

Edited by John Galloway

Facts On File

119 West 57th Street, New York, N.Y. 10019

Criminal Justice & The Burger Court

Published by Facts on File, Inc.,
119 West 57th Street, New York, N.Y. 10019.

Library of Congress Cataloging in Publication Data
Main entry under title:
Criminal justice & the Burger Court.
  (Checkmark books)
  Includes index.
    1. Criminal procedure—United States—Cases.
2. United States. Supreme Court. I. Galloway, John.
II. Facts on File, inc., New York.
KF9618.C67   345'.73'0502643   77-87239
ISBN 0-87196-231-4

9 8 7 6 5 4 3 2 1
PRINTED IN THE UNITED STATES OF AMERICA

Contents

Introduction

THE SUPREME COURT UNDER THE leadership of Chief Justice Earl Warren (1953-69) ushered in a new era in U.S. criminal law. In seizing the mantle of criminal law reform, the Warren Court proceeded in two parallel directions. (For a full review of these Warren Court activities, see the editor's 1973 FACTS ON FILE publication, *The Supreme Court & the Rights of the Accused*.)

First, in laying the groundwork for reform, the Warren Court applied the Bill of Rights to the state level in rendering the Bill of Rights a constitutional reality, in theory at least, in the local courthouse and police precinct. Previously, most provisions of the Bill of Rights concerning the rights of the accused had been interpreted to apply only on the federal level. In a series of decisions, the Warren Court interpreted the post-Civil War Fourteenth Amendment requirement that the *states* not deny anyone the "due process of law" as prohibiting the states from violating provisions in the Bill of Rights relating the rights of the accused.

Simultaneously with this development, the Warren Court gave additional new meaning to the Bill of Rights by interpreting many of its provisions in a broad, innovative fashion. In *Mapp v. Ohio* (1961), for example, the Court interpreted the Fourth Amendment requirement for a court-

1

issued search warrant as precluding the use in court of illegally obtained evidence. Five years later, in *Miranda v. Arizona*, the Court held the Fifth Amendment right against self incrimination and the Sixth Amendment right to an attorney as requiring the police to advise persons in custody of their right to remain silent and of their right to counsel. Failure to provide these warnings renders a confession inadmissable in court under *Miranda*.

The intense public reaction to these and other controversial decisions of the Warren Court gave rise to a conservative backlash that was reflected in the nomination by President Richard M. Nixon and President Gerald R. Ford of Supreme Court justices who to date have exhibited little enthusiasm for the bold, innovative ways of their Warren Court predecessors. The justices nominated to the Supreme Court by President Nixon and President Ford and the year of their appointment are as follows:

Chief Justice Warren E. Burger (1969)

Harry A. Blackmun (1970)

Lewis F. Powell, Jr. (1971)

William H. Rehnquist (1971)

John P. Stevens (1975)

The Nixon/Ford appointees along with Justices Bryon R. White and Potter Stewart, who frequently dissented from the Warren Court majority, have formed a new majority whose criminal law decisions have frequently provoked sharp dissents from two Warren Court holdovers, Thurgood Marshall and William J. Brennan, Jr.

A review of the leading criminal law decisions by the Burger Court demonstrates a hearty dislike of previous Warren Court holdings that is reflected in a tendency on the part of the new court to interpret these earlier decisions in a generally restrictive fashion while refusing thus far to overturn them directly. An exception to this generalization involves capital punishment, an area in which the Burger Court has moved ahead of the Warren Court in: (1) restricting the discretion previously accorded judges and juries in imposing the death penalty, (2) holding unconstitutional state mandatory death penalty provisions, and (3) barring the use of the death penalty for the rape of an adult woman.

The cases featured in this book illustrate the extent to which the Burger Court has held the line, or retreated (depending on one's view), from previous Warren Court decisions. These decisions reflect the attention paid by the Burger Court to confessions, the use in court of illegally seized evidence, the requirement for search warrants, and the presence of attorneys during police lineups and other pre-trial identification procedures. Those areas constitute the great bulk of the present court's involvement in the area of criminal law and as such provide an index for judging the court's work in this area.

JOHN GALLOWAY

Washington, D.C.
October, 1977

Capital Punishment

Death Penalty Ruled Invalid in 1972

The morality and utility of the death penalty has been debated in this country since the Nineteenth Century. The constitutionality of capital punishment, however, was first addressed by the Supreme Court in a series of historic decisions beginning in 1972 that (1) overturned existing death penalty provisions throught the U.S., (2) upheld the penalty of death for murder, (3) barred the use of mandatory death penalty provisions, (4) ruled that judges and juries can impose capital punishment only with "full disclosure of the basis for the death sentence," and (5) rejected the death penalty for rape of an adult woman.

The issue was joined by the Court in 1972 in a 5-4 decision in which five justices who had served under Chief Justice Earl Warren declared capital punishment, as currently administered in the U.S., to constitute "cruel and unusual punishment" as prohibited by the Constitution in the Eighth Amendment (part of the Bill of Rights) and the Fourteenth Amendment.* The decision, in the case of *Furman v. Georgia,*

*The Eighth Amendment prohibits the *federal government* from inflicting "cruel and unusual punishments." The Fourteenth Amendment adopted, in

5

saved from execution some 645 persons on death rows throughout the U.S. and overruled the death penalty provisions of 40 states, the District of Columbia and the federal government.

The nine justices all issued separate opinions, which together totalled 243 pages. The majority's disapproval of capital punishment centered on the relatively rare and arbitrary manner in which it was imposed. Justice Potter Stewart likened the imposition of the death penalty to being struck by lightning. The Constitution, he said, cannot tolerate a system that permits the death penalty to be so "wantonly and so freakishly imposed."

Two of the justices in the majority—Justices William J. Brennan, Jr., and Thurgood Marshall—went further in holding that capital punishment in and of itself constituted a cruel and unusual punishment:

In conceding that the framers of the Bill of Rights did not intend to outlaw legal executions when they passed the Eighth Amendment, Brennan noted that the court had held in 1958 that the Eighth Amendment "must draw its meaning from the evolving standards of decency that mark the progress of a maturing society." Accordingly, Brennan said, a punishment is "cruel and unusual" if "it does not comport with human dignity." He held that the principles on which such a determination should be made depend on whether a particular punishment is unnecessarily severe, arbitrary and excessive and on whether it is unacceptable to contemporary society. According to Brennan, the death penalty was deficient on all four criteria, most notably in the frequency in which it was imposed—fewer than fifty times a year in a nation of more than two hundred million people in which thousands of murders and rapes are committed annually. "When the

---

1868, prohibits a *state* from depriving any person "of life, liberty, or property without due process of law." The Supreme Court in 1962 held that the imposition of cruel and unusual punishments by a state government was tantamount to a denial of due process as prohibited by the Fourteenth Amendment. As a consequence, the Eighth Amendment is binding on both the federal and state level.

punishment of death is inflicted in a trivial number of cases in which it is legally available, the conclusion is virtually inescapable that it is being inflicted arbitrarily,'' he said. Moreover, the death penalty was unnecessarily severe, he asserted, since he saw no evidence that it served any purpose that could not be served as well by imprisonment. Brennan described as ''implausible'' the notion that a potential criminal would fail to commit a capital crime for fear of the death penalty.

Marshall used similar arguments, adding that the death penalty was ''morally unacceptable'' if for no other reason than that it most frequently was imposed on blacks, ''the poor, the ignorant and the underprivileged members of society.'' Marshall noted that of the 3,859 persons executed in the U.S. since 1930, 1,751 were white and 2,066 black. Of the 455 persons executed for rape during that period, 48 were white and 405 black.

The four dissenters were the four Nixon appointees—Chief Justice Warren Earl Burger and Justices Lewis F. Powell, Jr., Harry A. Blackmun and William H. Rehnquist. They emphasized in their separate dissents what they considered the proper role of the Supreme Court. In their view, public policy, to the extent possible, should be determined by legislators rather than judges. While ''over-reaching'' by the Legislative and Executive Branches might jeopardize individual rights, Rehnquist said, ''judicial overruling may result in sacrifice of the equally important right of the people to govern themselves.''

Blackmun, in his dissent, expressed the ''excruciating agony of the spirit'' faced by a justice whose deep-seated personal views cannot be reconciled with his reading of the Constitution. ''I yield to no one in the depth of my distaste, antipathy, and, indeed abhorrence, for the death penalty,'' he said. ''That distaste is buttressed by a belief that capital punishment serves no useful purpose that can be demonstrated. Were I a legislator, I would vote against the death penalty.'' Yet, he said, ''we should not allow our personal preferences as to the wisdom of legislative and congressional action, or our distaste for such action, to guide our judicial decision in cases such as these."

Burger, in a lengthy dissent, agreed that the Eighth Amendment should be interpreted with reference to society's "evolving standards of decency," but to Burger the crucial element in such a determination was the attitude of Congress and the state legislatures, which overwhelmingly favored some form of capital punishment. In " a democracy, the legislative judgment is presumed to embody the basic standards of decency prevailing in the society," he asserted. Burger, furthermore, did not accept the majority's contention that capital punishment was unconstitutional because of the relatively small number of instances in which it was imposed. That view, he said, "suggests that capital punishment can be made to satisfy the Eighth Amendment values if its rate of imposition is somehow multiplied." The majority opinions, he said, suggest that the flexible sentencing system created by the legislatures and carried out by judges and juries "has yielded more mercy than the Eighth Amendment can stand." One result of the majority ruling, Burger predicted, might be to encourage legislatures that want to maintain the death penalty to establish a mandatory death penalty for certain crimes. "I could more easily be persuaded that mandatory systems of death, without the intervening and ameliorating impact of lay jurors, are so arbitrary and doctrinaire that they violate the Constitution," he said.

Although the decision applied to all persons then awaiting execution, it involved the appeals of three Southern blacks who had been sentenced to death. In one case the crime was murder; in the other two cases the crime was rape.

In the aftermath of *Furman*, some 35 states moved to restore the death penalty in one of two ways. A number of states, including Florida, Texas and Georgia, imposed by statute standards designed to reduce the wide discretion previously available to judges and juries in deciding whether to impose the death penalty in an effort to meet the objections in *Furman* concerning the "wanton," "freakish," "discriminatory," and hence, cruel and unusual nature of the death penalty as previously employed. Other states, among them North Carolina and Louisiana, sought to restore the death penalty by making death mandatory for certain crimes, thus eliminating the wide ranging discretion held unconstitutional in *Furman*. In a series of decisions handed down in July 1976, the Supreme Court upheld the death penalty in Florida, Texas and Georgia while holding unconstitutional mandatory death penalty statutes in North Carolina and Louisiana.

Court Approval of Death Penalty Statutes

The Supreme Court, by a vote of 7-2 in three separate cases, upheld the death penalty provisions of three states and those states with similar statutes. The three cases, *Gregg v. Georgia, Profit v. Florida* and *Jurek v. Texas,* were decided July 2, 1976. Justices Brennan and Marshall, who had comprised part of the "liberal" bloc on the Warren Court, dissented in all three cases.

Gregg v. Georgia was the leading case. It involved a procedure by which Georgia sought to reduce the arbitrary discretion previously accorded juries in imposing the death penalty by means of a statute under which a person convicted of murder could receive a sentence either of death or of life imprisonment. Under the state's 1975 *post Furman* procedure, the sentence was defined as life imprisonment unless the jury, at a separate proceeding following the verdict, found unanimously and beyond a reasonable doubt at least one of ten statutorily defined "aggravating circumstance," such a murder by a person with a substantial history of previous convictions for serious assaults, or murder committed during the course of burglary or arson. Having determined an "aggravating circumstance," the jury, although not required to do so, could impose the death penalty. In such cases, Georgia law further required the state Supreme Court to review the sentence to determine whether the evidence supported the jury's finding of an aggravating circumstance and whether the imposition of the death penalty was excessive or disproportionate to the penalty imposed in similar cases.

The Supreme Court, in its review of the death sentence imposed in the case before it, upheld the Georgia procedure in distinguishing it from *Furman* on the ground that a Georgia jury could no longer "reach a finding of the defendant's guilt and then, without guidance or direction, decide whether he should live or die."

Justice Stewart, in the majority opinion, prefaced his review of the Georgia capital punishment procedure by rejecting the notion that capital punishment for the crime of murder is *per se* a "cruel and unusual punishment" in violation of the Constitution. Justices Brennan and Marshall, in dissent, argued that it is.

Court Overturns Mandatory Death Statutes

On the same day, July 2, 1976, in which it approved three state death penalty provisions as meeting the objections of *Furman*, the Supreme Court held unconstitutional the mandatory death penalty statutes of North Carolina and Louisiana and, by implication, similar statutes in other states.

By an identical 5-4 vote, the Court disallowed death penalty provisions that sought to reduce the discretion previously given juries in such cases by requiring the imposition of the death penalty for certain crimes. As stated by Justice Stewart in speaking for the Court in *Woodson v. North Carolina*, the Court faced "for the first time the question of whether a death sentence returned pursuant to a law imposing a mandatory death penalty for a broad category of homicidal offenses constitutes cruel and unusual punishment."

In ruling against such mandatory death penalty provisions, the majority held that the "fundamental respect for humanity requires considerations of the character and record of the individual offender and the circumstances of their particular offense as a constitutionally indispensable part of the process of inflicting the penalty of death."

In criticizing the failure of North Carolina to consider any and all possible mitigating factors, the Court held that the failure to do so was contrary to "civilized standards" and as such constituted a cruel and unusual punishment.

The leading dissent in the two cases was written by Justice Byron R. White in *Stanislaus Roberts v. Louisiana* on behalf of himself, Chief Justice Burger and Justices Blackmun and Rehnquist. The key to their dissent focused on the fact that *Furman* required only that juries not be accorded total discretion in imposing the death penalty and that elimination of such discretion through the imposition of mandatory death sentences satisfied the requirements of *Furman*.

In the case of *Gardner v. Florida*, the Supreme Court March 22, 1977, ruled that judges and juries can impose the death penalty only with "full disclosure of the basis for the death sentence." They cannot, the Court held, take a life—"a different kind of punishment than any other"—on the basis of secret information that neither the defendant nor his attorney has had an opportunity to deny or explain.

For different reasons, each of the nine justices voted to spare, at least temporarily, Daniel Wilbur Gardner, who had been sentenced to die by a Florida judge for killing his wife. Gardner, an alcoholic who had been drinking heavily prior to his wife's murder, was convicted by a Florida jury of first degree murder. In a separate sentencing hearing the same day, the trial judge instructed the jury to recommend, by majority vote, either death or life imprisonment.

Under state law, the jury was instructed to consider two factors: Was the crime "especially heinous, atrocious, or cruel" or was the crime mitigated by "the influence of extreme mental or emotional disturbance?" The jury recommended life imprisonment. The judge, however, on the basis of a pre-sentence investigation report received two weeks later, overruled the jury and sentenced Gardner to die because of the "heinous" nature of his crime and the absence of any mitigating circumstances.

The secrecy issue arose because the report contained material that neither Gardner nor his attorney were permitted to review. Justice Stevens, in the lead opinion, held that Gardner was thus "denied due process of law when the death sentence was imposed, at least in part, on the basis of information which he had no opportunity to deny or explain.''

Justices Brennan and Marshall objected to the decision to have the Florida courts reconsider Gardner's sentence. Believing the death penalty to be unconstitutional, they dissented from the Court's judgment to the extent that it ordered further proceedings that could lead to the imposition of the death penalty. Justice Marshall criticized the performance of the Florida Supreme Court in reviewing the trial judge's decision to sentence Gardner to death. He questioned the Florida Supreme Court's suggestion that the arbitrary nature of the judge's decision was sufficient to cause the Court to reconsider its previous decisions and to permit the death penalty on condition that the sentence not be imposed arbitrarily.

Justice Rehnquist dissented on the ground that the death penalty should have been upheld since a sentence procedure never before held unconstitutional ''cannot convert that sentence into a cruel and unusual punishment.''

Mandatory Death Penalty for Police Killers Overturned

In a 5-4 decision June 6, 1977, the Supreme Court ruled that states may not impose the death sentence on persons convicted of murdering a police officer. The decision paralleled a July 6, 1976 Supreme Court decision, *Washington v. Louisiana,* that invalidated a Louisiana statute requiring the death penalty in cases involving a police officer. The June 6, 1977 decision, *Harry Roberts v. Louisiana,* involved the same Louisiana law. The Court gave no reason for again considering the issue of whether mandatory death penalties were permissable for convicted police killers. It seemed likely, however, that several justices wanted to address the issue anew, in the hope possibly of getting a change in the law. Only four votes are needed to grant a Supreme Court review of a case.

In its June 6, 1977 ruling, the Court's unsigned opinion recognized a state's ''special interest'' in protecting police officers "who regularly must risk their lives." The opinion noted that 129 police officers were killed in the line of duty in 1975, compared with 57 in 1966.

But, the opinion said, it "is incorrect" to rule out the possibility in such slayings of any mitigating facts, including "the youth of the offender." In the case at hand, the offender, Harry Roberts, was 19 when sentenced to die for killing a New Orleans police officer in 1974.

The majority's list of possible mitigating circumstances also included "the absence of any prior conviction, the influence of drugs, alcohol or extreme emotional disturbance, and even the existence of circumstances which the offender reasonably believed provided a moral justification for his conduct."

In one of three dissenting opinions, Justice Rehnquist termed it "astonishing" that the majority could include in its list of possible mitigating circumstances those "reasonably believed" by the offender to provide "a moral justification" for his crime. "John Wilkes Booth may well have thought he was morally justified in murdering Abraham Lincoln, whom, while fleeing from the stage of Ford's Theater, he characterized as a 'tyrant,' " Rehnquist argued.

Justices Brennan and Marshall in joining with the majority, again noted their view that the death penalty is unconstitutional cruel and unusual punishment "in all circumstances." Justices Stewart, Powell and Stevens were also in the majority.

Court Bars Death Penalty for Rape

By a 7-2 vote in *Coker v. Georgia*, decided June 29, 1977, the Supreme Court rejected the death penalty for the rape of an adult woman as being "grossly disproportionate and excessive punishment" as forbidden by the Eighth Amendment's prohibition against cruel and unusual punishment.

Justice White, in speaking for the majority, emphasized that Georgia was the only state that authorized the death penalty for the rape of an adult woman and that in Georgia, juries imposed the death penalty in less than ten percent of such cases. That, according to the majority, was grounds for concluding that the death penalty for adult rape constituted excessive and disproportionate punishment.

Chief Justice Burger and Justice Rehnquist, in dissent, dismissed the relevance of the uniqueness of the Georgia statute as being indicative only of the uncertainty created by the Court in its 1972 *Furman v. North Carolina* decision that declared the death penalty, as then imposed by the majority of the states, unconstitutional.

The dissenting opinion took issue with the majority's view that the death penalty is disproportionate for a crime that does not entail the taking of life in view of the serious psychological and physical harm often suffered by rape victims. The dissenters further criticized the majority opinion for suggesting the unconstitutionality of the death penalty for other crimes that do not result in death, such as airplane hijacking or kidnapping.

Justice Powell, while agreeing that the death penalty was disproportionate in the case at hand, objected to ruling out the use of the death penalty for "outrageous cases of rape involving serious or lasting harm." Justices Brennan and Marshall, in short, concurring opinions, reiterated their view that capital punishment is unconstitutional in all circumstances.

ABRIDGMENTS OF CAPITAL PUNISHMENT DECISIONS

Furman v. Georgia (408 U.S. 238, June 29, 1972)

Justice William O. Douglas concurring:

...In each [of the three cases] the determination of whether the penalty should be death of a lighter punishment was left by the state to the descretion of the judge or of the jury. In each of the three cases the trial was to a jury. They are here on petitions for *certiorari* which we ganted limited to the question whether the imposition and execution of the death penalty constitutes "cruel and unusual punishments" within the meaning of the Eighth Amendment as applied to the states by the Fourteenth. I vote to vacate each judgment, believing that the exaction of the death penalty does violate the Eighth and Fourteenth Amendments....

There is increasing recognition of the fact that the basic theme of equal protection is implicit in "cruel and unusual" punishments. "A penalty...should be considered 'unusually' imposed if it is administered arbitrarily or disciminatorily."* The same authors add that "the extreme rarity with which applicable death penalty provisions are put to use raises a strong inference of arbitrariness." The President's Commission on Law Enforcement & Administration of Justice recently concluded: "Finally there is evidence that the imposition of the death sentence and the exercise of dispensing power by the courts and the executive follow discriminatory patterns. The death sentence is disproportionately imposed and carried out on the poor, the Negro, and the members of unpopular groups."

A study of capital cases in Texas from 1924 to 1968 reached the following conclusions: "Application of the death penalty is unequal: most of those executed were poor, young, and ignorant. Seventy-five of the 460 cases involved codefendants, who, under Texas law, were given separate trials. In several instances, where a white and a Negro were codefendants, the white was sentenced to

---

*Goldberg & Dershowitz, "Declaring the Death Penalty Unconstitutional," 83 *Harv. L. Rev.* 1773. 1790.

life imprisonment or a term of years, and the Negro was given the death penalty. Another ethnic disparity is found in the type of sentence imposed for rape. The Negro convicted of rape is far more likely to get the death penalty than a term sentence, whereas whites and Latins are far more likely to get a term sentence than the death penalty.''

Warden Lewis E. Lawes of Sing Sing said: ''Not only does capital punishment fail in its justification, but no punishment could be invented with so many inherent defects. It is an unequal punishment in the way it is applied to the rich and to the poor. The defendant of wealth and position never goes to the electric chair or to the gallows. Juries do not intentionally favor the rich, the law is theoretically impartial, but the defendant with ample means is able to have his case presented with every favorable aspect, while the poor defendant often has a lawyer assigned by the court. Sometimes such assignment is considered part of political patronage; usually the lawyer assigned has had no experience whatever in a capital case.''

Former Attorney General Ramsey Clark has said, ''It is the poor, the sick, the ignorant, the powerless and the hated who are executed.'' One searches our chronicles in vain for the execution of any member of the affluent strata of this society. . . .

Jackson, a black, convicted of the rape of a white woman, was 21 years old. A court-appointed psychiatrist said that Jackson was of average education and average intelligence, that he was not an imbecile or schizophrenic or psychotic, that his traits were the product of environmental influences, and that he was competent to stand trial. Jackson had entered the house after the husband left for work. He held scissors against the neck of the wife, demanding money. She could find none, and a struggle ensued for the scissors, a battle which she lost; and she was then raped, Jackson keeping the scissors pressed against her neck. While there did not appear to be any long-term traumatic impact on the victim, she was bruised and abrased in the struggle but was not hospitalized. Jackson was a convict who had escaped from a work gang in the area, a result of a three year sentence for auto theft. He was at large for three days and during that time had committed several other offenses—burglary, auto theft, and assault and battery.

Furman, a black, killed a householder while seeking to enter the home at night. Furman shot the deceased through a closed door. He was 26 years old and had finished the sixth grade in school. Pending trial, he was committed to the Georgia Central State Hospital for a psychiatric examination on his plea of insanity tendered by court-appointed counsel. The superintendent reported: that a unanimous staff diagnostic conference on the same date had concluded "that this patient should retain his present diagnosis of Mental Deficiency, Mild to Moderate, with Psychotic Episodes associated with Convulsive Disorder." . . .

Later he reported that the staff diagnosis was Mental Deficiency, Mild to Moderate, with Psychotic Episodes associated with Convulsive Disorder. He concluded, however, that Furman was "not psychotic at present, knows right from wrong and is able to cooperate with his counsel in preparing his defense."

Branch, a black, entered the rural home of a 65-year-old widow, a white, while she slept and raped her, holding his arm against her throat. Thereupon he demanded money and for thirty minutes or more the widow searched for money, finding little. As he left, Branch said if the widow told anyone what happened, he would return and kill her. The record is barren of any medical or psychiatric evidence showing injury to her as a result of Branch's attack.

He had previously been convicted of felony theft and found to be a borderline mentally deficient and well below the average IQ of Texas prison inmates. He had the equivalent of 5½ years of grade school education. He had a "dull intelligence" and was in the lower fourth percentile of his class.

We cannot say from facts disclosed in these records that these defendants were sentenced to death because they were black. Yet our task is not restricted to an effort to divine what motives impelled these death penalties. Rather we deal with a system of law and of justice that leaves to the uncontrolled discretion of judges or juries the determination whether defendants committing these crimes should die or be imprisoned. Under these laws no standards govern the selection of the penalty. People live or die, dependent on the whim of one man or of twelve. . . .

The high service rendered by the "cruel and unusual" punishment clause of the Eighth Amendment is to require legislatures to write penal laws that are evenhanded, nonselective and nonarbitrary and to require judges to see to it that general laws are not applied sparsely, selectively and spottily to unpopular groups.

A law that stated that anyone making more than $50,000 would be exempt from the death penalty and would plainly fall, as would a law that in terms said that blacks, those who never went beyond the fifth grade in school, or those who made less than $3,000 a year, or those who were unpopular or unstable should be the only people executed. A law which in the overall view reaches that result in practice has no more sanctity than a law which in terms provides the same.

Thus, these discretionary statutes are unconstitutional in their operation. They are pregnant with discrimination, and discrimination is an ingredient not compatible with the idea of equal protection of the laws that is implicit in the ban on "cruel and unusual" punishments.

Any law which is nondiscriminatory on its face may be applied in such a way as to violate the equal protection clause of the Fourteenth Amendment.... Such conceivably might be the fate of a mandatory death penalty, where equal or lesser sentences were imposed on the elite, a harsher one on the minorities or members of the lower castes. Whether a mandatory death penalty would otherwise be constitutional is a question I do not reach....

Justice Brennan concurring:

...Ours would indeed be a simple task were we required merely to measure a challenged punishment against those that history has long condemned.... Our task today is more complex. We know "that the words of the [cruel-and-unusual-punishments clause]...are not precise and that their scope is not static." We know, therefore, that the clause "must draw its meaning from the evolving standards of decency that mark the progress of a maturing society." *Trop v. Dulles* (1958).... That knowledge, of course, is but the beginning of the inquiry.

In *Trop v. Dulles*... it was said that "[t]he question is whether [a] penalty subjects the individual to a fate forbidden by the principle of civilized treatment guaranteed by the...[clause]." It was also said that a challenged punishment must be examined "in light of the basic prohibition against inhuman treatment" embodied in the clause.... It was said, finally, that: "The basic concept underlying the [clause]...is nothing less than the dignity of man. While the state has power to punish, the [clause]...stands to assure that this power be exercised within the limits of civilized standards."... At bottom, then, the cruel and unusual punishments clause prohibits the infliction of uncivilized and inhuman punishments. The state, even as it punishes, must treat its members with respect for their intrinsic worth as human beings. A punishment is "cruel and unusual," therefore, if it does not comport with human dignity.

This formulation, of course, does not of itself yield principles for assessing the constitutional validity of particular punishments. Nevertheless, even though [t]his court has had little occasion to give precise content to the [clause]," *ibid.*, there are principles recognized in our cases and inherent in the clause sufficient to permit a judicial determination whether a challenged punishment comports with human dignity.

The primary principle is that a punishment must not be so severe as to be degrading to the dignity of human beings. Pain, certainly, may be a factor in the judgment. The infliction of an extremely severe punishment will often entail physical suffering. See *Weems v. United States* [1910].... Yet the Framers also know "that there could be exercises of cruelty by laws other than those which inflicted bodily pain or mutilation" *id.* Even though "[t]here may be involved no physical mistreatment, no primitive torture," *Trop v. Dulles,* ... severe mental pain may be inherent in the infliction of a particular punishment. See *Weems v. United States....* That, indeed, was one of the conclusions underlying the holding of the plurality in *Trop v. Dulles* that the punishment of expatriation violates the clause....

More than the presence of pain, however, is comprehended in the judgment that the extreme severity of a punishment makes it degrading to the dignity of human beings. The barbaric punishments condemned by history, "punishments which inflict torture, such as the rack, the thumbscrew, the iron boot, the stretching of limbs and the like," are, of course, "attended with acute pain and suffering." *O'Neil v. Vermont...* (1892) (Field, J., dissenting). When we consider why they have been condemned, however, we realize that the pain involved is not the only reason. The true significance of these punishments is that they treat members of the human race as nonhumans, as objects to be toyed with and discarded. They are thus inconsistent with the fundamental premise of the clause that even the vilest criminal remains a human being possessed of common human dignity....

In determining whether a punishment comports with human dignity, we are aided also by a second principle inherent in the clause—that the state must not arbitrarily inflict a severe punishment. This principle derives from the notion that the state does not respect human dignity when, without reason, it inflicts upon some people a severe punishment that it does not inflict upon others. Indeed, the very words "cruel and unusual punishments" imply condemnation of the arbitrary infliction of severe punishments....

A third principle inherent in the clause is that a severe punishment must not be unacceptable to contemporary society. Rejection by society, of course, is a strong indication that a severe punishment does not comport with human dignity. In applying this principle, however, we must make certain that the judicial determination is as objective as possible....

The final principle inherent in the clause is that a severe punishment must not be excessive. A punishment is excessive under this principle if it is unnecessary: The indication of a severe punishment by the state cannot comport with human dignity when it is nothing more than the pointless infliction of suffering if there is a significantly less severe punishment adequate to achieve the purposes for which the punishment is inflicted....

The question, then, is whether the deliberate infliction of death is today consistent with the command of the clause that the state may not inflict punishments that do not comport with human dignity. I will analyze the punishment of death in terms of the principles set out above and the cumulative test to which they lead: It is a denial of human dignity for the state arbitrarily to subject a person to an unusually severe punishment that society has indicated it does not regard as acceptable and that cannot be shown to serve any penal purpose more effectively than a significantly less drastic punishment. Under these principles and this test, death is today a "cruel and unusual" punishment....

... Death is today an unusually severe punishment, unusual in its pain, in its finality and in its enormity. No other existing punishment is comparable to death in terms of physical and mental suffering. Although our information is not conclusive, it appears that there is no method available that guarantees an immediate and painless death. Since the discontinuance of flogging as a constitutionally permissible punishment, ... death remains as the only punishment that may involve the conscious infliction of physical pain. In addition, we know that mental pain is an inseparable part of our practice of punishing criminals by death, for the prospect of pending execution exacts a frightful toll during the inevitable long wait between the imposition of sentence and the actual infliction of death....

In comparison to all other punishments today, the deliberate extinguishment of human life by the state is uniquely degrading to human dignity. I would not hesitate to hold, on that ground alone, that death is today a "cruel and unusual" punishment, were it not that death is a punishment of long-standing usage and acceptance in this country. I therefore turn to the third principle that the state may not arbitrarily inflict an unusually severe punishment.

The outstanding characteristic of our present practice of punishing criminals by death is the infrequency with which we resort to it. The evidence is conclusive that death is not the ordinary punishment for any crime.

There has been a steady decline in the infliction of this punishment in every decade since the 1930s, the earliest period for which accurate statistics are available. In the 1930s, executions averaged 167 per year; in the 1940s, the average was 128; in the 1950s, it was 72; and in the years 1960-1962, it was 48. There have been a total of 46 executions since then, 36 of them in 1963-1964. Yet. . . . the numbers of capital crimes committed have increased greatly over the past four decades. . . .

When a country of over 200 million people inflicts an unusually severe punishment no more than fifty times a year, the inference is strong that the punishment is not being regularly and fairly applied. To dispel it would indeed require a clear showing of nonarbitrary infliction.

. . . [W]e know that thousands of murders and rapes are committed annually in states where death is an authorized punishment for those crimes. However the rate of infliction is characterized—as "freakishly" or "spectacularly" rare, or simply as rare—it would take the purest sophistry to deny that death is inflicted in only a minute fraction of these cases. How much rarer, after all, could the infliction of death be?

When the punishment of death is inflicted in a trivial number of the cases in which it is legally available, the conclusion is virtually inescapable that it is being inflicted arbitrarily. . . .

. . . When the rate of infliction is at this low level, it is highly implausible that only the worst criminals or the criminals who commit the worst crimes are selected for this punishment. No one has yet suggested a rational basis that could differentiate in those terms the few who die from the many who go to prison. . . .

The states' primary claim is that death is a necessary punishment because it prevents the commission of capital crimes more effectively than any less severe punishment. The first part of this claim is that the infliction of death is necessary to stop the individuals executed from committing further crimes. The sufficient answer to this is that if a criminal convicted of a capital crime poses a danger to society, effective administration of the state's pardon and parole laws can delay or deny his release from prison, and techniques of isolation can eliminate or minimize the danger while he remains confined.

The more significant argument is that the threat of death prevents the commission of capital crimes because it deters potential criminals who would not be deterred by the threat of imprisonment.

... It is not denied that many, and probably most, capital crimes cannot be deterred by the threat of punishment. Thus the argument can apply only to those who think rationally about the commission of capital crimes. Particularly is that true when the potential criminal, under this argument, must not only consider the risk of punishment but also distinguish between two possible punishments. The concern, then, is with a particular type of potential criminal, the rational person who will commit a capital crime knowing that the punishment is long-term imprisonment, which may well be for the rest of his life, but will not commit the crime knowing that the punishment is death. On the face of it, the assumption that such persons exist is implausible. . . .

In sum, the punishment of death is inconsistent with all four principles: Death is an unusually severe and degrading punishment; there is a strong probability that it is inflicted arbitrarily; its rejection by contemporary society is virtually total; and there is no reason to believe that it serves any penal purpose more effectively than the less severe punishment of imprisonment. The function of these principles is to enable a court to determine whether a punishment comports with human dignity. . . . Death, quite simply, does not. . . .

Justice Stewart concurring:

... These death sentences are cruel and unusual in the same way that being struck by lightning is cruel and unusual. For, of all the people convicted of rapes and murders in 1967 and 1968, many just as reprehensible as these, the petitioners, are among a capriciously selected random handful upon whom the sentence of death has in fact been imposed. . . . I simply conclude that the Eighth and Fourteenth Amendments cannot tolerate the infliction of a sentence of death under legal systems that permit this unique penalty to be so wantonly and so freakishly imposed.

Justice White concurring:

...I do not at all intimate that the death penalty is unconstitutional *per se* or that there is no system of capital punishment that would comport with the Eighth Amendment. That question...is not presented by these cases and need not be decided....

The narrower question to which I address myself concerns the constitutionality of capital punishment statutes under which (1) the legislature authorizes the imposition of the death penalty for murder or rape; (2) the legislature does not itself mandate the penalty....

The imposition and execution of the death penalty are obviously cruel in the dictionary sense. But the penalty has not been considered cruel and unusual punishment in the constitutional sense because it was thought justified by the social ends it was deemed to serve. At the moment that it ceases realistically to further these purposes, however, the emerging question is whether its imposition in such circumstances would violate the Eighth Admendment. It is my view that it would, for its imposition would then be the pointless and needless extinction of life with only marginal contributions to any discernible social or public purposes. A penalty with such negligible returns to the state would be patently excessive and cruel and unusual punishment violative of the Eighth Amendment.

It is also my judgment that this point has been reached with respect to capital punishment as it is presently administered under the statutes involved in these cases. Concededly, it is difficult to prove as a general proposition that capital punishment, however administered, more effectively serves the ends of the criminal law than does imprisonment. But however that may be, I cannot avoid the conclusion that as the statutes before us are now administered, the penalty is so infrequently imposed that the threat of execution is too attenuated to be of substantial service to criminal justice.

...I can do no more than state a conclusion based on ten years of almost daily exposure to the facts and circumstances of hundreds and hundreds of federal and state criminal cases involving crimes for which death is the authorized penalty. That conclusion...is that the death penalty is exacted with great infrequency even for the most atrocious crimes and that there is no meaningful basis for distinguishing the few cases in which it is imposed from the many cases in which it is not. The short of it is that the policy of vesting sentencing authority primarily in juries—a decision largely motivated by the desire to mitigate the harshness of the law and to bring community judgment to bear on the sentence as well as guilt or innocence—has so effectively achieved its aim that capital punishment within the confines of the statutes now before us has for all practical purposes run its course....

Justice Marshall concurring:

. . . [E]ven if capital punishment is not excessive, it nonetheless violates the Eighth Amendment because it is morally unacceptable to the people of the United States at this time in their history.

In judging whether or not a given penalty is morally acceptable, most courts have said that the punishment is valid unless "it shocks the conscience and sense of justice of the people."

Judge Frank once noted the problems inherent in the use of such a measuring stick: "[The court,] before it reduces a sentence as 'cruel and unusual,' must have reasonably good assurances that the sentence offends the 'common conscience.' And, in any context, such a standard—the community's attitude—is usually an unknowable. It resembles a slithery shadow, since one can seldom learn, at all accurately, what the community, or a majority, actually feels. Even a carefully taken 'public opinion poll' would be inconclusive in a case like this." While a public opinion poll obviously is of some assistance in indicating public acceptance or rejection of a specific penalty, its utility cannot be very great. This is because whether or not a punishment is cruel and unusual depends, not on whether its mere mention "shocks the conscience and sense of justice of the people," but on whether people who were fully informed as to the purposes of the penalty and its liabilities would find the penalty shocking, unjust, and unacceptable.

In other words, the question with which we must deal is not whether a substantial proportion of American citizens would today, if polled, opine that capital punishment is barbarously cruel, but whether they would find it to be so in the light of all information presently available.

This is not to suggest that with respect to this test of unconstitutionality people are required to act rationally; they are not. With respect to this judgment, a violation of the Eighth Amendment is totally dependent on the predictable subjective, emotional reactions of informed citizens.

It has often been noted that American citizens know almost nothing about capital punishment. Some of the conclusions arrived at in the preceding section and the supporting evidence would be critical to an informed judgment on the morality of the death penalty: *e.g.*, that the death penalty is no more effective a deterrent than life imprisonment, that convicted murderers are rarely executed but are usually sentenced to a term in prison; that convicted murderers usually are model prisoners and that they almost always become law-abiding citizens upon their release from prison; that the costs of executing a capital offender exceed the costs of imprisoning him for life; that while in prison, a convict under sentence of death performs none of the useful functions that life prisoners perform; that no attempt is made in the sentencing process to ferret out likely recidivists for execution; and that the death penalty may actually stimulate criminal activity.

This information would almost surely convince the average citizen that the death penalty was unwise, but a problem arises as to whether it would convince him that the penalty was morally reprehensible. This problem arises from the fact that the public's desire for retribution, even though this is a goal which the legislature cannot constitutionally pursue as its sole justification for capital punishment might influence the citizenry's view of the morality of capital punishment. The solution to the problem lies in the fact that no one has ever seriously advanced retribution as a legitimate goal of our society. Defenses of capital punishment are always mounted on deterrent or other similar theories. This should not be surprising. It is the people of this country who have urged in the past that prisons rehabilitate as well as isolate offenders, and it is the people who have injected a sense of purpose into our penology. I cannot believe that at this stage in our history, the American people would ever knowingly support purposeless vengeance. Thus, I believe that the great mass of citizens would conclude on the basis of the material already considered that the death penalty is immoral and therefore unconstitutional.

. . . I believe that the following facts would serve to convince even the most hesitant of citizens to condemn death as a sanction: capital punishment is imposed discriminatorily against certain identifiable classes of people; there is evidence that innocent people have been executed before their innocence can be proved; and the death penalty wreaks havoc with our entire criminal justice system. . . .

... [I]t has been said that "[i]t is usually the poor, the illiterate, the underprivileged, the member of the minority group—the man who, because he is without means, and is defended by a court appointed attorney—who becomes society's sacrificial lamb...." ... A total of 3,859 persons have been executed since 1930, of which 1,751 were white and 2,066 were Negro. . . . 1,664 of the executed murderers were white, and 1,630 were Negro. . . .48 whites and 405 Negroes were executed for rape. . . .Negroes were executed far more often than whites in proportion to their percentage of the population. Studies indicate that while the higher rate of execution among Negroes is partially due to a higher rate of crime, there is evidence of racial discrimination. . . .

There is also overwhelming evidence that the death penalty is employed against men and not women. Only 32 women have been executed since 1930, while 3,827 men have met a similar fate. . . .

It also is evident that the burden of capital punishment falls upon the poor, the ignorant and the underprivileged members of society. It is the poor and the members of minority groups who are least able to voice their complaints against capital punishment. Their impotence leaves them victims of a sanction which the wealthier, better-represented, just-as-guilty person can escape. So long as the capital sanction is used only against the forlorn, easily forgotten members of society, legislators are content to maintain the *status quo*. . . .

... [Americans] are unaware of the potential dangers of executing an innocent man. Our "beyond-a-reasonable-doubt" burden of proof in criminal cases is intended to protect the innocent, but we know it is not foolproof. Various studies have shown that people whose innocence is later convincingly established are convicted and sentenced to death.

Proving one's innocence after a jury finding of guilt is almost impossible. While reviewing courts are willing to entertain all kinds of collateral attacks where a sentence of death is involved, they very rarely dispute the jury's interpretation of the evidence. . . .If an innocent man has been found guilty, he must then depend on the good faith of the prosecutor's office to help him establish his innocence. There is evidence, however, that prosecutors do not welcome the idea of having convictions, which they labored hard to secure, overturned, and that their cooperation is highly unlikely.

No matter how careful courts are, the possibility of perjured testimony, mistaken honest testimony, and human error remain all to real. We have no way of judging how many innocent persons have been executed, but we can be certain that there were some. . . . Surely there will be more as long as capital punishment remains part of our penal law.

While it is difficult to ascertain with certainty the degree to which the death penalty is discriminatorily imposed or the number of innocent persons sentenced to die, there is one conclusion about the penalty that is universally accepted—*i.e.,* it "tends to distort the course of the criminal law." As Mr. Justice Frankfurter said: "I am strongly against capital punishment. . . . When life is at hazard in a trial, it sensationalizes the whole thing almost unwittingly; the effect on juries, the bar, the public, the judiciary, I regard as very bad. I think scientifically the claim of deterrence is not worth much. Whatever proof there may be in my judgment does not outweigh the social loss due to the inherent sensationalism of a trial for life." The deleterious effects of the death penalty are also felt otherwise than at trial. For example, its very existence "inevitably sabotages a social or institutional program of reformation." In short "[t]he presence of the death penalty, as the keystone of our penal system bedevils the administration of criminal justice all the way down the line and is the stumbling block in the path of general reform and of the treatment of crime and criminal."*

Assuming knowledge of all the facts presently available regarding capital punishment, the average citizen would, in my opinion, find it shocking to his conscience and sense of justice. For this reason alone capital punishment cannot stand. . . .

In striking down capital punishment, this court does not malign our system of government. On the contrary, it pays homage to it. Only in a free society could right triumph in difficult times and could civilization record its magnificent advancement. In recognizing the humanity of our fellow beings, we pay ourselves the highest tribute. We achieve "a major milestone in the long road up from barbarism" and join the approximately seventy other jurisdictions in the world which celebrate their regard for civilization and humanity by shunning capital punishment. . . .

---

*Dr. S. Glueck of Harvard University.

Chief Justice Burger, whom Blackmun, Powell and Rehnquist joined, dissenting:

. . . If we were possessed of legislative power, I would either join with Mr. Justice Brennan and Mr. Justice Marshall or, at the very least, restrict the use of capital punishment to a small category of the most heinous crimes. Our constitutional inquiry, however, must be divorced from personal feelings as to the morality and efficacy of the death penalty and be confined to the meaning and applicability of the uncertain language of the Eighth Amendment. There is no novelty in being called upon to interpret a constitutional provision that is less than self-defining, but of all our fundamental guarantees, the ban on "cruel and unusual punishments" is one of the most difficult to translate into judicially manageable terms. The widely divergent views of the amendment expressed in today's opinions reveal the haze that surrounds this constitutional command. . . .

Although the Eighth Amendment literally reads as prohibiting only those punishments that are both "cruel" and "unusual," history compels the conclusion that the Constitution prohibits all punishments of extreme and barbarous cruelty, regardless of how frequently or infrequently imposed. . . .

Counsel for petitioners properly concede that capital punishment was not impermissibly cruel at the time of the adoption of the Eighth Amendment. Not only do the records of the debates indicate that the founding fathers were limited in their concern to the prevention of torture, but it is also clear from the language of the Constitution itself that there was no thought whatever of the elimination of capital punishment. The opening sentence of the Fifth Amendment is a guarantee that the death penalty not be imposed "unless on a presentment or indictment of a grand jury." The double jeopardy clause of the Fifth Amendment is a prohibition against being "twice put in jeopardy of life" for the same offense. Similarly, the due process clause commands "due process of law" before an accused can be "deprived of life, liberty or property." Thus the explicit language of the Constitution affirmatively acknowledges the legal power to impose capital punishment; it does not expressly or by implication acknowledge the legal power to impose any of the various punishments that have been banned as cruel since 1791. Since the Eighth Amendment was adopted on the same day in 1791 as the Fifth Amendment, it hardly needs more to establish that the death penalty was not "cruel" in the constitutional sense at that time.

In the 181 years since the enactment of the Eighth Amendment, not a single decision of this court has cast the slightest shadow of a doubt on the constitutionality of capital punishment. In rejecting Eighth Amendment attacks on particular modes of execution, the court has more than once implicitly denied that capital punishment is impermissibly "cruel" in constitutional sense....

However, the inquiry cannot end here. For reasons unrelated to any change in intrinsic cruelty, the Eighth Amendment prohibition cannot fairly be limited to those punishments thought excessively cruel and barbarous at the time of the adoption of the Eighth Amendment. A punishment is inordinately cruel, in the sense we must deal with it in these cases, chiefly as perceived by the society so characterizing it. The standard of extreme cruelty is not merely descriptive but necessarily embodies a moral judgment. The standard itself remains the same, but its applicability must change as the basic mores of society change.... Nevertheless, the court up to now has never actually held that a punishment has become impermissibly cruel due to a shift in the weight of accepted social values; nor has the court suggested judicially manageable criteria for measuring such a shift in moral consensus.

The court's quiescence in this area can be attributed to the fact that in a democratic society, legislatures, not courts, are constituted to respond to the will and consequently the moral values of the people.... Accordingly, punishments such as branding and the cutting off of ears, which were commonplace at the time of the adoption of the Constitution, passed from the penal scene without judicial intervention because they became basically offensive to the people and the legislatures responded to this sentiment.

...The critical fact is that this court has never had to hold that a mode of punishment authorized by a domestic legislature was so cruel as to be fundamentally at odds with our basic notions of decency.... Judicial findings of impermissible cruelty have been limited, for the most part, to offensive punishments devised without specific authority by prison officials, not by legislatures.... The paucity of judicial decisions invalidating legislatively prescribed punishments is powerful evidence that in this country legislatures have in fact been responsive—albeit belatedly at times—to changes in social attitudes and moral values.

I do not suggest that the validity of legislatively authorized punishments presents no justiciable issue under the Eighth Amendment but rather that the primacy of the legislative role narrowly confines the scope of judicial inquiry. Whether or not provable, and whether or not true at all times, in a democracy the legislative judgment is presumed to embody the basic standards of decency prevailing in the society. This presumption can only be negated by unambiguous and compelling evidence of legislative default.

...There are no obvious indications that capital punishment offends the conscience of society to such a degree that our traditional deference to the legislative judgment must be abandoned. It is not a punishment such as burning at the stake that everyone would ineffably find to be repugnant to all civilized standards. Nor is it a punishment so roundly condemned that only a few aberrant legislatures have retained it on the statute books. Capital punishment is authorized by statute in forty states, the District of Columbia and in the federal courts for the commission of certain crimes. On four occasions in the last eleven years Congress has added to the list of federal crimes punishable by death....

One conceivable source of evidence that legislatures have abdicated their essentially barometric role with respect to community values would be public opinion polls, of which there have been many in the past decade addressed to the question of capital punishment. Without assessing the reliability of such polls, or intimating that any judicial reliance could ever be placed on them, it need only be noted that the reported results have shown nothing approximating the universal condemnation of capital punishment that might lead us to suspect that the legislatures in general have lost touch with current social values.

Counsel for petitioners rely on a different body of empirical evidence. They argue, in effect, that the number of cases in which the death penalty is imposed, as compared with the number of cases in which it is statutorily available, reflects a general revulsion toward the penalty that would lead to its repeal if only it were more generally and widely enforced. It cannot be gainsaid that by the choice of juries—and sometimes judges—the death penalty is imposed in far fewer than half the cases in which it is available. To go further and characterize the rate of imposition as "freakishly rare," as petitioners insist, is unwarranted hyperbole.... The rate of imposition does not impel the conclusion that capital punishment is now regarded as intolerably cruel or uncivilized.

It is argued that in those capital cases where juries have recommended mercy, they have given expression to civilized values and effectively renounced the legislative authorization for capital punishment. At the same time it is argued that where juries have made the awesome decision to send men to their deaths, they have acted arbitrarily and without sensitivity to prevailing standards of decency. This explanation for the infrequency of imposition of capital punishment is unsupported by known facts and is inconsistent in principle with everything this court has ever said about the functioning of juries in capital cases. . . .

. . . There are doubtless prisoners on death row who would not be there had they been tried before a different jury or in a different state. In this sense their fate has been controlled by a fortuitous circumstance. However, this element of fortuity does not stand as an indictment either of the general functioning of juries in capital cases or of the integrity of jury decisions in individual cases. There is no empirical basis for concluding that juries have generally failed to discharge in good faith the responsibility described in *Witherspoon* [*v. Illinois*, 1968]—that of choosing between life and death in individual cases according to the dictates of community values.

The rate of imposition of death sentences falls far short of providing the requisite unambiguous evidence that the legislatures of forty states and the Congress have turned their backs on current or evolving standards of decency in continuing to make the death penalty available. For if selective imposition evidences a rejection of capital punishment in those cases where it is not imposed, it surely evidences a correlative affirmation of the penalty in those cases where it is imposed. Absent some clear indication that the continued imposition of the death penalty on a selective basis is violative of prevailing standards of civilized conduct, the Eighth Amendment cannot be said to interdict its use. . . .

Today the court has not ruled that capital punishment is *per se* violative of the Eighth Amendment; nor has it ruled that the punishment is barred for any particular class or classes of crimes. The substantially similar concurring opinions of Mr. Justice Stewart and Mr. Justice White, which are necessary to support the judgment setting aside petitioners' sentences, stop short of reaching the ultimate question. The actual scope of the court's ruling, which I take to be embodied in these concurring opinions, is not entirely clear. This much, however, seems apparent: if the legislatures are to continue to authorize capital punishment of some crimes, juries and judges can no longer be permitted to make the sentencing determination in the same manner they have in the past. This approach—not urged in oral arguments or briefs—misconceives the nature of the constitutional command against "cruel and unusual

punishments,'' disregards controlling case law and demands a
rigidity in capital cases which, if possible of achievement, cannot be
regarded as a welcome change. Indeed the contrary seems to be the
case. . . .

The critical factor in the concurring opinions of both Mr. Justice
Stewart and Mr. Justice White is the infrequency with which the
penalty is imposed. This factor is taken not as evidence of society's
abhorrence of capital punishment—the inference that petitioners
would have the court draw—but as the earmark of a deteriorated
system of sentencing. It is concluded that petitioners' sentences must
be set aside, not because the punishment is impermissibly cruel, but
because juries and judges have failed to exercise their sentencing
discretion in acceptable fashion.

To be sure, there is a recitation cast in Eighth Amendment terms:
petitioners' sentences are "cruel" because they exceed that which the
legislatures have deemed necessary for all cases; petitioners'
sentences are "unusual" because they exceed that which is imposed
in most cases. This application of the words of the Eighth
Amendment suggests that capital punishment can be made to satisfy
Eighth Amendment values if its rate of imposition is somehow
multiplied; it seemingly follows that the flexible sentencing system
created by the legislatures, and carried out by juries and judges, has
yielded more mercy than the Eighth Amendment can stand. The
implications of this approach are mildly ironical. . . .

Justice Blackmun dissenting:

. . . Cases such as these provide for me an excruciating agony of
the spirit. I yield to no one in the depth of my distaste, antipathy,
and, indeed, abhorrence, for the death penalty. . . . For me, it violates childhood's training and life's experiences, and is not
compatible with the philosophical convictions I have been able to
develop. It is antagonistic to any sense of "reverence for life." Were
I a legislator, I would vote against the death penalty for the policy
reasons argued by counsel for the respective petitioners and
expressed and adopted in the several opinions filed by the justices
who vote to reverse these convictions. . . .

I do not sit on these cases, however, as a legislator responsive, at
least in part, to the will of constituents. Our task here, as must so
frequently be emphasized and re-emphasized, is to pass upon the
constitutionality of legislation that has been enacted and that is

challenged. This is the sole task for judges. We should not allow our personal preferences as to the wisdom of legislative and congressional action, or our distaste for such action, to guide our judicial decision in cases such as these. The temptations to cross that policy line are very great. In fact, as today's decision reveals, they are almost irresistible....

Although personally I may rejoice at the court's result, I find it difficult to accept or to justify as a matter of history, of law, or of constitutional pronouncement. I fear the court has overstepped. It has sought and has achieved an end.

Justice Powell dissenting:

...I now return to the overriding question in these cases: whether this court, acting in conformity with the Constitution, can justify its judgment to abolish capital punishment as heretofore known in this country. It is important to keep in focus the enormity of the step undertaken by the court today. Not only does it invalidate hundreds of state and federal laws, it deprives those jurisdictions of the power to legislate with respect to capital punishment in the future, except in a manner consistent with the cloudily outlined views of those justices who do not purport to undertake total abolition. Nothing short of an amendment to the United States Constitution can reverse the court's judgment. Meanwhile, all flexibility is foreclosed. The normal democratic process, as well as the opportunities for the several states to respond to the will of their people expressed through ballot referenda (as in Massachusetts, Illinois, and Colorado), is now shut off.

The sobering disadvantage of constitutional adjudication of this magnitude is the universality and permanence of the judgment. The enduring merit of legislative action is its responsiveness to the democratic process, and to revision and change: mistaken judgments may be corrected and refinements perfected. In England and Canada, critical choices were made after studies canvassing all competing views, and in those countries revisions may be made in light of experience....

...This is a classic case for the exercise of our oftannounced allegiance to judicial restraint. I know of no case in which greater gravity and delicacy have attached to the duty that this court is called on to perform whenever legislation—state or federal—is challenged on constitutional grounds. It seems to me that the sweeping judicial action undertaken today reflects a basic lack of faith and confidence in the democratic process. Many may regret, as I do, the failure of some legislative bodies to address the capital punishment issue with greater frankness of effectiveness. Many might decry their failure either to abolish the penalty entirely or selectively, or to establish standards for its enforcement. But impatience with the slowness, and even the unresponsiveness, of legislatures is no justification for judicial intrusion upon their historic powers. . . .

Justice Rehnquist dissenting:

The court's judgment today strikes down a penalty that our nation's legislators have thought necessary since our country was founded. My brothers Douglas, Brennan and Marshall would at one fell swoop invalidate laws enacted by Congress and forty of the fifty state legislatures and would consign to the limbo of unconstitutionality under a single rubric penalties for offenses as varied and unique as murder, piracy, mutiny, highjacking and desertion in the face of the enemy. My brothers Stewart and White, asserting reliance on a more limited rationale—the reluctance of judges and juries actually to impose the death penalty in the majority of capital cases—join in the judgment in these cases. Whatever its precise rationale, today's holding necessarily brings into sharp relief the fundamental question of the role of judicial review in a democratic society. How can government by the elected representatives of the people coexist with the power of the federal judiciary, whose members are constitutionally insulated from responsiveness to the popular will, to declare invalid laws duly enacted by the popular branches of government?

The answer, of course, is found in Hamilton's *Federalist Paper No. 78* and in Chief Justice Marshall's classic opinion in *Marbury v. Madison*...(1803). An oft told story since then, it bears summarization once more. Sovereignty resides ultimately in the people as a whole, and by adopting through their states a written Constitution for the nation, and subsequently adding amendments to that instrument, they have both granted certain powers to the national government and denied other powers to the national and the state governments. Courts are exercising no more than the judicial function conferred upon them by Art. III of the Constitution when they assess, in a case before them, whether or not a particular legislative enactment is within the authority granted by the Constitution to the enacting body, and whether it runs afoul of some limitation placed by the Constitution on the authority of that body. For the theory is that the people themselves have spoken in the Constitution, and therefore its commands are superior to the commands of the legislature, which is merely an agent of the people.

The founding fathers thus wisely sought to have the best of both worlds, the undeniable benefits of both democratic self-government and individual rights protected against possible excesses of that form of government.

The courts in cases properly before them have been entrusted under the Constitution with the last word, short of constitutional amendment, as to whether a law passed by the legislature conforms to the Constitution. But just because courts in general, and this court in particular, do have the last word, the admonition of Mr. Justice [Harlan Fiske] Stone in *United States v. Butler* [1936] must be constantly borne in mind: "[W]hile unconstitutional exercise of power by the executive and legislative branches of the government is subject to judicial restraint, the only check upon our own exercise of power is our own sense of self-restraint." . . .

Rigorous attention to the limits of this court's authority is likewise enjoined because of the natural desire that beguiles judges along with other human beings into imposing their own views of goodness, truth and justice upon others. Judges differ only in that they have the power, if not the authority, to enforce their desires. This is doubtless why nearly two centuries of judicial precedent from this court counsel the sparing use of that power. The most expansive reading of the leading constitutional cases does not remotely suggest that this court has been granted a roving commission, either by the founding fathers or by the framers of the Fourteenth Amendment, to strike down laws that are based upon notions of policy or morality suddenly found unacceptable by a majority of this court. . . .

If there can be said to be one dominant theme in the Constitution, perhaps more fully articulated in *The Federalist Papers* than in the instrument itself, it is the notion of checks and balances. The framers were well aware of the natural desire of office holders as well as others to seek to expand the scope and authority of their particular office at the expense of others. They sought to provide against success in such efforts by erecting adequate checks and balances in the form of grants of authority to each branch of the government in order to counteract and prevent usurpation on the part of the others.

This philosophy of the framers is best described by . . . James Madison, in *Federalist No. 51*: "In framing a government which is to be administered by men over men, the great difficulty lies in this: you must first enable the government to control the governed; and in the next place oblige it to control itself."

Madison's observation applies to the Judicial Branch with at least as much force as to the Legislative and Executive Branches. While overreaching by the Legislative and Executive Branches may result in the sacrifice of individual protections that the Constitution was designed to secure against action of the state, judicial overreaching may result in sacrifice of the equally important right of the people to govern themselves. The due process and equal protection clauses of the 14th Amendment were "never intended to destroy the states' power to govern themselves." Black, J., in *Oregon v. Mitchell* ...(1970).

The very nature of judicial review, as pointed out by Justice Stone in his dissent in the *Butler* case, makes the courts the least subject to Madisonian check in the event that they shall, for the best of motives, expand judicial authority beyond the limits contemplated by the framers. It is for this reason that judicial self-restraint is surely an implied, if not an expressed, condition of the grant of authority of judicial review. The court's holding these cases has been reached, I believe, in complete disregard of that implied condition.

Gregg v. Georgia (428 U.S. 153, July 2, 1976)

Judgment of the Court, and opinion of Justices Stewart, Powell and Stevens announced by Justice Stewart:

The issue in this case is whether the imposition of the sentence of death for the crime of murder under the law of Georgia violates the Eighth and Fourteenth Amendments.

The petitioner, Troy Gregg, was charged with committing armed robbery and murder. In accordance with Georgia procedure in capital cases, the trial was in two stages, a guilt stage and a sentencing stage. The evidence at the guilt trial established that on Nov. 21, 1973, the petitioner and a traveling companion, Floyd Allen, while hitchhiking north in Florida were picked up by Fred Simmons and Bob Moore. Their car broke down, but they continued north after Simmons purchased another vehicle with some of the cash he was carrying. While still in Florida, they picked up another hitchhiker, Dennis Weaver, who rode with them to Atlanta, where he was let out about 11 p.m. A short time later the four men interrupted their journey for a rest stop along the highway. The next morning the bodies of Simmons and Moore were discovered in a ditch nearby.

On Nov. 23, after reading about the shootings in an Atlanta newspaper, Weaver communicated with the Gwinnett County police and related information concerning the journey with the victims, including a description of the car. The next afternoon, the petitioner and Allen, while in Simmons' car, were arrested in Asheville, N.C. In the search incident to the arrest a .25-caliber pistol, later shown to be that used to kill Simmons and Moore, was found in the petitioner's pocket. After receiving the warnings required by *Miranda v. Arizona...*(1966) and signing a written waiver of his rights, the petitioner signed a statement in which he admitted shooting, then robbing Simmons and Moore. He justified the slayings on grounds of self-defense. The next day, while being transferred to Lawrenceville, Ga., the petitioner and Allen were taken to the scene of the shootings. Upon arriving there, Allen recounted the events leading to the slayings. His version of these events was as follows: After Simmons and Moore left the car, the petitioner stated that he intended to rob them. The petitioner then took his pistol in hand and positioned himself on the car to improve his aim. As Simmons and Moore came up an embankment toward the car, the petitioner fired three shots and the two men fell near a ditch. The petitioner, at close range, then fired a shot into the head of each. He robbed them of valuables and drove away with Allen.

A medical examiner testified that Simmons died from a bullet wound in the eye and that Moore died from bullet wounds in the cheek and in the back of the head.... Although Allen did not testify, a police detective recounted the substance of Allen's statements about the slayings and indicated that directly after Allen had made these statements the petitioner had admitted that Allen's account was accurate. The petitioner testified in his own defense. He confirmed that Allen had made the statements described by the detective, but denied their truth or ever having admitted to their accuracy. He indicated that he had shot Simmons and Moore because of fear and in self-defense, testifying they had attacked Allen and him, one wielding a pipe and the other a knife.

The trial judge submitted the murder charges to the jury on both felony-murder and nonfelony-murder theories. He also instructed on the issue of self-defense but declined to instruct on manslaughter. He submitted the robbery case to the jury on both an armed-robbery theory and on the lesser included offense of robbery by intimidation. The jury found the petitioner guilty of two counts of armed robbery and two counts of murder.

At the penalty stage, which took place before the same jury, neither the prosecutor nor the petitioner's lawyer offered any additional evidence. Both counsel, however, made lengthy arguments dealing generally with the propriety of capital punishment under the circumstances and with the weight of the evidence of guilt. The trial judge instructed the jury that it could recommend either a death sentence or a life prison sentence on each count. The judge further charged the jury that in determining what sentence was appropriate the jury was free to consider the facts and circumstances, if any, presented by the parties in mitigation or aggravation.

Finally, the judge instructed the jury that it "would not be authorized to consider [imposing] the penalty of death" unless it first found beyond a reasonable doubt one of these aggravating circumstances:

> "One—That the offense of murder was committed while the offender was engaged in the commission of two other capital felonies, to wit the armed robbery of [Simmons and Moore].
> "Two—That the offender committed the offense of murder for the purpose of receiving money and the automobile described in the indictment.
> "Three—The offense of murder was outrageously and wantonly vile, horrible and inhuman, and in that they [sic] involved the depravity of [the] mind of the defendant."

Finding the first and second of these circumstances, the jury returned verdicts of death on each count.

The Supreme Court of Georgia affirmed the convictions and the imposition of the death sentences for murder. . . . After reviewing the trial transcript and the record, including the evidence, and comparing the evidence and sentence in similar cases in accordance with the requirements of Georgia law, the court concluded that, considering the nature of the crime and the defendant, the sentences of death had not resulted from prejudice or any other arbitrary factor and were not excessive or disproportionate to the penalty applied in similar cases. The death sentences imposed for armed robbery, however, were vacated on the grounds that the death penalty had rarely been imposed in Georgia for that offense and that the jury improperly considered the murders as aggravating circumstances for the robberies after having considered the armed robberies as aggravating circumstances for the murders. . . .

We granted the petitioner's application for a writ of *certiorari* limited to his challenge to the imposition of the death sentences in this case as "cruel and unusual" punishment in violation of the Eighth and the Fourteenth Amendments. . . .

We address initially the basic contention that the punishment of death for the crime of murder is, under all circumstances, "cruel and unusual" in violation of the Eighth and Fourteenth Amendments of the Constitution. . . .

The Court on a number of occasions has both assumed and asserted the constitutionality of capital punishment. In several cases that assumption provided a necessary foundation for the decision, as the Court was asked to decide whether a particular method of carrying out a capital sentence would be allowed to stand under the Eighth Amendment. But until *Furman v. Georgia* . . ., the Court never confronted squarely the fundamental claim that the punishment of death always, regardless of the enormity of the offense or the procedure followed in imposing the sentence, is cruel and unusual punishment in violation of the Constitution. Although this issue was presented and addressed in *Furman*, it was not resolved by the Court. Four justices would have held that capital punishment is not unconstitutional *per se*; two justices would have reached the opposite conclusion; and three justices, while agreeing that the statutes then before the Court were invalid as applied, left open the question whether such punishment may ever be imposed. We now hold that the punishment of death does not invariably violate the Constitution. . . .

The imposition of the death penalty for the crime of murder has a long history of acceptance both in the United States and in England. The common-law rule imposed a mandatory death sentence on all convicted murderers. . . . And the penalty continued to be used into the Twentieth century by most American states, although the breadth of the common-law rule was diminished, initially by narrowing the class of murders to be punished by death and subsequently by widespread adoption of laws expressly granting juries the discretion to recommend mercy. . . .

It is apparent from the text of the Constitution itself that the existence of capital punishment was accepted by the Framers. At the time the Eighth Amendment was ratified, capital punishment was a common sanction in every state. Indeed, the First Congress of the United States enacted legislation providing death as the penalty for specified crimes.... The Fifth Amendment, adopted at the same time as the Eighth, contemplated the continued existence of the capital sanction by imposing certain limits on the prosecution of capital cases:

> "No person shall be held to answer for a capital, or otherwise infamous crime, unless on a presentment or indictment of a Grand Jury...; nor shall any person be subject for the same offense to be twice put in jeopardy of life or limb;...nor be deprived of life, liberty, or property, without due process of law...."

And the Fourteenth Amendment, adopted over three-quarters of a century later, similarly contemplates the existence of the capital sanction in providing that no state shall deprive any person of "life, liberty, or property" without due process of law.

For nearly two centuries, this Court, repeatedly and often expressly, had recognized that capital punishment is not invalid *per se*. In *Wilkerson* v. *Utah*..., where the Court found no constitutional violation in inflicting death by public shooting, it said:

> "Cruel and unusual punishments are forbidden by the Constitution, but the authorities referred to are quite sufficient to show that the punishment of shooting as a mode of executing the death penalty for the crime of murder in the first degree is not included in that category, within the meaning of the Eighth Amendement."

Rejecting the contention that death by electrocution was "cruel and unusual," the Court in *In re Kemmler*...reiterated:

> "(T)he punishment of death is not cruel, within the meaning of that word as used in the Constitution. It implies there something inhuman and barbarous, something more than the mere extinguishment of life."

Again, in *Louisiana ex rel. Francis* v. *Resweber*..., the Court remarked: "The cruelty against which the Constitution protects a convicted man is cruelty inherent in the method of punishment, not the necessary suffering involved in any method employed to extinguish life humanely." And in *Trop* v. *Dulles*..., Mr. Chief Justice (Earl) Warren, for himself and three other justices, wrote:

> "Whatever the arguments may be against capital punishment, both on moral grounds and in terms of accomplishing the

purposes of punishment...the death penalty has been
employed throughout our history, and, in a day when it is still
widely accepted, it cannot be said to violate the constitutional
concept of cruelty.''

Four years ago, the petitioners in *Furman* and its companion cases
predicated their argument primarily upon the asserted proposition
that standards of decency had evolved to the point where capital
punishment no longer could be tolerated. The petitioners in those
cases said, in effect, that the evolutionary process had come to an
end, and that standards of decency required that the Eighth
Amendment be construed finally as prohibiting capital punishment
for any crime regardless of its depravity and impact on society. This
view was accepted by two justices. Three other justices were
unwilling to go so far; focusing on the procedures by which
convicted defendants were selected for the death penalty rather than
on the actual punishment inflicted, they joined in the conclusion that
the statutes before the Court were constitutionally invalid.

The petitioners in the capital cases before the Court today renew
the "standards of decency" argument, but developments during the
four years since *Furman* have undercut substantially the assumptions upon which their argument rested. Despite the continuing
debate, dating back to the Nineteenth Century, over the morality
and utility of capital punishment, it is now evident that a large
proportion of American society continues to regard it as an
appropriate and necessary criminal sanction.

The most marked indication of society's endorsement of the death
penalty for murder is the legislative response to *Furman*. The legislatures of at least 35 states have enacted new statutes that provide
for the death penalty for at least some crimes that result in the death
of another person. And the Congress of the United States, in 1974,
enacted a statute providing the death penalty for aircraft piracy that
results in death. These recently adopted statutes have attempted to
address the concerns expressed by the Court in *Furman* primarily (i)
by specifying the factors to be weighed and the procedures to be
followed in deciding when to impose a capital sentence, or (ii) by
making the death penalty mandatory for specified crimes. But all of
the post-*Furman* statutes make clear that capital punishment itself
has not been rejected by the elected representatives of the people.

In the only statewide referendum occurring since *Furman* and
brought to our attention, the people of California adopted a
constitutional amendment that authorized capital punishment, in

effect negating a prior ruling by the Supreme Court of California... that the death penalty violated the California Constitution.

The jury also is a significant and reliable objective index of contemporary values because it is so directly involved.... The Court has said that "one of the most important functions any jury can perform in making...a selection [between life imprisonment and death for a defendant convicted in a capital case] is to maintain a link between contemporary community values and the penal system." *Witherspoon* v. *Illinois*...(1968). It may be true that evolving standards have influenced juries in recent decades to be more discriminating in imposing the sentence of death. But the relative infrequency of jury verdicts imposing the death sentence does not indicate rejection of capital punishment *per se*. Rather, the reluctance of juries in many cases to impose the sentence may well reflect the humane feeling that this most irrevocable of sanctions should be reserved for a small of number of extreme cases.... Indeed, the actions of juries in many states since *Furman* is fully compatible with the legislative judgments, reflected in the new statutes, as to the continued utility and necessity of capital punishment in appropriate cases. At the close of 1974 at least 254 persons had been sentenced to death since *Furman*, and by the end of March 1976, more than 460 persons were subject to death sentences.

As we have seen, however, the Eighth Amendment demands more than that a challenged punishment be acceptable to contemporary society. The Court also must ask whether it comports with the basic concept of human dignity at the core of the Amendment.... Although we cannot "invalidate a category of penalties because we deem less severe penalties adequate to serve the ends of penology," *Furman* v. *Georgia*...(Powell, J., dissenting), the sanction imposed cannot be so totally without penological justification that it results in the gratuitous infliction of suffering....

The death penalty is said to serve two principal social purposes: retribution and deterrence of capital crimes by prospective offenders.

In part, capital punishment is an expression of society's moral outrage at particularly offensive conduct. This function may be unappealing to many, but it is essential in an ordered society that asks its citizens to rely on legal processes rather than self-help to vindicate their wrongs.

"The instinct for retribution is part of the nature of man, and channeling that instinct in the administration of criminal justice serves an important purpose in promoting the stability of a society governed by law. When people begin to believe that organized society is unwilling or unable to impose upon criminal offenders the punishment they 'deserve,' then there are sown the seeds of anarchy—of self-help, vigilante justice, and lynch law." *Furman* v. *Georgia*...(Stewart, J., concurring). "Retribution is no longer the dominant objective of the criminal law," *Williams* v. *New York*...(1949), but neither is it a forbidden objective nor one inconsistent with our respect for the dignity of men. Indeed, the decision that capital punishment may be the appropriate sanction in extreme cases is an expression of the community's belief that certain crimes are themselves so grievous an affront to humanity that the only adequate response may be the penalty of death.

Statistical attempts to evaluate the worth of the death penalty as a deterrent to crimes by potential offenders have occasioned a great deal of debate. The results simply have been inconclusive. As one opponent of capital punishment has said:

"(A)fter all possible inquiry, including the probing of all possible methods of inquiry, we do not know, and for systematic and easily visible reasons cannot know, what the truth about this 'deterrent' effect may be....

"The inescapable flaw is...that social conditions in any state are not constant through time, and that social conditions are not the same in any two states. If an effect were observed (and the observed effects, one way or another, are not large) then one could not at all tell whether any of this effect is attributable to the presence or absence of capital punishment. A 'scientific'— that is to say, a soundly based—conclusion is simply impossible, and no methodological path out of this tangle suggests itself." C. Black, *Capital Punishment: the Inevitability of Caprice and Mistake* 25-26 (1974).

Although some of the studies suggest that the death penalty may not function as a significantly greater deterrent than lesser penalties, there is no convincing empirical evidence either supporting or refuting this view. We may nevertheless assume safely that there are murderers, such as those who act in passion, for whom the threat of death has little or no deterrent effect. But for many others, the death penalty undoubtedly is a significant deterrent. There are carefully contemplated murders, such as murder for hire, where the possible penalty of death may well enter into the cold calculus that precedes the decision to act. And there are some categories of murder, such as murder by a life prisoner, where other sanctions may not be adequate.

The value of capital punishment as a deterrent of crime is a complex factual issue the resolution of which properly rests with the legislatures, which can evaluate the results of statistical studies in terms of their own local conditions and with a flexibility of approach that is not available to the courts.... Indeed, many of the post-*Furman* statutes reflect just such a responsible effort to define those crimes and those criminals for which capital punishment is not probably an effective deterrent.

In sum, we cannot say that the judgment of the Georgia legislature that capital punishment may be necessary in some cases is clearly wrong. Considerations of federalism, as well as respect for the ability of a legislature to evaluate, in terms of its particular state, the moral consensus concerning the death penalty and its social utility as a sanction, require us to conclude, in the absence of more convincing evidence, that the infliction of death as a punishment for murder is not without justification and thus is not unconstitutionally severe.

Finally, we must consider whether the punishment of death is disproportionate in relation to the crime for which it is imposed. There is no question that death as a punishment is unique in its severity and irrevocability.... When a defendant's life is at stake, the Court has been particularly sensitive to insure that every safeguard is observed.... But we are concerned here only with the imposition of capital punishment for the crime of murder, and when a life has been taken deliberately by the offender, we cannot say that the punishment is invariably disproportionate to the crime. It is an extreme sanction, suitable to the most extreme of crimes.

We hold that the death penalty is not a form of punishment that may never be imposed, regardless of the circumstances of the offense, regardless of the character of the offender, and regardless of the procedure followed in reaching the decision to impose it....

We now turn to consideration of the constitutionality of Georgia's capital-sentencing procedures. In the wake of *Furman*, Georgia amended its capital punishment statute, but chose not to narrow the scope of its murder provisions.... Thus, now as before *Furman*, in

Georgia "[a] person commits murder when he unlawfully and with malice aforethought, either express or implied, causes the death of another human being.". . . All persons convicted of murder "shall be punished by death or by imprisonment for life.". . .

Georgia did act, however, to narrow the class of murderers subject to capital punishment by specifying ten statutory aggravating circumstances, one of which must be found by the jury to exist beyond a resonable doubt before a death sentence can ever be imposed. In addition, the jury is authorized to consider any other appropriate aggravating or mitigating circumstances. . . . The jury is not required to find any mitigating circumstance in order to make a recommendation of mercy that is binding on the trial court, . . . but it must find a *statutory* aggravating circumstance before recommending a sentence of death.

These procedures require the jury to consider the circumstances of the crime and the criminal before it recommends sentence. No longer can a Georgia jury do as *Furman's* jury did: reach a finding of the defendant's guilt and then, without guidance or direction, decide whether he should live or die. Instead, the jury's attention is directed to the specific circumstances of the crime: Was it committed in the course of another capital felony? Was it committed for money? Was it committed upon a peace officer or judicial officer? Was it committed in a particularly heinous way or in a manner that endangered the lives of many persons? In addition, the jury's attention is focused on the characteristics of the person who committed the crime: Does he have a record of prior convictions for capital offenses? Are there any special facts about this defendant that mitigate against imposing capital punishment (*e. g.*, his youth, the extent of his cooperation with the police, his emotional state at the time of the crime). As a result, while some jury discretion still exists "the discretion to be exercised is controlled by clear and objective standards so as to produce non-discriminatory application." *Coley* v. *State* [Georgia Supreme Court, 1974]. . . .

As an important additional safeguard against arbitrariness and caprice, the Georgia statutory scheme provides for automatic appeal of all death sentences to the state's Supreme Court. That court is required by statute to review each sentence of death and determine whether it was imposed under the influence of passion or prejudice, whether the evidence supports the jury's finding of a statutory aggravating circumstance, and whether the sentence is disproportionate compared to those sentences imposed in similar cases. . . .

In short, Georgia's new sentencing procedures require as a prerequisite to the imposition of the death penalty, specific jury findings as to the circumstances of the crime or the character of the defendant. Moreover to guard further against a situation comparable to that presented in Furman, the Supreme Court of Georgia compares each death sentence with the sentences imposed on similarly situated defendants to ensure that the sentence of death in a particular case is not disproportionate. On their face these procedures seem to satisfy the concerns of *Furman*. No longer should there be "no meaningful basis for distinguishing the few cases in which [the death penalty] is imposed from the many cases in which it is not.". . . [*Furman*] (White, J., concurring).

The petitioner contends, however, that the changes in the Georgia sentencing procedures are only cosmetic, that the arbitrariness and capriciousness condemned by *Furman* continue to exist in Georgia—both in traditional practices that still remain and in the new sentencing procedures adopted in response to *Furman*.

First, the petitioner focuses on the opportunities for discretionary action that are inherent in the processing of any murder case under Georgia law. He notes that the state prosecutor has unfettered authority to select those persons whom he wishes to prosecute for a capital offense and to plea bargain with them. Further, at the trial the jury may choose to convict a defendant of a lesser included offense rather than find him guilty of a crime punishable by death, even if the evidence would support a capital verdict. And finally, a defendant who is convicted and sentenced to die may have his sentence commuted by the governor of the state and the Georgia Board of Pardons & Paroles.

The existence of these discretionary stages is not determinative of the issues before us. At each of these stages an actor in the criminal justice system makes a decision which may remove a defendant from consideration as a candidate for the death penalty. *Furman*, in contrast, dealt with the decision to impose the death sentence on a specific individual who had been convicted of a capital offense. Nothing in any of our cases suggests that the decision to afford an individual defendant mercy violates the Constitution. *Furman* held only that, in order to minimize the risk that the death penalty would be imposed on a capriciously selected group of offenders, the decision to impose it had to be guided by standards so that the sentencing authority would focus on the particularized circumstances of the crime and the defendant.

The petitioner further contends that the capital-sentencing procedures adopted by Georgia in response to *Furman* do not eliminate the dangers of arbitrariness and caprice in jury sentencing that were held in *Furman* to be violative of the eighth and Fourteenth Amendments. He claims that the statute is so broad and vague as to leave juries free to act as arbitrarily and capriciously as they wish in deciding whether to impose the death penalty. While there is no claim that the jury in this case relied upon a vague or overbroad provision to establish the existence of a statutory aggravating circumstance, the petitioner looks to the sentencing system as a whole (as the Court did in *Furman* and we do today) and argues that it fails to reduce sufficiently the risk of arbitrary infliction of death sentences. Specifically, Gregg urges that the statutory aggravating circumstances are too broad and too vague, that the sentencing procedure allows for arbitrary grants of mercy, and that the scope of the evidence and argument that can be considered at the presentence hearing is too wide. . . .

The petitioner next argues that the requirements of *Furman* are not met here because the jury has the power to decline to impose the death penalty even if it finds that one or more statutory aggravating circumstances are present in the case. This contention misinterprets *Furman*. . . . Moreover, it ignores the role of the Supreme Court of Georgia which reviews each death sentence to determine whether it is proportional to other sentences imposed for similar crimes. Since the proportionality requirement on review is intended to prevent caprice in the decision to inflict the penalty, the isolated decision of a jury to afford mercy does not render unconstitutional death sentences imposed on defendants who were sentenced under a system that does not create a substantial risk of arbitrariness or caprice.

The petitioner objects, finally, to the wide scope of evidence and argument allowed at presentence hearings. We think that the Georgia court wisely has chosen not to impose unnecessary restrictions on the evidence that can be offered at such a hearing and to approve open and far-ranging argument. . . . So long as the evidence introduced and the arguments made at the presentence hearing do not prejudice a defendant, it is preferable not to impose restrictions. We think it desirable for the jury to have as much information before it as possible when it makes the sentencing decision. . . .

Finally, the Georgia statute has an additional provision designed to assure that the death penalty will not be imposed on a capriciously selected group of convicted defendants. The new sentencing procedures require that the State Supreme Court review every death sentence to determine whether it was imposed under the influence of passion, prejudice, or any other arbitrary factor, whether the evidence supports the findings of a statutory aggravating circumstance, and "[w]hether the sentence of death is excessive or disproportionate to the penalty imposed in similar cases, considering both the crime and the defendant.". . . In performing its sentence-review function, the Georgia court has held that "if the death penalty is only rarely imposed for an act or it is substantially out of line with sentences imposed for other acts it will be set aside as excessive.". . . The court on another occasion stated that "we view it to be our duty under the similarity standard to assure that no death sentence is affirmed unless in similar cases throughout the state the death penalty has been imposed generally. . . ."

It is apparent that the Supreme Court of Georgia has taken its review responsibilities seriously. In *Coley*, it held that "[t]he prior cases indicate that the past practice among juries faced with similar factual situations and like aggravating circumstances has been to impose only the sentence of life imprisonment for the offense of rape, rather than death.". . . It thereupon reduced Coley's sentence from death to life imprisonment. Similarly, although armed robbery is a capital offense under Georgia law, . . . the Georgia court concluded that the death sentences imposed in this case for that crime were "unusual in that they are rarely imposed for [armed robbery]. Thus, under the test provided by statute, . . . they must be considered to be excessive or disproportionate to the penalties imposed in similar cases.". . . The court therefore vacated Gregg's death sentences for armed robbery and has followed a similar course in every other armed robbery death penalty case to come before it. . . .

The provision for appellate review in the Georgia capital-sentencing system serves as a check against the random or arbitrary imposition of the death penalty. In particular, the proportionality review substantially eliminates the possibility that a person will be sentenced to die by the action of an aberrant jury. If a time comes when juries generally do not impose the death sentence in a certain kind of murder case, the appellate review procedures assure that no defendant convicted under such circumstances will suffer a sentence of death.

The basic concern of *Furman* centered on those defendants who were being condemned to death capriciously and arbitrarily. Under the procedures before the Court in that case, sentencing authorities were not directed to give attention to the nature or circumstances of the crime committed or to the character or record of the defendant. Left unguided, juries imposed the death sentence in a way that could only be called freakish. The new Georgia sentencing procedures, by contrast, focus the jury's attention on the particularized characteristics of the individual defendant. While the jury is permitted to consider any aggravating or mitigating circumstances, it must find and identify at least one statutory aggravating factor before it may impose a penalty of death. In this way the jury's discretion is channeled. No longer can a jury wantonly and freakishly impose the death sentence; it is always circumscribed by the legislative guidelines. In addition, the review function of the Supreme Court of Georgia affords additional assurance that the concerns that prompted our decision in *Furman* are not present to any significant degree in the Georgia procedure applied here.

For the reasons expressed in this opinion, we hold that the statutory system under which Gregg was sentenced to death does not violate the Constitution. Accordingly, the judgment of the Georgia Supreme Court is affirmed.

Justice Brennan dissenting:

The cruel and unusual punishment clause "must draw its meaning from the evolving standards of decency that mark the progress of a maturing society" [*Trop* v. *Dulles*, 1958]. The opinions of Mr. Justice Stewart, Mr. Justice Powell, and Mr. Justice Stevens today hold that "evolving standards of decency" require focus not on the essence of the death penalty itself but primarily upon the procedures employed by the state to single out persons to suffer the penalty of death. Those opinions hold further that, so viewed, the clause invalidates the mandatory infliction of the death penalty but not its infliction under sentencing procedures that Mr. Justice Stewart, Mr. Justice Powell, and Mr. Justice Stevens conclude adequately safeguard against the risk that the death penalty was imposed in an arbitrary and capricious manner.

In *Furman* v. *Georgia*. . . (concurring), I read "evolving standards of decency" as requiring focus upon the essence of the death penalty itself and not primarily or solely upon the procedures under which the determination to inflict the penalty upon a particular person was made. . . . That continues to be my view. For the clause forbidding cruel and unusual punishments under our constitutional system of government embodies in unique degree moral principles restraining the punishments that our civilized society may impose on those persons who transgress its laws. . . .

This Court inescapably has the duty, as the ultimate arbiter of the meaning of our Constitution, to say whether, when individuals condemned to death stand before our bar, "moral concepts" require us to hold that the law has progressed to the point where we should declare that the punishment of death, like punishments on the rack, the screw, and the wheel, is no longer morally tolerable in our civilized sociey. My opinion in *Furman* v. *Georgia* concluded that our civilization and the law had progressed to this point and that therefore the punishment of death, for whatever crime and under all circumstances, is "cruel and unusual" in violation of the Eighth and Fourteenth Amendments of the Constitution. I shall not again canvass the reasons that led to that conclusion. I emphasize only that foremost among the "moral concepts" recognized in our cases and inherent in the clause is the primary moral principle that the state, even as it punishes, must treat its citizens in a manner consistent with their intrinsic worth as human beings—a punishment must not be so severe as to be degrading to human dignity. A judicial determination whether the punishment of death comports with human dignity is therefore not only permitted but compelled by the clause. . . .

I do not understand that the Court disagrees that "[i]n comparison to all other punishments today. . .the deliberate extinguishment of human life by the state is uniquely degrading to human dignity.". . .For three of my brethren hold today that mandatory infliction of the death penalty constitutes the penalty cruel and unusual punishment. I perceive no principled basis for this limiation. Death for whatever crime and under all circumstances "is truly an awesome punishment. The calculated killing of a human being by the state involves, by its very nature, a denial of the executed person's humanity. . . . An executed person has indeed 'lost the right to have rights.' ". . .Death is not only an unusually severe punishment, unusual in its pain, in its finality, and in its enormity, but it serves no penal purpose more effectively than a less severe punishment; therefore the principle inherent in the clause that prohibits pointless infliction of excessive punishment when less severe punishment can adequately achieve the same purposes invalidates the punishment....

The fatal constitutional infirmity in the punishment of death is that it treats "members of the human race as nonhumans, as objects to be toyed with and discarded. [It is] thus inconsistent with the fundamental premise of the clause that even the vilest criminal remains a human being possessed of common human dignity."...

As such it is a penalty that "subjects the individual to a fate forbidden by the principle of civilized treatment guaranteed by the [clause]." I therefore would hold, on that ground alone, that death is today a cruel and unusual punishment prohibited by the clause. "Justice of this kind is obivously no less shocking than the crime itself, and the new 'official' murder, far from offering redress for the offense committed against society, adds instead a second defilement to the first."...

Justice Marshall dissenting:

In *Furman* v. *Georgia*,... I set forth at some length my views on the basic issue presented to the Court in these cases. The death penalty, I concluded, is a cruel and unusual punishment prohibited by the Eighth and Fourteenth Amendments. That continues to be my view....

In *Furman* I concluded that the death penalty is constitutionally invalid for two reasons. First, the death penalty is excessive.... And second, the American people, fully informed as to the purposes of the death penalty and its liabilities, would in my view reject it as morally unacceptable....

Since the decision in *Furman*, the legislatures of 35 states have enacted new statutes authorizing the imposition of the death sentence for certain crimes, and Congress has enacted a law providing the death penalth for air piracy resulting in death. ... I would be less than candid if I did not acknowledge that these developments have a signficant bearing on a realistic assement of the moral acceptability of the death penalty to the American people. But if the constitutionality of the death penalty turns, as I have urged, on the opinion of an *informed* citizenry, then even the enactment of new death statutes cannot be viewed as conclusive. In *Furman*, I observed that American people are largely unaware of the information critical to a judgment on the morality of the death penalty, and concluded that if they were better informed they would consider it shocking, unjust, and unacceptable.... A recent study, conducted after the enactment of the post-*Furman* statutes, has confirmed that the American people know little about the death penalty, and that the opinions of an informed public would differ significantly from those of a public unaware of the consequences and effects of the death penalty.*

Even assuming, however, that the post-*Furman* enactment of statutes authorizing the death penalty renders the prediction of the views of an informed citizenry an uncertain basis for a constitutional decision, the enactment of those statutes has no bearing whatsoever on the conclusion that the death penalty is unconstitutional because it is excessive. An excessive penalty is invalid under the cruel and unusual punishments clause "even though popular sentiment may favor" it. [*Furman v. North Carolina*].... The inquiry here, then, is simply whether the death penalty is necessary to accomplish the legitimate legislative purposes in punishment, or whether a less severe penalty—life imprisonment—would do as well....

The two purposes that sustain the death penalty as nonexcessive in the Court's view are general deterrence and retribution. In *Furman*, I canvassed the relevant data on the deterrent effect of capital punishment. ... The state of knowledge at that point, after literally centuries of debate, was summarized as follows by a United Nations Committee:

> "It is generally agreed between the retentionists and abolitionists, whatever their opinions about the validity of comparative studies of deterrence, that the data which now exist show no correlation between the existence of capital punishment and lower rates of capital crime."

The available evidence, I concluded in *Furman*, was convincing that "capital punishment is not necessary as a deterrent to crime in our society."...

The Solicitor General in his *amicus* brief in these cases relies heavily on a study by Isaac Ehrlich,† reported a year after *Furman*,

---

*I. Ehrlich, *The Deterrent Effect of Capital Punishment: A Question of Life and Death* (Working Paper No. 18, National Bureau of Economic Research, Nov. 1973); Ehrlich, "The Deterrent Effect of Capital Punishment: A Question of Life and Death," 65 *Am. Econ. Rev.* 397 (June 1975).

†Ehrlich, *op. cit.*

to support the contention that the death penalty does deter murder. Since the Ehrlich study was not available at the time of *Furman* and since it is the first scientific study to suggest that the death penalty may have a deterrent effect, I will briefly consider its import.

The Ehrlich study focused on the relationship in the nation as a whole between the homicide rate and "execution risk"—the fraction of persons convicted of murder who were actually executed. Comparing the differences in homicide rate and execution risk for the years 1933 to 1969, Ehrlich found that increases in execution risk were associated with increases in the homicide rate. But when he employed the statistical technique of multiple regression analysis to control for the influence of other variables posited to have an impact on the homicide rate, Ehrlich found a negative correlation between changes in the homicide rate and changes in execution risk. His tentative conclusion was that for the period from 1933 to 1967 each additional execution in the United States might have saved eight lives.

The methods and conclusions of the Ehrlich study have been severely criticized on a number of grounds. It has been suggested, for example, that the study is defective because it compares execution and homicide rates on a nationwide, rather than a state-by-state, basis. The aggregation of data from all states—including those that have abolished the death penalty—obscures the relationship between murder and execution rates. Under Ehrlich's methodology, a decrease in the execution risk in one state combined with an increase in the murder rate in another state would, all other things being equal, suggest a deterrent effect that quite obviously would not exist. Indeed, a deterrent effect would be suggested if, once again all other things being equal, one state abolished the death penalty and experienced no change in the murder rate, while another State experienced an increase in the murder rate.

The most compelling criticism of the Ehrlich study is that its conclusions are extremely sensitive to the choice of the time period included in the regression analysis. Analysis of Ehrlich's data reveals that all empirical support for the deterrent effect of capital punishment disappears when the five most recent years are removed from his time series—that is to say, whether a decrease in the execution risk corresponds to an increase or a decrease in the murder rate depends on the ending point of the sample period. This finding has cast severe doubts on the reliability of Ehrlich's tentative conclusions. Indeed, a recent regression study, based on Ehrlich's theoretical model but using cross-section state data for the years

1950 and 1960, found no support for the conclusion that executions act as a deterrent.

The Ehrlich study, in short, is of little, if any, assistance in assessing the deterrent impact of the death penalty. . . . The evidence I reviewed in *Furman* remains convincing, in my view, that "capital punishment is not necessary as a deterrent to crime in our society.". . . The justification for the death penalty must be found elsewhere.

The other principal purpose said to be served by the death penalty is retribution. The notion that retribution can serve as a moral justification for the sanction of death. . . [is a] notion that I find to be the most disturbing aspect of today's unfortunate decisions.

The concept of retribution is a multifaceted one, and any discussion of its role in the criminal law must be undertaken with caution. On one level, it can be said that the notion of retribution or reprobation is the basis of our insistence that only those who have broken the law be punished, and in this sense the notion is quite obviously central to a just system of criminal sanctions. But our recognition that retribution plays a crucial role in determining who may be punished by no means requires approval of retribution as a general justification for punishment. It is the question whether retribution can provide a moral justification for punishment—in particular, capital punishment—that we must consider.

My Brothers Stewart, Powell, and Stevens offer the following explanation of the retributive justification for capital punishment:

> " 'The instinct for retribution is part of the nature of man, and channeling that instinct in the administration of criminal justice serves an important purpose in promoting the stability of a society governed by law. When people begin to believe that organized society is unwilling or unable to impose upon criminal offenders the punishment they 'deserve,' then there are sown the seeds of anarchy—of self-help, vigilante justice, and lynch law.' " . . . [Q]uoting from *Furman v. Georgia.* . . .

This statement is wholly inadequate to justify the death penalty. As my Brother Brennan stated in *Furman*, "[t]here is no evidence whatever that utilization of imprisonment rather than death encourages private blood feuds and other disorders.". . . It simply defies belief to suggest that the death penalty is necessary to prevent the American people from taking the law into their own hands.

In a related vein, it may be suggested that the expression of moral outrage through the imposition of the death penalty serves to reinforce basic moral values—that it marks some crimes as particularly offensive and therefore to be avoided. The argument is akin to a deterrence argument, but differs in that it contemplates the individual's shrinking from antisocial conduct, not because he fears punishment, but because he has been told in the strongest possible way that the conduct is wrong. This contention, like the previous one, provides no support for the death penalty. It is inconceivable that any individual concerned about conforming his conduct to what society says is "right" would fail to realize that murder is "wrong" if the penalty were simply life imprisonment.

The foregoing contentions—that society's expression of moral outrage through the imposition of the death penalty pre-empts the citizenry from taking the law into its own hands and reinforces moral values—are not retributive in the purest sense. They are essentially utilitarian in that they portray the death penalty as valuable because of its beneficial results. These justifications for the death penalty are inadequate because the penalty is, quite clearly I think, not necessary to the accomplishment of those results....

The death penalty, unnecessary to promote the goal of deterrence or to further any legitimate notion of retribution, is an excessive penalty forbidden by the Eighth and Fourteenth Amendments. I respectfully dissent from the Court's judgment upholding the sentences of death imposed upon the petitioners in these cases.

Woodson v. North Carolina (428 U.S. 282, July 2, 1976)

Judgment of the Court and opinion of Justices Stewart, Powell and Stevens, announced by Justice Stewart:

The petitioners were convicted of first-degree murder as the result of their participation in an armed robbery of a convenience food store, in the course of which the cashier was killed and a customer was seriously wounded. There were four participants in the robbery: the petitioners James Tyrone Woodson and Luby Waxton and two others, Leonard Tucker and Johnnie Lee Carroll. At the petitioners' trial Tucker and Carroll testified for the prosecution after having been permitted to plead guilty to lesser offenses; the petitioners testified in their own defense.

The evidence for the prosecution established that the four men had been discussing a possible robbery for some time. On the fatal day Woodson had been drinking heavily. About 9:30 p.m., Waxton and Tucker came to the trailer where Woodson was staying. When

Woodson came out of the trailer, Waxton struck him in the face and threatened to kill him in an effort to make him sober up and come along on the robbery. The three proceeded to Waxton's trailer where they met Carroll. Waxton armed himself with a nickel-plated derringer, and Tucker handed Woodson a rifle. The four then set out be automobile to rob the store. Upon arriving at their destination Tucker and Waxton went into the store while Carroll and Woodson remained in the car as lookouts. Once inside the store, Tucker purchased a package of cigarettes from the woman cashier. Waxton then also asked for a package of cigarettes, but as the cashier approached him he pulled the derringer out of his hip pocket and fatally shot her at point-blank range. Waxton then took the money tray from the cash register and gave it to Tucker, who carried it out of the store, pushing past an entering customer as he reached the door. After he was outside, Tucker heard a second shot from inside the store, and shortly thereafter Waxton emerged, carrying a handful of paper money. Tucker and Waxton got in the car and the four drove away.

The petitioners' testimony agreed in large part with this version of the circumstances of the robbery. It differed diametrically in one important respect: Waxton claimed that he never had a gun, and that Tucker had shot both the cashier and the customer.

During the trial Waxton asked to be allowed to plead guilty to the same lesser offenses to which Tucker had pleaded guilty, but the solicitor refused to accept the pleas. Woodson, by contrast, maintained throughout the trial that he had been coerced by Waxton, that he was therefore innocent, and that he would not consider pleading guilty to any offense.

The petitioners were found guilty on all charges, and, as was required by statute, sentenced to death. The Supreme Court of North Carolina affirmed. . . . We granted *certiorari*, . . . to consider whether the imposition of the death penalties in this case comports with the Eighth and Fourteenth Amendments to the United States Constitution. . . .

At the time of this Court's decision in *Furman v. Georgia*, . . . North Carolina law provided that in cases of first-degree murder, the jury in its unbridled discretion could choose whether the convicted defendant should be death or to life imprisonment. After the *Furman* decision the Supreme Court of North Carolina . . . held unconstitutional the provision of the death penalty statute that gave the jury the option of returning a verdict of guilty without capital punishment, but held further that this provision was severable so that the statute survived as a mandatory death penalty law.

The North Carolina General Assembly in 1974 followed the court's lead and enacted a new statute that was essentially unchanged from the old one except that it made the death penalty mandatory. . . .

It was under this statute that the petitioners, who committed their crime on June 3, 1974, was tried, convicted, and sentenced to death.

North Carolina, unlike Florida, Georgia, and Texas, has thus responded to the *Furman* decision by making death the mandatory sentence for all persons convicted of first-degree murder. In ruling on the constitutionality of the sentences imposed on the petitioners under this North Carolina statute, the Court now addresses for the first time the question whether a death sentence returned pursuant to a law imposing a mandatory death penalty for a broad category of homicidal offenses constitutes cruel and unusual punishment within the meaning of the Eighth and Fourteenth Amendments. The issue, like that explored in *Furman*, involves the procedure employed by the state to select persons for the unique and irreversible penalty of death. . . .

In order to provide a frame for assessing the relevancy of these factors in this case we begin by sketching the history of mandatory death penalty statutes in the United States. At the time the Eighth Amendment was adopted in 1791, the states uniformly followed the common-law practice of making death the exclusive and mandatory sentence for certain specified offenses. Although the range of capital offenses in the American Colonies was quite limited in comparison to the more than 200 offenses then punishable by death in England, the Colonies at the time of the Revolution imposed death sentences on all persons convicted of any of a considerable number of crimes, typically including at a minimum, murder, treason, piracy, arson, rape, robbery, burglary, and sodomy. As at common law, all homicides that were not involuntary, provoked, justified, or excused constituted murder and were automatically punished by death. Almost from the outset jurors reacted unfavorably to the harshness of mandatory death sentences. The states initially responded to this expression of public dissatisfaction with mandatory statutes by limiting the classes of capital offenses.

This reform, however, left unresolved the problem posed by the not infrequent refusal of juries to convict murderers rather than subject them to automatic death sentences. In 1794, Pennsylvania attempted to alleviate the undue severity of the law by confining the mandatory death penalty to "murder of the first degree" encompassing all "wilful, deliberate and premeditated" killings. . . . Other jurisdictions, including Virginia and Ohio, soon enacted similar measures, and within a generation the practice spread to most of the states.

Despite the broad acceptance of the division of murder into degrees, the reform proved to be an unsatisfactory means of identifying persons appropriately punishable by death. Although its failure was due in part to the amorphous nature of the controlling concepts of willfulness, deliberateness, and premeditation, a more fundamental weakness of the reform soon became apparent. Juries continued to find the death penalty inappropriate in a significant number of first-degree murder cases and refused to return guilty verdicts for that crime.

The inadequacy of distinguishing between murderers solely on the basis of legislative criteria narrowing the definition of the capital offense led the states to grant juries sentencing discretion in capital cases. Tennessee in 1838, followed by Alabama in 1841, and Louisiana in 1846, were the first states to abandon mandatory death sentences in favor of discretionary death penalty statutes. This flexibility remedied the harshness of mandatory statutes by permitting the jury to respond to mitigating factors by withholding the death penalty. By the turn of the century, 23 states and the federal government had made death sentences discretionary for first-degree murder and other capital offenses. During the next two decades 14 additional states replaced their mandatory death penalty statutes. Thus, by the end of World War I, all but eight states, Hawaii, and the District of Columbia either had adopted discretionary death penalty schemes or abolished the death penalty altogether. By 1963, all of these remaining jurisdictions had replaced their automatic death penalty statutes with discretionary jury sentencing.

The history of mandatory death penalty statutes in the United States thus reveals that the practice of sentencing to death all persons convicted of a particular offense has been rejected as unduly harsh and unworkably rigid. The two crucial indicators of evolving standards of decency respecting the imposition of punishment in our society—jury determinations and legislative enactments—both point conclusively to the repudiation of automatic death sentences. At least since the Revolution, American jurors have, with some regularity, disregarded their oaths and refused to convict defendants where a death sentence was the automatic consequence of a guilty verdict. As we have seen, the initial movement to reduce the number of capital offenses and to separate murder into degrees was prompted in part by the reaction of jurors as well as by reformers who objected to the imposition of death as the penalty for any crime. Nineteenth Century journalists, statesmen, and jurists repeatedly observed that jurors were often deterred from convicting palpably guilty men of first-degree murder under mandatory statutes. Thereafter, continuing evidence of jury reluctance to convict persons of capital offenses in mandatory death penalty jurisdictions resulted in legislative authorization of descretionary jury sentencing—by Congress for federal crimes in 1897, by North Carolina in 1949, and by Congress for the District of Columbia in 1962.

As we have noted today in *Gregg v. Georgia*,...legislative measures adopted by the people's chosen representatives weigh heavily in ascertaining contemporary standards of decency. The consistent course charted by the state legislatures and by Congress since the middle of the past century demonstrates that the aversion of jurors to mandatory death penalty statutes is shared by society at large.

Still further evidence of the incompatibility of mandatory death penalties with contemporary values is provided by the results of jury sentencing under discretionary statutes. In *Witherspoon v. Illinois* ...(1968), the Court observed that "one of the most important functions any jury can perform" in exercising its descretion to choose "between life imprisonment and capital punishment" is "to maintain a link between contemporary community values and the penal system." . . . Various studies indicate that even in first-degree murder cases juries with sentencing discretion do not impose the death penalty "with any great frequency." H. Kalven & H. Zeisel, *The American Jury* 436 (1966). The actions of sentencing juries suggest that under contemporary standards of decency death is viewed as an inappropriate punishment for a substantial portion of convicted first-degree murders. . . .

Although it seems beyond dispute that, at the time of the *Furman* decision in 1972, mandatory death penalty statutes had been renounced by American juries and legislatures, there remains the question whether the mandatory statutes adopted by North Carolina and a number of other states following *Furman* evince a sudden reversal of societal values regarding the imposition of capital punishment. In view of the persistent and unswerving legislative rejection of mandatory death penalty statutes beginning in 1838 and continuing for more than 130 years until *Furman*, it seems evident that the post-*Furman* enactments reflect attempts by the states to retain the death penalty in a form consistent with the Constitution, rather than a renewed societal acceptance of mandatory death sentencing. The fact that some states have adopted mandatory measures following *Furman* while others have legislated standards to guide jury discretion appears attributable to diverse readings of this Court's multi-opinioned decision in that case. . . .

It is now well established that the Eighth Amendment draws much of its meaning from "the evolving standards of decency that mark the progress of a maturing society." *Trop v. Dulles*. . . . As the above discussion makes clear, one of the most significant developments in our society's treatment of capital punishment has been the rejection of the common-law practice of inexorably imposing a death sentence upon every person convicted of a specified offense. North Carolina's mandatory death penalty statute for first-degree murder departs markedly from contemporary standards respecting the imposition of the punishment of death and thus cannot be applied consistently with the Eighth and Fourteenth Amendments' requirement that the state's power to punish "be exercised within the limits of civilized standards." [*Trop v. Dulles*]. . .

A separate deficiency of North Carolina's mandatory death sentence statute is its failure to provide a constitutionally tolerable response to *Furman's* rejection of unbridled jury discretion in the imposition of capital sentences. Central to the limited holding in *Furman* was the conviction that the vesting of standardless sentencing power in the jury violated the Eighth and Fourteenth Amendments. . . . It is argued that North Carolina has remedied the inadequacies of the death penalty statutes held unconstitutional in *Furman* by withdrawing all sentencing descretion from juries in capital cases. But when one considers the long and consistent American experience with the death penalty in first-degree murder cases, it becomes evident that mandatory statutes enacted in response to *Furman* have simply papered over the problem of unguided and unchecked jury discretion.

As we have noted. . ., there is general agreement that American juries have persistently refused to convict a significant portion of persons charged with first-degree murder of that offense under mandatory death penalty statutes. The North Carolina study commission . . . reported that juries in that state "[q]uite frequently" were deterred from rendering guilty verdicts of first-degree murder because of the enormity of the sentence automatically imposed. Moreover, as a matter of historic fact, juries operating under discretionary sentencing statutes have consistently returned death sentences in only a minority of first-degree murder cases. In view of the historic record, it is only reasonable to assume that many juries under mandatory statutes will continue to consider the grave consequences of a conviction in reaching a verdict. North Carolina's mandatory death penalty statute provides no standards to guide the jury in its inevitable exercise of the power to determine which first-degree murderers shall live and which shall die. And there is no way under the North Carolina law for the judiciary to check arbitrary and capricious exercise of that power through a review of death sentences. Instead of rationalizing the sentencing process, a mandatory scheme may well exacerbate the problem identified in *Furman* by resting the penalty determination of the particular jury's willingness to act lawlessly. While a mandatory death penalty statute may reasonably be expected to increase the number of persons sentenced to death, it does not fulfill *Furman*'s basic requirement by replacing arbitrary and wanton jury discretion with objective standards to guide, regularize, and make rationally reviewable the process for imposing a sentence of death.

A third constitutional shortcoming of the North Carolina statute is its failure to allow the particularized consideration of relevant aspects of the character and record of each convicted defendant before the imposition upon him of a sentence of death. In *Furman*, members of the Court acknowledged what cannot fairly be denied—that death is a punishment different from all other sanctions in kind rather than degree.... A process that accords no significance to relevant facets of the character and record of the individual offender or the circumstances of the particular offense excludes from consideration in fixing the ultimate punishment of death the possibility of compassionate or mitigating factors stemming from the diverse frailties of humankind. It treats all persons convicted of a designated offense not as uniquely individual human beings, but as members of a faceless, undifferentiated mass to be subjected to the blind infliction of the penalty of death.

This Court has previously recognized that "[f]or the determination of sentences, justice generally requires consideration of more than the particular acts by which the crime was committed and that there be taken into account the circumstances of the offense together with the character and propensities of the offender." *Pennsylvania ex rel. Sullivan v. Ashe*...(1937). Consideration of both the offender and the offense in order to arrive at a just and appropriate sentence has been viewed as a progressive and humanizing development.... While the prevailing practice of individualizing sentencing determinations generally reflects simply enlightened policy rather than a constitutional imperative, we believe that in capital cases the fundamental respect for humanity underlying the Eighth Amendment. . . requires consideration of the character and record of the individual offender and the circumstances of the particular offense as a constitutionally indispensable part of the process of inflicting the penalty of death.

This conclusion rests squarely on the predicate that the penalty of death is qualitatively different from a sentence of imprisonment.... Death, in its finality, differs more from life imprisonment than a 100-year prison term differs from one of only a year or two. Because of that qualitative difference, there is a corresponding difference in the need for reliability in the determination that death is the appropriate punishment in a specific case.

For the reasons stated, we conclude that the death sentences imposed upon the petitioners under North Carolina's mandatory death sentence statute violated the Eighth and Fourteenth Amendments and therefore must be set aside. The judgment of the Supreme Court of North Carolina is reversed insofar as it upheld the death sentences imposed upon the petitioners, and the case is remanded for further proceedings not inconsistent with this opinion.

Gardner v. Florida (March 22, 1977)

Judgment of the Court and opinion of Justice Stevens, joined by Justices Stewart and Powell:

... We consider the justifications offered by the state for a capital sentencing procedure which permits a trial judge to impose the death sentence on the basis of confidential information which is not disclosed to the defendant or his counsel.

The state first argues that an assurance of confidentiality to potential sources of information is essential to enable investigators to obtain relevant but sensitive disclosures from persons unwilling to comment publicly about a defendant's background or character. The availability of such information, it is argued, provides the person who prepares the report with greater detail on which to base a sentencing recommendation and, in turn, provides the judge with a better basis for his sentencing decision. But consideration must be given to the quality, as well as the quantity, of the information on which the sentencing judge may rely. Assurances of secrecy are conducive to the transmission of confidences which may bear no closer relation to fact than the average rumor or item of gossip, and may imply a pledge not to attempt independent verification of the information received. The risk that some of the information accepted in confidence may be erroneous, or may be misinterpreted, by the investigator or by the sentencing judge, is manifest.

If, as the state argues, it is important to use such information in the sentencing process, we must assume that in some case it will be decisive in the judge's choice between a life sentence and a death sentence. If it tends to tip the scales in favor of life, presumably the information would be favorable and there would be no reason why it should not be disclosed. On the other hand, if it is the basis for a death sentence, the interest in reliability plainly outweighs the state's interest in preserving the availability of comparable information in other cases.

The state also suggests that full disclosure of the presentence report will unnecessarily delay the proceeding. We think the likelihood of significant delay is overstated because we must presume that reports prepared by professional probation officers, as the Florida, procedure requires, are generally reliable. In those cases in which the accuracy of a report is contested, the trial judge can avoid delay by disregarding the disputed material. Or if the disputed matter is of critical importance, the time invested in ascertaining the truth would surely be well spent if it makes the difference between life and death.

The state further urges that full disclosure of presentence reports, which often include psychiatric and psychological evaluations, will occasionally disrupt the process of rehabilitation. The argument, if valid, would hardly justify withholding the report from defense counsel. Moreover, whatever force that argument may have in noncapital cases, it has absolutely no merit in a case in which the judge has decided to sentence the defendant to death. Indeed, the extinction of all possibility of rehabilitation is one of the aspects of the death sentence that makes it different in kind from any other sentence a state may legitimately impose.

Finally, Florida argues that trial judges can be trusted to exercise their discretion in a responsible manner, even though they may base their decisions on secret information. However acceptable that argument might have been before *Furman v. Georgia* it is now clearly foreclosed. Moreover, the argument rests on the erroneous premise that the participation of counsel is superfluous to the process of evaluating the relevance and significance of aggravating and mitigating facts. Our belief that debate between adversaries is often essential to the truth-seeking function of trials requires us also to recognize the importance of giving an opportunity to comment on facts which may influence the sentencing decision in capital cases.

Even if it were permissible to withhold a portion of the report from a defendant, and even from defense counsel, pursuant to an express finding of good cause for nondisclosure, it would nevertheless be necessary to make the full report a part of the record to be reviewed on appeal. Since the state must administer its capital sentencing procedures with an even hand, see *Proffitt v. Florida...* (July 2, 1976),... it is important that the record on appeal disclose to the reviewing court the considerations which motivate the death sentence in every case in which it is imposed. Without full disclosure of the basis for the death sentence, the Florida capital sentencing procedure would be subject to the defects which resulted in the holding of unconstitutionality in *Furman v. Georgia....*

We conclude that petitioner was denied due process of law when the death sentence was imposed, at least in part, on the basis of information which he had no opportunity to deny or explain.

There remains only the question of what disposition is now proper. Petitioner's conviction, of course, is not tainted by the error in the sentencing procedure. The state argues that we should merely remand the case to the Florida Supreme Court with directions to have the entire presentence report made a part of the record to enable that court to complete its reviewing function. That procedure, however, could not fully correct the error. For it is possible that full disclosure, followed by explanation or argument by defense counsel would have caused the trial judge to accept the jury's advisory verdict. Accordingly, the death sentence is vacated and the case is remanded to the Florida Supreme Court with directions to order further proceedings at the trial court level not inconsistent with this opinion.

Justice Marshall, dissenting:

Last term, this Court carefully scrutinized the Florida procedures for imposing the death penalty and concluded that there were sufficient safeguards to insure that the death sentence would not be "wantonly" and "freakishly" imposed. *Proffitt v. Florida...*

(1976). This case, however, belies that hope. While I continue to believe that the death penalty is unconstitutional in all circumstances, see *Furman v. Georgia*...(1972); *Gregg v. Georgia*... (Marshall, J., dissenting), and therefore would remand this case for resentencing to a term of years; nevertheless, now that Florida may legally take a life, we must insist that it be in accordance with the standards enunciated by this Court. In this case I am appalled at the extent to which Florida has deviated from the procedures upon which this Court expressly relied. It is not simply that the trial judge, in overriding the jury's recommendation of life imprisonment, relied on undisclosed portions of the presentence report. Nor is it merely that the Florida Supreme Court affirmed the sentence without discussing the omission and without concern that it did not even have the entire report before it. Obviously that alone is enough to deny due process and require reversal as the Court now holds. But the blatant desregard exhibited by the courts below for the standards devised to regulate imposition of the death penalty calls into question the very basis for this Court's approval of that system in *Proffitt.*

In *Proffitt v. Florida*...(1976), this Court gave its approval to the death penalty statute of Florida, but very carefully spelled out its reasons for doing so. The Court noted in particular that "[t]he Florida Supreme Court has stated,...that '[i]n order to sustain a sentence of death following a jury recommendation of life, the facts suggesting a sentence of death should be so clear and convincing that virtually no reasonable person could differ'...and that the Florida "statute requires that if the trial court imposes a sentence of death, 'it shall set forth in writing its findings upon which the sentence of death is based as to the facts (a) [t]hat sufficient [statutory] aggravating circumstances exist...and (b) [t]hat there are insufficient [statutory] circumstances...to outweigh the aggravating circumstances.'..."

After studying the performance of the Florida Supreme Court in reviewing death cases, this Court satisfied itself that these guarantees were genuine and that "the Florida Court has undertaken responsibly to perform its function of death sentence review with a maximum of rationality and consistency,"—...and "has in effect adopted the type of proportionality review mandated by the Georgia statute" upheld in *Gregg v. Georgia*...(1976). ... The majority placed great emphasis on this factor, reasoning that "because of its statewide jurisdiction, [the Florida Supreme Court] can assure consistency, fairness, and rationality in the evenhanded operation of the state law." ...

In the present case, however, the Florida Supreme Court engaged in precisely the "cursory or rubber stamp review" that this Court trusted would not occur.... The jury, after considering the evidence, recommended a life sentence:

> "We, the Jury, have heard evidence, under the sentencing procedure in the above cause, as to whether aggravating circumstances which were so defined in the Court's charge, existed in the capital offense here involved, and whether sufficient mitigating circumstances are defined in the Court's charge to outweigh such aggravating circumstances, do find and advise that the mitigating circumstances do outweigh the aggravating circumstances.
>
> "We therefore advise the Court that a *life* sentence should be imposed herein upon the defendant by the Court." ...

The judge, however, ignored the jury's findings. His statutorily required written findings consisted of:

> "... the undersigned concludes and determines that aggravating circumstances exist, to wit: The capital felony was especially heinous, atrocious or cruel; and that such aggravating circumstances outweighs the mitigating circumstance, to wit: none; and based upon the records of such trial and sentencing proceedings makes the following findings of facts, to wit:
>
> "1. That the victim died as a result of expecially heinous, atrocious and cruel acts committed by the defendant, the nature and extent of which are reflected by the testimony of Dr. William H. Shutze, District Medical Examiner of the Fifth Judicial Circuit of the State of Florida, as follows: [followed by a list of eleven injuries to the deceased]." ...

The Florida Supreme Court affirmed with two justices dissenting. The *per curiam* consisted of a statement of the facts of the murder, a verbatim copy of the trial judge's "findings," a conclusion that no new trial was warranted, and the following "analysis":

> "Upon considering all the mitigating and aggravating circumstances and careful review of the entire record in the cause, the trial court imposed the death penalty for the commission of afore-described atrocious and heinous crime.

"Accordingly, the judgment and sentence of the Circuit Court are hereby affirmed.

"It is so ordered."

From this quotation, which includes the entire legal analysis of the opinion, it is apparent that the Supreme Court undertook none of the analysis it had previously proclaimed to be its duty. The opinion does not say that the Supreme Court evaluated the propriety of the death sentence. It merely says the trial judge did so. Despite its professed obligation to do so, the Supreme Court thus failed "to determine independently" whether death was the appropriate penalty. The Supreme Court also appears to have done nothing "to guarantee" consistency with other death sentences. Its opinion makes no comparison with the facts in other similar cases. Nor did it consider whether the trial judge was correct in overriding the jury's recommendation. There was no attempt to ascertain whether the evidence sustaining death was "so clear and convincing that virtually no reasonable person could differ." Indeed, it is impossible for me to believe that that standard can be met in this case.

As the Court notes..., there are two mitigating factors that could apply to this case and apparently were found applicable by the jury—"The capital felony was committed while the defendant was under the influence of extreme mental or emotional disturbance" and "[t]he capacity of the defendant to appreciate the criminality of his conduct or to conform his conduct to the requirements of law was substantially impaired." ... The purpose of these two categories is, as Justice Ervin observed in dissent below, " 'to protect that person who, while legally answerable for his actions, may be deserving of some mitigation of sentence because of his mental state.' ..."

I agree with Justice Ervin that petitioner is such a person. It is undisputed that he had been drinking virtually the entire day and night prior to the killing. Both court-appointed psychiatrists found that petitioner was an alcoholic and that "had he not been under the influence of alcohol at the time of the alleged crime, he would have been competent, knowing right from wrong and being capable of adhering to the right." ... Furthermore, his actions after the murder—falling asleep with his wife's dead body, seeking his mother-in-law's help the next morning because his wife did not appear to be breathing properly, weeping when he realized she might be dead, and waiting for the police to come with no attempt to escape—are consistent with his being temporarily mentally impaired at the time of the crime. In light of these facts, it is not surprising that the jury found that the mitigating circumstances outweighed the aggravating.

Clearly, this is not a case where the evidence suggesting death is "so clear and convincing that virtually no reasonable person could differ." Had the Florida Supreme Court examined the evidence in the manner this Court trusted it would, I have no doubt that the jury recommendation of life imprisonment would have been reinstated. As Justice Ervin observed:

> "This was a crime of passion in a marital setting in which the excessive use of alcohol was a material factor resulting in the homicide. As I read our statutes, this type of crime does not merit the death penalty because the discretion exercised to impose that penalty here extends beyond the discretion the statutes repose in governmental officials for such purpose. I do not believe that the statutes contemplate that a crime of this nature is intended to be included in the heinous category warranting the death penalty. A drunken spree in which one of the spouses is killed traditionally has not resulted in the death penalty in this state." . . .

In *Proffitt*, a majority of this Court was led to believe that Florida had established capital sentencing procedures that would "assure that the death penalty would not be imposed in an arbitrary or capricious manner." . . . This case belies that promise and suggests the need to reconsider that assessment.

Stanislaus Roberts v. Louisiana (428 U.S. 325, July 2, 1976)

Dissenting opinion of Justice White, joined by Chief Justice Burger, and Justices Blackmun and Rehnquist:

The difference between a jury having and not having the lawful discretion to spare the life of the defendant is apparent and fundamental. It is undeniable that the unfettered discretion of the jury to save the defendant from death was a major contributing factor in the developments which led us to invalidate the death penalty in *Furman v. Georgia*. This factor Louisiana has now sought to eliminate by making the death penalty compulsory upon a verdict of guilty in first-degree murder cases. As I see it, we are now in no position to rule that the state's present law, having eliminated the overt discretionary power of juries, suffers from the same constitutional infirmities which led this Court to invalidate the Georgia death penalty statute in *Furman* v. *Georgia*.

Harry Roberts v. Louisiana (June 6, 1977)

The unsigned opinion of the Court:

Petitioner Harry Roberts was indicted, tried, and convicted of the first-degree murder of Police Officer Dennis McInerney, who at the time of his death was engaged in the performance of his lawful duties. As required by Louisiana statute, petitioner was sentenced to death. ... On appeal, the Supreme Court of Louisiana affirmed his conviction and sentence. ... Roberts then filed a petition for a writ of *certiorari* in this Court. The petition presented the question whether Louisiana's mandatory death penalty could be imposed pursuant to his conviction of first-degree murder. ...

Shortly before that petition was filed, we held in another case (involving a different petitioner named Roberts) that Louisiana could not enforce its mandatory death penalty for a conviction of first-degree murder. ... *Stanislaus Roberts v. Louisiana*... [1976]. In the plurality opinion in that case, the precise question presented in this case was explicitly answered.

This precise question was again answered by the Court in *Washington v. Louisiana*... (1976). The petitioner in the *Washington* case had killed a policeman and was tried and sentenced to death under the same provision of the Louisiana statute as was the petitioner in the present case. We vacated the death sentence, holding: "The imposition and carrying out of the death penalty [in this case] constitute cruel and unusual punishment in violation of the Eighth and Fourteenth Amendments. ..."

Recognizing that this Court had already decided that a mandatory death sentence could not be imposed for the crime that Harry Roberts committed, the Attorney General of Louisiana initially conceded that "under this Court's decision in *Stanislaus Roberts v. Louisiana*..., [the sentence of death in the present case] cannot be carried out unless, of course, this Court grants Louisiana's application for rehearing and modifies its former holding." . . . The Court nevertheless granted *certiorari* on Nov. 8, 1976. . . . and on Nov. 29 limited the grant to the question [w]hether the imposition and carrying out of the sentence of death for the crime of first-degree murder of a police officer under the law of Louisiana violates the Eighth and Fourteenth Amendments to the Constitution of the United States."

In *Woodson v. North Carolina,* . . . this Court held that ". . . the fundamental respect for humanity underlying the Eighth Amendment. . . requires consideration of the character and record of the individual offender and the circumstances of a particular offense as a constitutionally indispensable part of the process of inflicting the penalty of death." in *Roberts v. Louisiana* we made clear that this principle applies even where the crime of first-degree murder is narrowly defined.

To be sure, the fact that the murder victim was a peace officer performing his regular duties may be regarded as an aggravating circumstance. There is a special interest in affording protection to these public servants who regularly must risk their lives in order to guard the safety of other persons and property. But it is incorrect to suppose that no mitigating circumstances can exist when the victim is a police officer. Circumstances such as the youth of the offender, the absence of any prior conviction the influence of drugs, alcohol or extreme emotional disturbance, and even the existence of circumstances which the offender reasonably believed provided a moral justification for his conduct are all examples of mitigating facts which might attend the killing of a peace officer and which are considered relevant in other jurisdictions.

As we emphasized repeatedly in *Roberts* and its companion cases decided last Term, it is essential that the capital sentencing decision allow for consideration of whatever mitigating circumstances may be relevant to either the particular offender or the particular offense. Because the Louisiana statute does not allow consideration of particularized mitigating factors, it is unconstitutional.

Accordingly, we hold that the death sentence imposed upon this petitioner violates the Eighth and Fourteenth Amendments and must be set aside. The judgment of the Supreme Court of Louisiana is reversed insofar as it upholds the death sentence upon petitioner. The case is remanded for further proceedings not inconsistent with this opinion.

Justice Rehnquist dissenting, joined by Justice White:

The Court today holds that the State of Louisiana is not entitled to vindicate its substantial interests in protecting the foot soldiers of an ordered society by mandatorily sentencing their murderers to death. This is so even though the state has demonstrated to a jury in a fair trial, beyond a reasonable doubt, that a particular defendant was the murderer, and that he committed the act while possessing "a specific intent to kill, or to inflict great bodily harm upon, a fireman or a peace officer who was engaged in the performance of his lawful duties...." ... That holding would have shocked those who drafted the Bill of Rights on which it purports to rest, and would commend itself only to the most imaginative observer as being required by today's "evolving standards of decency."

I am unable to agree that a mandatory death sentence under such circumstances violates the Eighth Amendment's proscription against "cruel and unusual punishment." I am equally unable to see how this limited application of the mandatory death statute violates even the scope of the Eighth Amendment as seen through the eyes of last term's plurality in *Stanislaus Roberts v. Louisiana*. ... Nor does the brief *per curiam* opinion issued today demonstrate why the application of a mandatory death sentence to the criminal who intentionally murders a peace officer performing his official duties should be considered "cruel and unusual punishment" in light of either the view of society when the Eighth Amendment was passed. *Gregg v. Georgia*...(1976); the "objective indicia that reflect the public attitude" ...; or even the more generalized "basic concept of human dignity" test relied upon last term by the plurality in striking down several more general mandatory statutes. ...

Five terms ago, in *Furman v. Georgia*...(1972), this Court invalidated the then-current system of capital punishments, condemning jury discretion as resulting in "freakish" punishment. The Louisiana Legislature has conscientiously determined, in an effort to respond to that holding, that the death sentence would be made mandatory upon the conviction of particular types of offenses, including, as in the case before us, the intentional killing of a peace officer while in the performance of his duties. ... I am no more persuaded now than I was then that a mandatory death sentence for all, let alone for a limited class of, persons who commit premeditated murder constitutes "cruel and unusual punishment" under the Eighth and Fourteenth Amendments. . . .

This interest of the state, I think, entitled the Louisiana Legislature, in its considered judgment, to make the death penalty mandatory for those convicted of the intentional murder of a police officer. I had thought the plurality had conceded that this response—this need for a mandatory penalty—could be permissible when focusing on the crime, not the criminal, it wrote last term,. . . [*Gregg v. Louisiana*], that

> "the decision that capital punishment may be the appropriate sanction in extreme cases is an expression of the community's belief that certain *crimes* are themselves so grievous an affront to humanity that the only adequate response may be the penalty of death." (Emphasis added.)

I am quite unable to decipher why the Court today concludes that the intentional murder of a police officer is not one of these "certain crimes" The Court's answer appears to lie in its observation that "it is incorrect to suppose that no mitigating circumstances can exist when the victim is a police officer." . . . The Court, however, has asked the wrong question. The question is not whether mitigating factors might *exist*, but, rather, whether whatever "mitigating" factors that might exist are of sufficient *force* so as to constitutionally require their consideration as counterweights to the admitted aggravating circumstance. Like Mr. Justice White, I am unable to believe that a state is not entitled to determine that the premeditated murder of a peace officer is so heinous and intolerable a crime that no combination of mitigating factors can overcome the demonstration "that the criminal's character is such that he deserves death." . . .

As an example of a mitigating factor which, presumably, may "overcome" the aggravating factor inherent in the murder of a peace officer, the Court today gives us the astonishing suggestion of "the existence of circumstances which the offender reasonably believed provided a moral justification for his conduct. . . ." . . . I cannot believe that states are constitutionally required to allow a defense, even at the sentencing stage, which depends on nothing more than the convict's moral belief that he was entitled to kill a peace officer in cold blood. John Wilkes Booth may well have thought he was morally justified in murdering Abraham Lincoln, whom, while fleeing from the stage of Ford's Theater, he characterized as a "tyrant"; I am appalled to believe that the Constitution would have *required* the government to allow him to argue that as a "mitigating factor" before it could sentence him to death if he were found guilty. I am equally appalled that a state should be required to instruct a jury that such individual beliefs must or should be considered as a possible balancing factor against the admittedly proper aggravating factor.

The historical and legal content of the "cruel and unusual punishment" clause was stretched to the breaking point by the plurality's opinion in the *Stanislaus Roberts* case last Term. Today this judicially created superstructure, designed and erected more than 180 years after the Bill of Rights was adopted, is tortured beyond permissible limits of judicial review. There is nothing in the Constitution's prohibition against cruel and unusual punishment which disables a legislature from imposing a mandatory-death sentence on a defendant convicted after a fair trial of deliberately murdering a police officer.

Coker v. Georgia (June 29, 1977)

Justice White announcing the judgment of the Court, joined by Justices Stewart, Blackmun and Stevens:

Georgia Code (1972) provides that "[a] person convicted of rape shall be punished by death or by imprisonment for life, or by imprisonment for not less than 20 years." Punishment is determined by a jury in a separate sentencing proceeding in which at least one of the statutory aggravating circumstances must be found before the death penalty may be imposed. Petitioner Coker was convicted of rape and sentenced to death. Both conviction and sentence were affirmed by the Georgia Supreme Court. Coker was granted a writ of *certiorari*, . . . limited to the single claim, rejected by the Georgia court, that the punishment of death for rape violates the Eighth Amendment, which proscribes "cruel and unusual punishments" and which must be observed by the states as well as the Federal Government. *Robinson* v. *California*. . . (1962).

While serving various sentences for murder, rape, kidnapping, and aggravated assault, petitioner escaped from the Ware Correctional Institution near Waycross, Ga., on Sept. 2, 1974. At approximately 11 p.m. that night, petitioner entered the house of Allen and Elnita Carver through an unlocked kitchen door. Threatening the couple with a "board," he tied up Mr. Carver in the bathroom, obtained a knife from the kitchen, and took Mr. Carver's money and the keys to the family car. Brandishing the knife and saying "you know what's going to happen to you if you try anything, don't you," Coker then raped Mrs. Carver. Soon thereafter, petitioner drove away in the Carver car, taking Mrs. Carver with him. Mr. Carver, freeing himself, notified the police; and not long thereafter petitioner was apprehended. Mrs. Carver was unharmed.

Petitioner was charged with escape, armed robbery, motor vehicle theft, kidnapping, and rape. Counsel was appointed to represent him. Having been found competent to stand trial, he was tried. The jury returned a verdict of guilty, rejecting his general plea of insanity. A sentencing hearing was then conducted in accordance with the procedures dealt with at length in *Gregg* v. *Georgia*... (1976), where this Court sustained the death penalty for murder when imposed pursuant to statutory procedures. The jury was instructed that it could consider as aggravating circumstances whether the rape had been committed by a person with a prior record of conviction for a capital felony and whether the rape had been committed in the course of committing another capital felony, namely, the armed robbery of Allen Carver. The court also instructed, pursuant to statute, that even if aggravating circumstances were present, the death penalty need not be imposed if the jury found they were outweighed by mitigating circumstances, that is, circumstances not constituting justification or excuse for the offense in question, "but which, in fairness and mercy, may be considered as extenuating or reducing the degree" of moral culpability or punishment.... The jury's verdict on the rape count was death by electrocution. Both aggravating circumstances on which the court instructed were found to be present by the jury.

Furman v. *Georgia*...(1972) and the Court's decisions last term in *Gregg* v. *Georgia*...; *Proffitt* v. *Florida*...(1976); *Jurek* v. *Texas*...(1976); *Woodson* v. *North Carolina*...(1976); and *Roberts* v. *Lousiana*...(1976), make unnecessary the recanvassing of certain critical aspects of the controversy about the constitutionality of capital punishment. It is now settled that the death penalty is not invariably cruel and unusual punishment within the meaning of the Eighth Amendment; it is not inherently barbaric or an unacceptable mode of punishment for crime; neither is it always disproportionate to the crime for which it is imposed. It is also established that imposing capital punishment, at least for murder, in accordance with the procedures provided under the Georgia statutes saves the sentence from the infirmities which led the Court to invalidate the prior Georgia capital punishment statute in *Furman* v. *Georgia*. . . .

In sustaining the imposition of the death penalty in *Gregg*, however, the Court firmly embraced the holdings and dicta from prior cases, *Furman* v. *Georgia*. . .; *Robinson* v. *California*. . . (1962); *Trop* v. *Dulles*. . .(1958); and *Weems* v. *United States*. . . (1910), to the effect that the Eighth Amendment bars not only those punishments that are "barbaric" but also those that are "excessive" and unconstitutional if it (1) makes no measurable contribution to acceptable goals of punishment and hence is nothing more than the purposeless and needless imposition of pain and suffering; or (2) is grossly out of proportion to the severity of the crime. A punishment might fail the test on either ground. Furthermore, these Eighth Amendment judgments should not be, or appear to be, merely the subjective views of individual justices; judgment should be informed by objective factors to the maximum possible extent. To this end, attention must be given to the public attitudes concerning a particular sentence—history and precedent, legislative attitudes, and the response of juries reflected in their sentencing decisions are to be consulted. In *Gregg*, after giving due regard to such sources, the Court's judgment was that the death penalty for the deliberate murder was neither the purposeless imposition of severe punishment nor a punishment grossly disproportionate to the crime. But the Court reserved the question of the constitutionality of the death penalty when imposed for other crimes. . . .

That question, with respect to rape of an adult woman, is now before us. We have concluded that a sentence of death is grossly disproportionate and excessive punishment for the crime of rape and is therefore forbidden by the Eighth Amendment as cruel and unusual punishment.

As advised by recent cases, we seek guidance in history and from the objective evidence of the country's present judgment concerning the acceptability of death as a penalty for rape of an adult woman. At no time in the last 50 years has a majority of the states authorized death as a punishment for rape. In 1925, 18 states, the District of Columbia, and the Federal Government authorized capital punishment for the rape of an adult female. By 1971 just prior to the decision in *Furman* v. *Georgia* that number had declined, but not substantially, to 16 states plus the Federal Government. *Furman* then invalidated most of the capital punishment statutes in this country, including the rape statutes, because, among other reasons, of the manner in which the death penalty was imposed and utilized under those laws.

With their death penalty statutes for the most part invalidated, the states were faced with the choice of enacting modified capital punishment laws in an attempt to satisfy the requirements of *Furman* or of being satisfied with life imprisonment as the ultimate punishment for *any* offense. Thirty-five states immediately reinstituted the death penalty for at least limited kinds of crime. ... This public judgment as to the acceptability of capital punishment, evidenced by the immediate, post-*Furman* legislative reaction in a large majority of the states, heavily influenced the Court to sustain the death penalty for murder in *Gregg* v. *Georgia.* ...

But if the "most marked indication of a society's endorsement of the death penalty for murder is the legislative response to *Furman*," *Gregg* v. *Georgia,* ..., it should also be a telling datum that the public judgment with respect to rape, as reflected in the statutes providing the punishment for that crime, has been dramatically different. In reviving death penalty laws to satisfy *Furman's* mandate, none of the states that had not previously authorized death for rape chose to include rape among capital felonies. Of the 16 states in which rape had been a capital offense, only three provided the death penalty for rape of an adult woman in their revised statutes —Georgia, North Carolina, and Louisiana. In the latter two states, the death penalty was mandatory for those found guilty, and those laws were invalidated by *Woodson* and *Roberts.* When Louisiana and North Carolina, responding to those decisions, again revised their capital punishment laws, they reenacted the death legislatures that to our knowledge have amended or replaced their death penalty statutes since July 2, 1976, including four states (in addition to Louisiana and North Carolina) that had authorized the death sentence for rape prior to 1972 and had reacted to *Furman* with mandatory statutes, included rape among the crimes for which death was an authorized punishment.

Georgia argues that 11 of the 16 states that authorized death for rape in 1972 attempted to comply with *Furman* by enacting arguably mandatory death penalty legislation and that it is very likely that aside from Louisiana and North Carolina, these States simply chose to eliminate rape as a capital offense rather than to *require* death for *each* and *every* instance of rape. The argument is not without force; but four of the 16 states did not take the mandatory course and also did *not* continue rape of an adult woman as a capital offense. Further, as we have indicated, the legislatures of six of the 11 arguably mandatory states have revised their death penalty laws since *Woodson* and *Roberts* without enacting a new death penalty for rape. And this is to say nothing of 19 other states that enacted no mandatory, post-*Furman* statutes and chose not to sentence rapists to death.

It should be noted that Florida, Mississippi, and Tennessee also authorized the death penalty in some rape cases, but only where the victim was a child and the rapist an adult. The Tennessee statute has since been invalidated because the death sentence was mandatory. . . . The upshot is that Georgia is the sole jurisdiction in the United States at the present time that authorizes a sentence of death when the rape victim is an adult woman, and only two other jurisdictions provide capital punishment when the victim is child.

It was also observed in *Gregg* that "[t]he jury. . . is a significant and reliable index of contemporary values because it is so directly involved". . . and that it is thus important to look to the sentencing decisions that juries have made in the course of assessing whether capital punishment is an appropriate penalty for the crime being tried. Of course, the jury's judgment is meaningful only where the jury has an appropriate measure of choice as to whether the death penalty is to be imposed. As far as execution for rape is concerned, this is now true only in Georgia and in Florida; and in the latter state, capital punishment is authorized only for the rape of children.

According to the factual submissions in this Court, out of all rape convictions in Georgia since 1973—and that total number has not been tendered—63 cases had been reviewed by the Georgia Supreme Court as of the time of oral argument; and of these, six involved a death sentence, one of which was set aside, leaving five convicted rapists now under sentence of death in the State of Georgia. Georgia juries have thus sentenced rapists to death six times since 1973. This obviously is not a negligible number; and the state argues that as a practical matter juries simply reserve the extreme sanction for extreme cases of rape and that recent experience surely does not prove that jurors consider the death penalty to be a disproportionate punishment for every conceivable instance of rape, no matter how aggravated. Nevertheless, it is true that in the vast majority of cases, at least nine out of 10, juries have not imposed the death sentence.

These recent events evidencing the attitude of state legislatures and sentencing juries do not wholly determine this controversy, for the Constitution contemplates that in the end our own judgment will be brought to bear on the question of the acceptability of the death penalty under the Eighth Amendment. Nevertheless, the legislative rejection of capital punishment for rape strongly confirms our own judgment, which is that death is indeed a disproportionate penalty for the crime of raping an adult woman.

We do not discount the seriousness of rape as a crime. It is highly reprehensible, both in a moral sense and in its almost total contempt for the personal integrity and autonomy of the female victim and for the latter's privilege of choosing those with whom intimate relationships are to be established. Short of homicide, it is the "ultimate violation of self." It is also a violent crime because it normally involves force, or the threat of force or intimidation, to overcome the will and the capacity of the victim to resist. Rape is very often accompanied by physical injury to the female and can also inflict mental and psychological damage. Because it undermines the community's sense of security, there is public injury as well.

Rape is without a doubt deserving of serious punishment; but in terms of moral depravity and of the injury to the person and to the public, it does not compare with murder, which does involve the unjustified taking of human life. Although it may be accompanied by another crime, rape by definition does not include the death or even the serious injury to another person. The murderer kills; the rapist, if no more than that, does not. Life is over for the victim of the murderers; for the rape victim, life may not be nearly so happy as it was, but it is not over and normally is not beyond repair. We have the abiding conviction that the death penalty, which "is unique in its severity and revocability,"... is an excessive penalty for the rapist who, as such, does not take human life.

This does not end the matter; for under Georgia law, death may not be imposed for any capital offense, including rape, unless the jury or judge finds one of the statutory aggravating circumstances and then elects to impose that sentence.... For the rapist to be executed in Georgia, it must therefore be found not only that he committed rape but also that one or more of the following aggravating circumstances were present: (1) that the rape was committed by a person with a prior record of conviction for a capital felony; (2) that the rape was committed while the offender was engaged in the commission of another capital felony, or aggravated battery; or (3) the rape "was outrageously or wantonly vile, horrible or inhuman in that it involved torture, depravity of mind, or aggravated battery to the victim." Here, the first two of these aggravating circumstances were alleged and found by the jury.

Neither of these circumstances, nor both of them together, change our conclusion that the death sentence imposed on Coker is a disproportionate punishment for rape. Coker had prior convictions for capital felonies—rape, murder and kidnapping—but these prior convictions do not change the fact that the instant crime being punished is a rape not involving the taking of life.

It is also true that the present rape occurred while Coker was committing armed robbery, a felony for which the Georgia statutes authorize the death penalty. But Coker was tried for the robbery offense as well as for rape and received a separate life sentence for this crime; the jury did not deem the robbery itself deserving of the death penalty, even though accompanied by the aggravating circumstance, which was stipulated, that Coker had been convicted of a prior capital crime.

We note finally that in Georgia a person commits murder when he unlawfully and with malice aforethought, either express or implied, causes the death of another human being. He also commits that crime when in the commission of a felony he causes the death of another human being, irrespective of malice. But even where the killing is deliberate, it is not punishable by death absent proof of aggravating circumstances. It is difficult to accept the notion, and we do not, that the rape, with or without aggravating circumstances, should be punished more heavily than the deliberate killer as long as the rapist does not himself take the life of his victim. The judgment of the Georgia Supreme Court upholding the death sentence is reversed and the case is remanded to that court for further proceedings not inconsistent with this opinion.

Chief Justice Burger dissenting, joined by Justice Rehnquist:

In a case such as this, confusion often arises as to the Court's proper role in reaching a decision. Our task is not to give effect to our individual views on capital punishment; rather, we must determine what the Constitution permits a state to do under its reserved powers. In striking down the death penalty imposed upon the petitioner in this case, the Court has overstepped the bounds of proper constitutional adjudication by substituting its policy judgment for that of the state legislature. I accept that the Eighth Amendment's concept of disproportionality bars the death penalty for minor crimes. But rape is not a minor crime; hence the cruel and unusual punishment clause does not give the members of this Court license to engraft their conceptions of proper public policy onto the considered legislative judgments of the states. Since I cannot agree that Georgia lacked the constitutional power to impose the penalty of death for rape, I dissent from the Court's judgment.

On Dec. 5, 1971, the petitioner, Ehrlich Anthony Coker, raped and then stabbed to death a young woman. Less than eight months later Coker kidnapped and raped a second young woman. After twice raping this 16-year-old victim, he stripped her, severely beat her with a club, and dragged her into a wooded area where he left her for dead. He was apprehended and pleaded guilty to offenses stemming from these incidents. He was sentenced by three separate courts to three life terms, two 20-year terms, and one eight-year term of imprisonment. Each judgment specified that the sentences it imposed were to run consecutively rather than concurrently. Approximately one and one-half years later, on Sept. 2, 1974, petitioner escaped from the state prison where he was serving these sentences. He promptly raped another 16-year-old woman in the presence of her husband, abducted her from her home, and threatened her with death and serious bodily harm. It is this crime for which the sentence now under review was imposed.

The Court today holds that the State of Georgia may not impose the death penalty on Coker. In so doing, it prevents the state from imposing any effective punishment upon Coker for his latest rape. The Court's holding, moreover, bars Georgia from guaranteeing its citizens that they will suffer no further attacks by this habitual rapist. In fact, given the lengthy sentences Coker must serve for the crimes he has already committed, the Court's holding assures that petitioner—and others in his position—will henceforth feel no compunction whatsoever about committing further rapes as frequently as he may be able to escape from confinement and indeed even within the walls of the prison itself. To what extent we have left states "elbow room" to protect innocent persons from depraved human beings like Coker remains in doubt. ...

The plurality...acknowledges the gross nature of the crime of rape. A rapist not only violates a victim's privacy and personal integrity, but inevitably causes serious psychological as well as physical harm in the process. The long-range effect upon the victim's life and health is likely to be irreparable... Rape is not a mere physical attack—it is destructive of the human personality. The remainder of the victim's life may be gravely affected, and this in turn may have a serious detrimental effect upon her husband and any children she may have. I therefore wholly agree with Mr. Justice White's conclusion as far as it goes—that "[s]hort of homicide, [rape] is the 'ultimate violation of the self.' "... Victims may recover from the physical damage of knife or bullet wounds, or a beating with fists or a club, but recovery from such a gross assault on the human personality is not healed by medicine or surgery. To speak blandly, as the plurality does, of rape victims which are "unharmed," or, as the concurrence, to classify the human outrage of rape in terms of "excessively brutal..." versus "moderately brutal," takes too little account of the profound suffering the crime imposes upon the victims and their loved ones. ...

The plurality opinion bases its analysis, in part, on the fact that "Georgia is the sole jurisdiction in the United States at the present time that authorizes the sentence of death when the rape victim is an adult woman.'"... Surely, however, this statistic cannot be deemed determinative, or even particularly revelant. As the opinion concedes,...two other states—Louisiana and North Carolina—have enacted death penalty statutes for adult rape since this Court's 1972 decision in *Furman* v. *Georgia*. ... If the Court is to rely on some "public opinion" process, does this not suggest the beginning of a "trend?"

...[I]t is myopic to base sweeping constitutional principles upon the narrow experience of the past five years. Considerable uncertainty was introduced into this area of the law by this Court's *Furman* decision. A large number of states found their death penalty statutes invalidated; legislatures were left in serious doubt by the expressions vacillating between discretionary and mandatory death penalties, as to whether this Court would sustain *any* statute imposing death as a criminal sanction. Failure of more states to enact statutes imposing death for rape of an adult woman may thus reflect hasty legislative compromise occasioned by time pressures following *Furman*, a desire to wait on the experience of those states which did enact such statutes, or simply an accurate forecast of today's holding. ...

The question of whether the death penalty is an appropriate punishment for rape is surely an open one. It is arguable that many prospective rapists would be deterred by the possibility that they could suffer death for their offense; it is also arguable that the death penalty would have only minimal deterrent effect. It may well be that rape victims would become more willing to report the crime and aid in the apprehension of the criminals if they knew that community disapproval of rapists was sufficiently strong to inflict the extreme penalty; or perhaps they would be reluctant to cooperate in the prosecution of rapists if they knew that a conviction might result in the imposition of the death penalty. Quite possibly, the occasional, well-publicized execution of egregious rapists may cause citizens to feel greater security in their daily lives; or, on the contrary, it may be that members of a civilized community will suffer the pangs of a heavy conscience because such punishment will be perceived as excessive. We cannot know which among this range of possibilities is correct, but today's holding forecloses the very exploration we have said federalism was intended to foster. It is difficult to believe that Georgia would long remain alone in punishing rape by death if the next decade demonstrated a drastic reduction in its incidence of rape, an increased cooperation by rape victims in the apprehension and prosecution of rapists, and a greater confidence in the rule of law on the part of the populace.

In order for Georgia's legislative program to develop it must be given time to take effect so that data may be evaluated for comparison with the experience of states which have not enacted death penalty statutes. Today, the Court repudiates the state's solemn judgment on how best to deal with the crime of rape before anyone can know whether the death penalty is an effective deterrent for one of the most horrible of all crimes. And this is done a few short years after Justice Powell's excellent statement:

> "In a period in our country's history when the frequency of [rape] is increasing alarmingly, it is indeed a grave event for the Court to take from the states whatever deterrent and retributive weight the death penalty retains." *Furman* v. *Georgia*... (Powell, J., dissenting). ...

To deprive states of this authority as the Court does, on the basis that "the current judgment with respect to the death penalty for rape...weighs very heavily on the side of rejecting capital punishment as a suitable penalty for raping an adult woman,"...is impermissibly rash. The current judgment of some members of this Court has undergone significant change in the short time since

Furman. Social change on great issues generally reveals itself in small increments, and the "current judgment" of many states could well be altered on the basis of Georgia's experience, were we to allow its statute to stand.

The subjective judgment that the death penalty is simply disproportionate for the crime of rape is even more disturbing than the "objective" analysis discussed *supra.* The plurality's conclusion on this point is based upon the bare fact that murder necessarily results in the physical death of the victim, while rape does not. . . . However, no member of the Court explains why this distinction has relevance, much less constitutional significance. It is, after all, not irrational—nor constitutionally impermissible—for a legislature to make the penalty more severe than the criminal act it punishes in the hope it would deter wrongdoing. . . .

. . . Until now, the issue under the Eighth Amendment has not been the state of any particular victim after the crime, but rather whether the punishment imposed is grossly disproportionate to the evil committed by the perpetrator. See, *Gregg* v. *Georgia.* . .*Furman* v. *Georgia.* . .(Powell, J., dissenting). As a matter of constitutional principle, that test cannot have the primitive simplicity of "life for life, eye for eye, tooth for tooth." Rather states must be permitted to engage in a more sophisticated weighing of values in dealing with criminal activity which consistently poses serious danger of death or grave bodily harm. If innocent life and limb is to be preserved I see no constitutional barrier in punishing by death all who engage in such activity, regardless of whether the risk comes to fruition in any particular instance. . . .

Only one year ago the Court held it constitutionally permissible to impose the death penalty for the crime of murder, provided that certain procedural safeguards are followed. . . . Today, the Court readily admits that "[s]hort of homicide, [rape] is the 'ultimate violation of self.' ". . .

. . . Rape thus is not a crime "light-years" removed from murder in the degree of its heinousness; it certainly poses a serious potential danger to the life and safety of innocent victims—apart from the devastating psychic consequences. It would seem to follow therefore that, affording the states proper leeway under the broad standard of the Eighth Amendment, murder is properly punishable by death, rape should be also, if that is the considered judgment of the legislators.

The Court's conclusion to the contrary is very disturbing indeed. The clear implication of today's holding appears to be that the death penalty may be properly imposed only as to crimes resulting in death of the victim. This casts serious doubt upon the unconstitutional validity of statutes imposing the death penalty for a variety of conduct which, though dangerous, may not necessarily result in any immediate death, *e.g.*, treason, airplane hijacking, and kidnapping. In the respect, today's holding does even more harm than is initially apparent. We cannot avoid judicial notice that crimes such as airplane hijacking, kidnapping, and mass terrorist activity constitute a serious and increasing danger to the safety of the public. It would be unfortunate indeed if the effect of today's holding were to inhibit states and the Federal Government from experimenting with various remedies—including possibly imposition of the penalty of death—to prevent and deter such crimes.

Some sound observations, made only a few years ago, deserve repetition:

> "Our task here, as must so frequently be emphasized and re-emphasized, is to pass upon the constitutionality of legislation that has been enacted and that is challenged. This is the sole task for judges. We should not allow our personal preferences as to the wisdom of legislative and congressional action, or our distaste for such action, to guide our judicial decision in cases such as these. The temptations to cross that policy line are very great. In fact, as today's decision reveals, they are almost irresistible." *Furman* v. *Georgia*...(Blackmun, J., dissenting).

Whatever our individual views as to the wisdom of capital punishment, I cannot agree that it is constitutionally impermissible for a state legislature to make the "solemn judgment" to impose such penalty for the crime of rape. Accordingly, I would leave to the states the task of legislating in this area of the law.

Justice Powell concurring in part and dissenting in part:

I concur in the judgment of the Court on the facts of this case, and also in its reasoning supporting the view that ordinarily death is disproportionate punishment for the crime of raping an adult woman. Although rape invariably is a reprehensible crime, there is no indication that petitioner's offense was committed with excessive brutality or that the victim sustained serious or lasting injury. The plurality, however, does not limit its holding to the case before us or to similar cases. Rather, in an opinion that ranges well beyond what is necessary, it holds that capital punishment *always*—regardless of the circumstances—is a disproportionate penalty for the crime of rape.

The Georgia statute, sustained in *Gregg* v. *Georgia*...(1976), specifies aggravating circumstances that may be considered by the jury when appropriate. With respect to the crime of rape, only three such circumstances are specified: (i) the offense was committed by a person with a prior record of conviction for a capital felony; (ii) the offense was committed while the offender was engaged in another capital felony or in aggravated battery; and (iii) the offense was "outrageously or wantonly vile, horrible or inhuman in that it involved torture, depravity of mind, or an aggravated battery to the victim."... Only the third circumstance describes in general the offense of aggravated rape, often identified as a separate and more heinous offense than rape. ... That third circumstance was not submitted to the jury in this case, as the evidence would not have supported such a finding. It is therefore quite unnecessary for the plurality to write in terms so sweeping as to foreclose each of the 50 state legislatures from creating a narrowly defined substantive crime of aggravated rape punishable by death. ...

Today, in a case that does not require such an expansive pronouncement, the plurality draws a bright line between murder and all rapes—regardless of the degree of brutality of the rape or the effect upon the victim. I dissent because I am not persuaded that such a bright line is appropriate. ... The deliberate viciousness of the rapist may be greater than that of the murderer. Rape is never an act committed accidentally. Rarely can it be said to be unpremeditated. There also is wide variation in the effect on the victim. The plurality opinion says that "[l]ife is over for the victim of the murderer; for the rape victim, life may not be nearly so happy as it was, but it is not over and normally is not beyond repair."... But there is indeed "extreme variation" in the crime of rape. Some victims are so grievously injured physically or psychologically that life *is* beyond repair.

Thus it may be that the death penalty is not disproportionate punishment for the crime of aggravated rape. Final resolution of the question must await careful inquiry into objective indicators of society's "evolving standards of decency," particularly legislative enactments and the responses of juries in capital cases. ... The plurality properly examines these indicia, which do support the conclusion that society finds the death penalty unacceptable for the crime of rape in the absence of excessive brutality or severe injury. But it has not been shown that society finds the penalty disproportionate for all rapists. In a proper case a more discriminating inquiry than the plurality undertakes well might discover that both juries and legislatures have reserved the ultimate penalty for the case of an outrageous rape resulting in serious, lasting harm to the victim. I would not prejudge the issue. To this extent, I respectfully dissent.

Confessions

Disagreement on Pre-Trial Admissions

One of the key areas of disagreement between the Warren and Burger Courts concerns pre-trial confessions. In 1966, the Warren Court, in one of the most controversial decisions in the history of the Supreme Court, ruled, 5-4, that a confession could not be used in court if the suspect, once in police custody, had not been informed of his right to an attorney and of his right to remain silent.

In 1977 the Burger Court refused a request by 22 states to overrule *Miranda*. Prior to this, however, the Burger Court had previously limited *Miranda* in holding: (1) that a defendant who takes the witness stand can be contradicted by what he previously told the police even though the suspect had not been informed of his *Miranda* rights, (2) that the police may attempt again to question a suspect following the suspect's initial decision to invoke his right to remain silent, (3) that the *Miranda* doctrine extends only to instances in which a person is in custody and thus does not apply in grand jury proceedings or when a person is questioned by government agents at home.

Burger Court Limits Miranda Rule

In a 5-4 decision handed down Feb. 23, 1971, in *Harris v. New York*, the Burger Court ruled that statements made to police officers by a suspect not informed of his *Miranda* rights can be used in court to impugn the defendant's courtroom testimony. The effect of *Harris,* therefore, is to discourage defendants from taking the witness stand lest they be confronted with pre-trial statements that cannot be excluded under *Miranda*. Chief Justice Burger wrote the majority opinion, which acknowledged that Harris' confession could not be used in court as evidence of his guilt. But it stated that Harris' confessional statements, nevertheless, could be used to judge the truthfulness of his testimony at his trial.

During his trial, Viven Harris had testified that he had not sold narcotics to an undercover police officer as charged. Yet, when arrested, Harris had admitted to having made two such sales. The decision of the trial judge to admit evidence concerning Harris' pretrial admission of guilt for the purpose of enabling the jury to judge the truthfulness of his courtroom testimony was upheld by the court on the ground that "the shield provided by *Miranda* cannot be perverted into a license to use perjury by way of a defense, free from the risk of confrontation with prior inconsistent utterances."

Justice Brennan, dissenting, called it "monstrous that courts should aid or abet the law-breaking police officer." According to Brennan, "the court today tells the police that they may freely interrogate an accused incommunicado and without counsel and know that although any statement they obtain in violation of *Miranda* can't be used on the state's direct case, it may be introduced if the defendant has the temerity to testify in his own defense. This goes far toward undoing much of the progress made in conforming police methods to the Constitution."

Police Permitted to Try Again to Question Suspect

The Burger Court, in a 6-2 decision handed down Dec. 9, 1975 in *Michigan v. Mosley*, ruled that the police may again seek to question a suspect following his initial decision to invoke his *Miranda* rights. Justices Brennan and Marshall, holdovers from the Warren Court, dissented.

Richard Bert Mosley had been arrested in connection with a pair of robberies. Following his arrest, Mosley, on being given the required *Miranda* warnings, stated that he did not wish to be questioned. At this point the interrogation was ended, and Mosley was locked up pending arraignment. Two hours later, another police officer told Mosley that he had been implicated by his alleged partner in a murder that had nothing to do with the crimes for which he had been arrested. After again being given his *Miranda* warnings, Mosley confessed to the murder and was ultimately sentenced to life imprisonment.

The key issue in the case concerned a passage in *Miranda* that held that "[o]nce warnings have been given, the subsequent procedure is clear. If the individual indicates in any manner, at any time prior to or during questioning that he wishes to remain silent, the interrogation must cease. *Miranda* did not, however, state the circumstances, if any, in which the police could resume questioning a suspect who claimed his *Miranda* rights.

The majority, in an opinion by Justice Stewart, stated that *Miranda* obviously could not be read to mean that a suspect who availed himself of his right to remain silent could never again be questioned by the police. Thus, the majority concluded "that the admissability of statements obtained after the person in custody has decided to remain silent depends under *Miranda* on whether his 'right to cut off questioning' was 'scrupulously honored,' " as required by *Miranda*. The confession obtained in this particular instance, the Court said, met this requirement since the police did *not* fail "to honor a decision of a person in custody to cut off questioning, either by refusing to discontinue the interrogation upon request or by persisting in repeated efforts to wear down his resistance and make him change his mind."

Justice Brennan, in a strong dissenting opinion joined by Justice Marshall, claimed that the majority opinion "virtually empties *Miranda* of principle, for plainly the decision encourages police asked to cease interrogation to continue the suspect's detention until the police station's coercive atmosphere does its work and the suspect responds to resumed questioning."

The two Warren Court holdovers, in citing *Harris v. New York*, claimed that this latest "distortion of *Miranda's* constitutional principles can be viewed only as yet another step in the erosion" and "ultimate overruling of *Miranda's* enforcement of the privilege against self-incrimination." The prudent course for the Court to have taken, they said, would have been for it to have fashioned a rule prohibiting the police to resume questioning a suspect who claimed his *Miranda* rights until the arrival of his attorney.

Court Refuses to Extend Miranda

In two 1976 decisions, *Beckwith v. U.S.* and *U.S. v. Mandujano*, the Court refused to require that *Miranda* warnings to be given to persons questioned at home by Internal Revenue Service criminal investigators or to persons ordered to appear before a grand jury. Writing for the majority in *Beckwith*, Chief Justice Burger held that *Miranda* was not appropriate in the case of persons questioned at home because of the lack of compulsion inherent in such situations.

Justice Brennan, the lone dissenter in the case, argued that "Interrogation under conditions that have the practical consequence of compelling the taxpayer to make disclosures, and interrogation in 'custody' having the same consequence, are in my view peas from the same pod."

Court Spurns States' Plea to Void Miranda

In a much publicized decision, the Supreme Court March 22, 1977 declined a request by 22 states that it overturn *Miranda*. By a 5-4 vote, the Court ruled in favor of the defendant in an Iowa child-murder case that the states' had sought to turn into a *Miranda* test case. The Court did so without considering the *Miranda* issue *per se* in finding other grounds on which to base its decision in *Brewer v. Williams*.

The case involved one Robert Williams. He had been found guilty of murdering a 10-year old girl who had been abducted from a YMCA, where she had gone with her family to watch her brother wrestle. Soon after the girl's disappearance, Williams, who had recently escaped from a mental hospital, was seen in the lobby of the YMCA carrying some clothing and a large bundle wrapped in a blanket. A 14-year-old boy, who helped Williams by opening the doors of the building and of Williams' car, saw two legs protruding from the bundle. A warrant was issued that day for Williams' arrest.

Two days later, an attorney notified the Des Moines police that he had just received a telephone call from Williams and that he had advised Williams to surrender to the Davenport police. On surrendering to the police in Davenport, Williams was given his *Miranda* warnings and was permitted to speak with his lawyer in Des Moines. In the presence of the Des Moines Chief of Police and a Detective Leaming, the attorney advised Williams that Des Moines police officers would transport him from Davenport to Des Moines and that they had agreed not to question him during the 160-mile drive.

At no time during the journey did Williams agree to be interrogated. During the trip, Detective Leaming, knowing Williams to be deeply religious, suggested to Williams that he show where he had left the girl's body in order to provide the girl with a "Christian burial." Williams then directed the police to the girl's body.

Justice Stewart, delivering the opinion of the Court, held that it was not necessary to review *Miranda* in determining whether Williams had been coerced into making his admission. According to Stewart, the case focused on Williams' being denied his right to an attorney while under interrogation. "Despite Williams' express and implicit assertions of his right to counsel, Detective Leaming proceeded to elicit incriminating statements from Williams," Stewart stated. This denial of counsel, Stewart concluded, justified ordering that Williams be granted a new trial.

Justice Marshall, in a concurring opinion, said that he doubted that Williams—even with a new trial—would go free despite "blood-curdling" cries by the dissenting justices in the case. Even if Williams were freed, Marshall said, it would be because of Detective Leaming's "intentional police misconduct."

The majority decision was vigorously dissented to by Chief Justice Burger, who called the decision "intolerable in any society which purports to call itself an organized society." It continues, he said, "on the much criticized course of punishing the public for the mistakes and misdeeds of law enforcement officers, instead of punishing the officer directly, if in fact he is guilty of wrongdoing." According to Burger, Williams, in telling the police where he buried the girl's body, "acted voluntarily and with full awareness of his constitutional rights."

ABRIDGMENTS OF CONFESSION DECISIONS

Harris v. New York (401 U.S. 222, Feb. 23, 1971)

Chief Justice Burger delivering the opinion of the Court:

We granted the writ in this case to consider petitioner's claim that a statement made by him to police under circumstances rendering it inadmissible to establish the prosecution's case in chief under *Miranda v. Arizona*...may not be used to impeach his credibility.

The State of New York charged petitioner in a two-count indictment with twice selling heroin to an undercover police officer. At a subsequent jury trial the officer was the state's chief witness, and he testified as to details of the two sales. A second officer verified collateral details of the sales, and a third offered testimony about the chemical analysis of the heroin.

Petitioner took the stand in his own defense. He admitted knowing the undercover police officer but denied a sale on Jan. 4. He admitted making a sale of contents of a glassine bag to the officer on Jan. 6 but claimed it was baking powder and part of a scheme to defraud the purchaser.

On cross-examination petitioner was asked *seriatim* whether he had made specified statements to the police immediately following his arrest on Jan. 7—statements that partially contradicted petitioner's direct testimony at trial. In response to the cross-examination, petitioner testified that he could not remember virtually any of the questions or answers recited by the prosecutor. At the request of petitioner's counsel, the written statement from which the prosecutor had read questions and answers in his impeaching process was placed in the record for possible use on appeal; the statement was not shown to the jury.

The trial judge instructed the jury that the statements attributed to petitioner by the prosecution could be considered only in passing on petitioner's credibility and not as evidence of guilt. In closing summations, both counsel argued the substance of the impeaching statements. The jury then found petitioner guilty of the second count of the indictment. [No agreement was reached on the first count. That count was later dropped by the state.]...

At trial, the prosecution made no effort in its case in chief to use the statements allegedly made by petitioner, conceding that they were inadmissible under *Miranda*. ... The transcript of the interrogation used in the impeachment, but not given to the jury, shows that no warning of a right to appointed counsel was given before questions were put to petitioner when he was taken into custody. Petitioner makes no claim that the statements made to the police were coerced or involuntary.

Some comments in the *Miranda* opinion can indeed be read as indicating a bar to use of an uncounseled statement for any purpose, but discussion of that issue was not at all necessary to the court's holding and cannot be regarded as controlling. *Miranda* barred the prosecution from making its case with statements of an accused made while in custody prior to having or effectively waiving counsel. It does not follow from *Miranda* that evidence inadmissible against an accused in the prosecution's case in chief is barred for all purposes, provided of course that the trustworthiness of the evidence satisfies legal standards. ...

... The conflict between petitioner's testimony in his own behalf concerning the events of Jan. 7 contrasted sharply with what he told the police shortly after his arrest. The impeachment process here undoubtedly provided valuable aid to the jury in assessing petitioner's credibility, and the benefits of this process should not be lost, in our view, because of the speculative possibility that impermissible police conduct will be encouraged thereby. Assuming that the exclusionary rule has a deterrent effect on proscribed police conduct, sufficient deterrence flows when the evidence in question is made unavailable to the prosecution in its case in chief.

Every criminal defendant is privileged to testify in his own defense, or to refuse to do so. But that privilege cannot be construed to include the right to commit perjury. ... Having voluntarily taken the stand, petitioner was under an obligation to speak truthfully and accurately, and the prosecution here did no more than utilize the traditional truth-testing devices of the adversary process. Had inconsistent statements been made by the accused to some third person, it could hardly be contended that the conflict could not be laid before the jury by way of cross-examination and impeachment.

The shield provided by *Miranda* cannot be perverted into a license to use perjury by way of a defense, free from the risk of confrontation with prior inconsistent utterances. We hold, therefore, that petitioner's credibility was appropriately impeached by use of his earlier conflicting statements.

Justice Brennan, whom Douglas and Marshall joined, dissenting:

It is conceded that the question-and-answer statement used to impeach petitioner's direct testimony was, under *Miranda v. Arizona,* . . . constitutionally inadmissible as part of the state's direct case against petitioner. I think that the Constitution also denied the state the use of the statement on cross-examination to impeach the credibility of petitioner's testimony given in his own defense. . . .

The state's case against Harris depended upon the jury's belief of the testimony of the undercover agent that petitioner "sold" the officer heroin on Jan. 4 and again on Jan. 6. Petitioner took the stand and flatly denied having sold anything to the officer on Jan. 4. He countered the officer's testimony as to the Jan. 6 sale with testimony that he had sold the officer two glassine bags containing what appeared to be heroin, but that actually the bags contained only baking powder intended to deceive the officer in order to obtain $12. The statement contradicted petitioner's direct testimony as to the events of both days. The statement's version of the events on Jan. 4 was that the officer had used petitioner as a middleman to buy some heroin from a third person with money furnished by the officer. The version of the events on Jan. 6 was that petitioner had again acted for the officer in buying two bags of heroin from a third person for which petitioner received $12 and a part of the heroin. Thus, it is clear that the statement was used to impeach petitioner's direct testimony not on collateral matters but on matters directly related to the crimes for which he was on trial. . . .

The objective of deterring improper police conduct is only part of the larger objective of safeguarding the integrity of our adversary system. The "essential mainstay" of that system, *Miranda v. Arizona,* . . . is the privilege against self-incrimination, which for that reason has occupied a central place in our jurisprudence since before the nation's birth. Moreover, "we may view the historical development of the privilege as one which groped for the proper scope of governmental power over the citizen. . . . All these policies point to one overriding thought: the constitutional foundation underlying the privilege is the respect of government . . . must accord to the dignity and integrity of its citizens." *Ibid.* These values are plainly jeopardized if an exception against admission of tainted statements is made for those used for impeachment purposes. Moreover, it is monstrous that courts should aid or abet the law-breaking police officer. It is abiding truth that ''[n]othing can destroy a government more quickly than its failure to observe its own laws, or worse, its disregard of the charter of its own existence.'' *Mapp v. Ohio.* . . . Thus, even to the extent that *Miranda* was aimed at deterring police practices in disregard of the Constitution, I fear that today's holding will seriously undermine the achievement of that objective. . . .

Michigan v. Mosley (423 U.S. 96, Dec. 9, 1975)

Justice Stewart delivering the opinion of the Court:

The respondent, Richard Bert Mosley, was arrested in Detroit, Mich., in the early afternoon of April 8, 1971, in connection with robberies that had recently occurred at the Blue Goose Bar and the White Tower Restaurant on that city's lower east side. The arresting officer, Detective James Cowie of the Armed Robbery Section of the Detroit Police Department, was acting on a tip implicating Mosely and three other men in the robberies. After effecting the arrest, Detective Cowie brought Mosely to the Robbery, Breaking & Entering Bureau of the Police Department, located on the fourth floor of the departmental headquarters building. The officer advised Mosely of his rights under this Court's decision in *Miranda v. Arizona*. . . and had him read and sign the department's constitutional rights notification certificate. After filling out the necessary arrest papers, Cowie began questioning Mosley about the robbery of the White Tower Restaurant. When Mosley said he did not want to answer any questions about the robberies, Cowie promptly ceased the interrogation. The completion of the arrest papers and the questioning of Mosely together took approximately 20 minutes. At no time during the questioning did Mosely indicate a desire to consult with a lawyer, and there is no claim that the procedures followed to this point did not fully comply with the strictures of the *Miranda* opinion. Mosley was then taken to a ninth-floor cell block.

Shortly after 6 p.m., Detective Hill of the Detroit Police Department Homicide Bureau brought Mosley from the cell block to the fifth-floor office of the Homicide Bureau for questioning about the fatal shooting of a man named Leroy Williams. Williams had been killed on Jan. 9, 1971, during a holdup attempt outside the 101 Ranch Bar in Detroit. Mosley has not been arrested on this charge or interrogated about it by Detective Cowie. Before questioning Mosley about this homicide, Detective Hill carefully advised him of his *"Miranda* rights." Mosely read the notification form both silently and aloud, and Detective Hill then read and explained the warnings to him and had him sign the form. Mosley at first denied any involvement in the Williams murder, but after the officer told him that Anthony Smith had confessed to participating in the slaying and had named him as the "shooter," Mosley made a statement implicating himself in the homicide. The interrogation by Detective Hill lasted approximately 15 minutes, and at no time during its course did Mosley ask to consult with a lawyer or indicate that he did not want to discuss the homicide. In short, there is no claim that the procedures followed during Detective Hill's interrogation of Mosley, standing alone, did not fully comply with the strictures of the *Miranda* opinion.

Mosley was subsequently charged in a one-count information with first-degree murder. Before the trial he moved to suppress his incriminating statement on a number of grounds, among them the claim that under the doctrine of the *Miranda* case it was constitutionally impermissible for Detective Hill to question him about the Williams murder after he had told Detective Cowie that he did not want to answer any questions about the robberies. The trial court denied the motion to suppress after an evidentiary hearing, and the incriminating statement was subsequently introduced in evidence against Mosley at his trial. The jury convicted Mosley of first-degree murder, and the court imposed a mandatory sentence of life imprisonment. . . .

In the *Miranda* case this Court promulgated a set of safeguards to protect the there-delineated constitutional rights of persons subjected to custodial police interrogation. In sum, the Court held in that case that unless law enforcement officers give certain specified warnings before questioning a person in custody, and follow certain specified procedures during the course of any subsequent interrogation, any statement made by the person in custody cannot over his objection be admitted in evidence against him as a defendant at trial, even though the statement may in fact be wholly voluntary. . . .

Neither party in the present case challenges the continuing validity of the *Miranda* decision, or of any of the so-called guidelines it established to protect what the Court there said was a person's constitutional privilege against compulsory self-incrimination. The issue in this case, rather, is whether the conduct of the Detroit police that led to Mosley's incriminating statement did in fact violate the *Miranda* "guidelines," so as to render the statement inadmissible in evidence against Mosley at his trial. Resolution of the question turns almost entirely on the interpretation of a single passage in the *Miranda* opinion, upon which the Michigan appellate court relied in finding a *per se* violation of *Miranda*:

"Once warnings have been given, the subsequent procedure is clear. If the individual indicates in any manner, at any time prior to or during questioning, that he wishes to remain silent, the interrogation must cease. At this point he has shown that he intends to exercise his Fifth Amendment privilege; any statement taken after the person invokes his privilege cannot be other than the product of compulsion, subtle or otherwise. Without the right to cut off questioning, the setting of in-custody interrogation operates on the individual to overcome free choice in producing a statement after the privilege has been once invoked." . . .

This passage states that "the interrogation must cease" when the person in custody indicates that "he wishes to remain silent." It does not state under what circumstances, if any, a resumption of questioning is permissible. The passage could be literally read to mean that a person who has invoked his "right to silence" can never again be subjected to custodial interrogation by any police officer at any time or place on any subject. Another possible construction of the passage would characterize "any statement taken after the person invokes his privilege" as "the product of compulsion" and would therefore mandate its exclusion from evidence, even if it were volunteered by the person in custody without any further interrogation whatever. Or the passage could be interpreted to require only the immediate cessation of questioning, and to permit a resumption of interrogation after a momentary respite.

It is evident that any of these possible literal interpretations would lead to absurd and unintended results. To permit the continuation of custodial interrogation after a momentary cessation would clearly frustrate the purposes of *Miranda* by allowing repeated rounds of questioning to undermine the will of the person being questioned. At the other extreme, a blanket prohibition against the taking of voluntary statements or a permanent immunity from further interrogation, regardless of the circumstances, would transform the *Miranda* safeguards into wholly irrational obstacles to legitimate police investigative activity, and deprive suspects of an opportunity to make informed and intelligent assessments of their interests. Clearly, therefore, neither this passage nor any other passage in the *Miranda* opinion can sensibly be read to create a *per se* proscription of indefinite duration upon any further questioning by any police officer on any subject, once the person in custody has indicated a desire to remain silent.

A reasonable and faithful interpretation of the *Miranda* opinion must rest on the intention of the Court in that case to adopt "fully effective means. . . to notify the person of his right of silence and to assure that the exercise of the right will be scrupulously honored. . . ." . . . The critical safeguard identified in the passage at issue is a person's "right to cut off questioning." . . . Through the exercise of his option to terminate questioning he can control the time at which questioning occurs, the subjects discussed, and the duration of the interrogation. The requirement that law enforcement authorities must respect a person's exercise of that option counteracts the coercive pressures of the custodial setting. We therefore conclude that the admissibility of statements obtained after the person in custody has decided to remain silent depends under *Miranda* on whether his "right to cut off questioning" was "scrupulously honored."

A review of the circumstances leading to Mosley's confession reveals that his "right to cut off questioning" was fully respected in this case. Before his initial interrogation, Mosley was carefully advised that he was under no obligation to answer any questions and could remain silent if he wished. He orally acknowledged that he understood the *Miranda* warnings and then signed a printed notification-of-rights form. When Mosley stated that he did not want to discuss the robberies, Detective Cowie immediately ceased the interrogation and did not try either to resume the questioning or in any way to persuade Mosely to reconsider his position. After an interval of more than two hours, Mosley was questioned by another police officer at another location about an unrelated holdup murder. He was given full and complete *Miranda* warnings at the outset of the second interrogation. He was thus reminded again that he could remain silent and could consult with a lawyer, and was carefully given a full and fair opportunity to exercise these options. The subsequent questioning did not undercut Mosley's previous decision not to answer Detective Cowie's inquiries. Detective Hill did not resume the interrogation about the White Tower Restaurant robbery or inquire about the Blue Goose Bar robbery, but instead focused exclusively on the Leroy Williams homicide, a crime different in nature and in time and place of occurrence from the robberies for which Mosley had been arrested and interrogated by Detective Cowie. Although it is not clear from the record how much Detective Hill knew about the earlier interrogation, his questioning of Mosley about an unrelated homicide was quite consistent with a reasonable interpretation of Mosley's earlier refusal to answer any questions about the robberies.

This is not a case, therefore, where the police failed to honor a decision of a person in custody to cut off questioning, either by refusing to discontinue the interrogation upon request or by persisting in repeated efforts to wear down his resistance and make him change his mind. In contrast to such practices, the police here immediately ceased the interrogation, resumed questioning only after the passage of a significant period of time and the provision of a fresh set of warnings, and restricted the second interrogation to a crime that had not been a subject of the earlier interrogation. ...

For these reasons, we conclude that the admission in evidence of Mosley's incriminating statement did not violate the principles of *Miranda* v. *Arizona*. Accordingly, the judgment of the Michigan Court of Appeals is vacated, and the case is remanded to that court for further proceedings not inconsistent with this opinion.

Justice Brennan, joined by Justice Marshall, dissenting:

... [T]he process of eroding *Miranda* rights, begun with *Harris* v. *New York*...(1971), continues with today's holding that police may renew the questioning of a suspect who has once exercised his right to remain silent, provided the suspect's right to cut off questioning has been "scrupulously honored." Today's distortion of *Miranda's* constitutional principles can be viewed only as yet another step in the erosion and, I suppose, ultimate overruling of *Miranda's* enforcement of the privilege against self-incrimination.

The *Miranda* guidelines were necessitated by the inherently coercive nature of in-custody questioning. As in *Escobedo* v. *Illinois*...(1964), "we sought a protective device to dispel the compelling atmosphere of the interrogation." ... We "concluded that without proper safeguards the process of in-custody interrogation of persons suspected or accused of crime contains inherently compelling pressures which work to undermine the individual's will to resist and to compel him to speak where he would not otherwise do so freely." . . . To assure safeguards that promised to dispel the "inherently compelling pressures" of in-custody interrogation, a prophylatic rule was fashioned to supplement the traditional determination of voluntariness on the facts of each case. *Miranda* held that any confession obtained when not preceded by the required warnings or an adequate substitute safeguard was *per se* inadmissible in evidence. . . . Satisfaction of this prophylatic rule, therefore, was necessary, though not sufficient, for the admission of a confession. *Certiorari* was expressly granted in *Miranda* "to give concrete constitutional guidelines for law enforcement agencies and courts to follow," . . . that is, clear, objective standards that might be applied to avoid the vagaries of the traditional voluntariness test.

The task that confronts the Court in this case is to satisfy the *Miranda* approach by establishing "concrete constitutional guidelines" governing the resumption of questioning a suspect who, while in custody, has once clearly and unequivocally "indicate[d] . . . that he wishes to remain silent. . . . " As the Court today continues to recognize, under *Miranda*, the cost of assuring voluntariness by procedural tests, independent of any actual inquiry into voluntariness, is that some voluntary statements will be excluded. . . . Thus the consideration in the task confronting the Court is not whether voluntary statements will be excluded, but whether the procedures approved will be sufficient to assure with reasonable certainty that a confession is not obtained under the influence of the complusion inherent in interrogation and detention. The procedures approved by the Court today fail to provide that assurance. . . .

Observing that the suspect can control the circumstances of interrogation "[t]hrough the exercise of his option to terminate questioning," the Court concludes "that the admissibility of statements obtained after the person in custody has decided to remain silent depends . . . on whether his 'right to cut off questioning' was 'scrupulously honored.'" . . . But scrupulously honoring exercises of the right to cut off questioning is only meaningful insofar as the suspect's will to exercise that right remains wholly unfettered. The Court's formulation thus assumes the very matter at issue here: whether renewed questioning following a lengthy period of detention acts to overbear the suspect's will, irrespective of giving the *Miranda* warnings a second time (and scrupulously honoring them), thereby rendering inconsequential any failure to exercise the right to remain silent. For the Court it is enough conclusorily to assert that "[t]he subsequent questioning did not undercut Mosley's previous decision not to answer Detective Cowie's inquiries." . . . Under *Miranda*, however, Mosley's failure to exercise the right upon renewed questioning is presumptively the consequence of an overbearing in which detention and that subsequent questioning played central roles.

I agree that *Miranda* is not to be read, on the one hand, to impose an absolute ban on resumption of questioning "at any time or place on any subject," . . . or on the other hand, "to permit a resumption of interrogation after a momentary respite." . . . But this surely cannot justify adoption of a vague and ineffective procedural standard that falls somewhere between those absurd extremes, for *Miranda* in flat and unambiguous terms requires that questioning "cease" when a suspect exercises the right to remain silent. *Miranda's* terms, however, are not so uncompromising as to preclude the fashioning of guidelines to govern this case. Those guidelines must, of course, necessarily be sensitive to the reality that "[a]s a practical matter, the compulsion to speak in the isolated setting of the police station may well be greater than in courts or other official investigations, where there are often impartial observers to guard against intimidation or trickery." . . .

The fashioning of guidelines for this case is an easy task. Adequate procedures are readily available. Michigan law requires that the suspect be arraigned before a judicial officer "without unnecessary delay," certainly not a burdensome requirement. Alternatively, a requirement that resumption of questioning should await appointment and arrival of counsel for the suspect would be an acceptable and readily satisfied precondition to resumption. *Miranda* expressly held that "[t]he presence of counsel . . . would be the adequate protective device necessary to make process of police interrogation conform to the dictates of the privilege [against self-incrimination]." . . . The Court expendiently bypasses that alternative in its search for circumstances where renewed questioning would be permissible. . . .

Beckwith v. U.S. (425 U.S. 341, April 21, 1976)

Chief Justice Burger delivering the opinion of the Court:

The important issue presented in this case is whether a special agent of the Internal Revenue Service, investigating potential criminal income tax violations, must, in an interview with a taxpayer, not

in custody, give the warnings called for by this Court's decision in
Miranda v. *Arizona*. . . .
The District Court conducted a thorough inquiry into the facts
surrounding the interview of petitioner before ruling on his motion
to suppress the statements at issue. After a considerable amount of
investigation, two special agents of the Intelligence Division of the
Internal Revenue Service met with petitioner in a private home where
petitioner occasionally stayed. The senior agent testified that they
went to see petitioner at this private residence at 8 a. m. in order to
spare petitioner the possible embarrassment of being interviewed at
his place of employment which opened at 10 a. m. Upon their
arrival, they identified themselves to the person answering the door
and asked to speak to petitioner. The agents were invited into the
house and, when petitioner entered the room where they were
waiting, they introduced themselves and, according to the testimony
of the senior agent, Beckwith then excused himself for a period in
excess of five minutes, to finish dressing. Petitioner then sat down at
the dining room table with the agents; they presented their
credentials and stated they were attached to the Intelligence Division
and that one of their functions was to investigate the possibility of
criminal tax fraud. They then informed petitioner that they were
assigned to investigate his federal income tax liability for the years
1966 through 1971. The senior agent then read to petitioner
from a printed card the following:

> "As a special agent, one of my functions is to investigate the
> possibility of criminal violations of the Internal Revenue laws,
> and related offenses.
> "Under the Fifth Amendment to the Constitution of the United
> States, I cannot compel you to answer any questions or to
> submit any information if such answer or information might
> tend to incriminate you in any way. I also advise you that
> anything which you say and any information which you submit
> may be used against you in any criminal proceeding which may
> be undertaken. I advise you further that you may, if you wish,
> seek the assistance of an attorney before responding." . . .

Petitioner acknowledged that he understood his rights. The agents
then interviewed him until about 11 o'clock. The agents described
the conversation as "friendly" and "relaxed." The petitioner noted
that the agents did not "press" him on any question he could not or
chose not to answer.
Prior to the conclusion of the interview, the senior agent requested
that petitioner permit the agents to inspect certain records.

Petitioner indicated that they were at his place of employment. The agents asked if they could meet him there later. Having traveled separately from petitioner, the agents met petitioner approximately 45 minutes later and the senior agent advised the petitioner that he was not required to furnish any books or records; petitioner, however, supplied the books to the agents.

Prior to trial, petitioner moved to suppress all statements he made to the agents or evidence derived from those statements on the ground that petitioner had not been given the warnings mandated by *Miranda.* . . .

An interview with government agents in a situation such as the one shown by this record simply does not present the elements which the *Miranda* Court found so inherently coercive as to require its holding. Although the "focus" of an investigation may indeed have been on Beckwith at the time of the interview in the sense that it was his tax liability which was under scrutiny, he hardly found himself in the custodial situation described by the *Miranda* Court as the basis for *Miranda* specifically defined "focus," for its purposes, as "questioning initiated by law enforcement officers *after* a person has been taken into custody or otherwise deprived of his freedom of action in any significant way." . . . (Emphasis supplied.) It may well be true as petitioner contends, that the "starting point" for the criminal prosecution was the information obtained from petitioner and the records exhibited by him. But this amounts to no more than saying that a tax return signed by a taxpayer can be the "starting point" for a prosecution.

We recognize, or course, that noncustodial interrogation might possibly in some situations, by virtue of some special circumstances, be characterized as one where "the behavior of. . .law enforcement officials was such as to overbear petitioner's will to resist and bring about confessions not freely self-determined. . . ." *Rogers* v. *Richmond*. . .(1961). When such a claim is raised, it is the duty of an appellate court, including this Court, "to examine the entire record and make an independent determination of the ultimate issue of voluntariness." *Davis* v. *North Carolina*. . .(1966). Proof that some kind of warnings were given or that none were given would be relevant evidence only on the issue of whether the questioning was in fact coercive. . . .

Justice Brennan dissenting:

I respectfully dissent. In my view the District Court should have granted petitioner's motion to suppress all statements made by him to the agents because the agents did not give petitioner the warnings mandated by *Miranda* v. *Arizona*...(1966). The Court affirms the conviction on the ground that "[a]lthough the 'focus' of an investigation may indeed have been on Beckwith at the time of the interview in the sense that it was his tax liability which was under scrutiny, he hardly found himself in the *custodial* situation described by the *Miranda* Court as the basis for its holding." ... (Emphasis is supplied). But the fact that Beckwith had not been taken into formal "custody" is not determinative of the question whether the agents were required to give him the *Miranda* warnings. I agree with the Court of Appeals for the Seventh Circuit that the warnings are also mandated when the taxpayer is, as here, interrogated by Intelligence Division agents of the Internal Revenue Serivce in surroundings where, as in the case of the subject in "custody," the practical compulsion to respond to questions about his tax returns is comparable to the psychological pressures described in *Miranda*. ... Interrogation under conditions that have the practical consequence of compelling the taxpayer to make disclosures, and interrogation in "custody" having the same consequence, are in my view peas from the same pod. ...

Brewer v. Williams (March 23, 1977)

Justice Stewart delivering the opinion of the Court:

An Iowa trial jury found the respondent, Robert Williams, guilty of murder. The judgment of conviction was affirmed in the Iowa Supreme Court by a closely divided vote. In a subsequent *habeas corpus* proceeding a federal district court ruled that under the United States Constitution Williams is entitled to a new trial, and a divided Court of Appeals for the Eighth Circuit agreed. The question before us is whether the District Court and the Court of Appeals were wrong.

On the afternoon of Dec. 24, 1968, a 10-year-old girl named Pamela Powers went with her family to the YMCA in Des Moines, Iowa, to watch a wrestling tournament in which her brother was participating. When she failed to return from a trip to the washroom, a search for her began. The search was successful.

Robert Williams, who had recently escaped from a mental hospital, was a resident of the YMCA. Soon after the girl's disappearance Williams was seen in the YMCA lobby carrying some clothing and a large bundle wrapped in a blanket. He obtained help from a 14-year-old boy in opening the street door of the YMCA and the door to his automobile parked outside. When Williams placed the bundle in the front seat of his car the boy "saw two legs in it and they were skinny and white." Before anyone could see what was in the bundle Williams drove away. His abandoned car was found the following day in Davenport, Iowa, roughly 160 miles east of Des Moines. A warrant was then issued in Des Moines for his arrest on a charge of abduction.

On the morning of Dec. 26, a Des Moines lawyer named Henry McKnight went to the Des Moines police station and informed the officers present that he had just received a long distance call from Williams, and that he had advised Williams to turn himself in to the Davenport police. Williams did surrender that morning to the police in Davenport, and they booked him on the charge specified in the arrest warrant and gave him the warnings required by *Miranda* v. *Arizona.* . . . The Davenport police then telephoned their counterparts in Des Moines to inform them that Williams had surrendered. McKnight, the lawyer, was still at the Des Moines police headquarters, and Williams conversed with McKnight on the telephone. In the presence of the Des Moines Chief of Police and a Police Detective named Leaming, McKnight advised Williams that Des Moines police officers would be driving to Davenport to pick him up, that the officers would not interrogate him or mistreat him, and that Williams was not to talk to the officers about Pamela Powers until after consulting with McKnight upon his return to Des Moines. As a result of these conversations, it was agreed between McKnight and the Des Moines police officials that Detective Leaming and a fellow officer would drive to Davenport to pick up Williams, that they would bring him directly back to Des Moines, and that they would not question him during the trip.

In the meantime Williams was arraigned before a judge in Davenport on the outstanding arrest warrant. The judge advised him of his *Miranda* rights and committed him to jail. Before leaving the courtroom, Williams conferred with a lawyer named Kelly, who advised him not make any statements until consulting with McKnight back in Des Moines.

Detective Leaming and his fellow officer arrived in Davenport about noon to pick up Williams and return him to Des Moines. Soon after their arrival they met with Williams and Kelly, who, they understood, was acting as Williams' lawyer. Detective Leaming repeated the *Miranda* warnings, and told Williams:

"...we both know that you're being represented here by Mr. Kelly and you're being represented by Mr. McKnight in Des Moines, and...I want you to remember this because we'll be visiting between here and Des Moines."

Williams then conferred again with Kelly alone, and after this conference Kelly reiterated to Detective Leaming that Williams was not to be questioned about the disappearance of Pamela Powers until after he had consulted with McKnight back in Des Moines. When Leaming expressed some reservations, Kelly firmly stated that the agreement with McKnight was to be carried out—that there was to be no interrogation of Williams during the automobile journey to Des Moines. Kelly was denied permission to ride in the police car back to Des Moines with Williams and the two officers.

The two detectives, with Williams in their charge, then set out on the 160-mile drive. At no time during the trip did Williams express a willingness to be interrogated in the absence of an attorney. Instead, he stated several times that "[w]hen I get to Des Moines and see Mr. McKnight, I am going to tell you the whole story." Detective Leaming knew that Williams was a former mental patient, and knew also that he was deeply religious.

The detective and his prisoner soon embarked on a wide-ranging conversation covering a variety of topics, including the subject of religion. Then, not long after leaving Davenport and reaching the interstate highway, Detective Leaming delivered what has been referred to in the briefs and oral arguments as the "Christian burial speech." Addressing Williams as "Reverend," the detective said:

"I want to give you something to think about while we're traveling down the road. ... Number one, I want you to observe the weather conditions, it's raining, it's sleeting, it's freezing, driving is very treacherous, visibility is poor, it's going to be dark early this evening. They are predicting several inches of snow for tonight, and I feel that you yourself are the only person that knows where this little girl's body is, that you yourself have only been there once, and if you get a snow on top of it you yourself may be unable to find it. And, since we will be going right past the area on the way into Des Moines, I feel that we could stop and locate the body, that the parents of this little girl should be entitled to a Christian burial for the little girl who was snatched away from them on Christmas Eve and murdered. And I feel we should stop and locate it on the way in rather than waiting until morning and trying to come back out after a snow storm and possibly not being able to find it at all."

Williams asked Detective Leaming why he thought their route to Des Moines would be taking them past the girl's body, and Leaming responded that he knew the body was in the area of Mitchellville—a town they would be passing on the way to Des Moines.* Leaming then stated: "I do not want you to answer me. I don't want to discuss it further. Just think about it as we're riding down the road."

As the car approached Grinnell, a town approximately 100 miles west of Davenport, Williams asked whether the police had found the victim's shoes. When Detective Leaming replied that he was unsure, Williams directed the officers to a service station where he said he had left the shoes; a search for them proved unsuccessful. As they continued towards Des Moines, Williams asked whether the police had found the blanket, and directed the officers to a rest area where he said he had disposed of the blanket. Nothing was found. The car continued towards Des Moines, and as it approached Mitchellville, Williams said that he would show the officers where the body was. He then directed the police to the body of Pamela Powers.

Williams was indicted for first-degree murder. Before trial, his counsel moved to suppress all evidence relating to or resulting from any statements Williams had made during the automobile ride from Davenport to Des Moines. After an evidentiary hearing the trail judge denied the motion. He found that "an agreement was made between defense and counsel and the police officials to the effect that the defendant was not to be questioned on the return trip to Des Moines," and that the evidence in question had been elicited from Williams during "a critical stage in the proceedings requiring the presence of counsel on his request." The judge ruled, however, that Williams had "waived his right to have an attorney present during the giving of such information."

The evidence in question was introduced over counsel's continuing objection at the subsequent trial. The jury found Williams guilty of murder, and the judgment of conviction was affirmed by the Iowa Supreme Court, a bare majority of whose members agreed with the trial court that Williams had "waived his right to the presence of his counsel" on the automobile ride from Davenport to Des Moines.

---

*The fact of the matter, of course, was that Detective Leaming possessed no such knowledge.

... The four dissenting justices expressed the view that "when counsel and police have agreed defendant is not to be questioned until counsel is present and defendant has been advised not to talk and repeatedly has stated he will tell the whole story after he talks with counsel, the state should be required to make a stronger showing of intentional voluntary waiver than was made here.". . .

Williams then petitioned for a writ of *habeas corpus* in the United States District Court for the Southern District of Iowa. Counsel for the state and for Williams stipulated "that the case would be submitted on the record of facts and proceedings in the trial court, without taking of further testimony." The District Court made findings of fact as summarized above, and concluded as a matter of law that the evidence in question had been wrongly admitted at Williams' trial. This conclusion was based on three alternative and independent grounds: (1) that Williams had been denied his constitutional right to the assistance of counsel; (2) that he had been denied the constitutional protections defined by this Court's decisions in *Escobedo* v. *Illinois*. . . and *Miranda* v. *Arizona*. . .; and (3) that in any event, his self-incriminatory statements on the automobile trip from Davenport to Des Moines had been involuntarily made. Further, the District Court ruled that there had been no waiver by Williams of the constitutional protections in question. . . .

The Court of Appeals for the Eighth Circuit, with one judge dissenting, affirmed this judgment. . . and denied a petition for rehearing en banc. We granted *certiorari* to consider the constitutional issues presented. . . .

Specifically, there is no need to review in this case the doctrine of *Miranda* v. *Arizona*,. . . a doctrine designed to secure the constitutional privilege against compulsory self-incrimination. . . . It is equally unnecessary to evaluate the ruling of the District Court that Williams' self-incriminating statements were, indeed, involuntarily made. . . . For it is clear that the judgment before us must in any event be affirmed upon the ground that Williams was deprived of a different constitutional right—the right to the assistance of counsel.

This right, guaranteed by the Sixth and Fourteenth Amendments, is indispensable to the fair administration of our adversary system of criminal justice. Its vital need at the pretrial stage has perhaps nowhere been more succinctly explained than in Mr. Justice Sutherland's memorable words for the Court 44 years ago in *Powell* v. *Alabama*. . . :

"[D]uring perhaps the most critical period of the proceedings against these defendants, that is to say, from the time of their arraignment until the beginning of their trial, when consultation, thoroughgoing investigation and preparation were vitally important, the defendants did not have the aid of counsel in any real sense, although they were as much entitled to such aid during that period as at the trial itself."

There has occasionally been a difference of opinion within the Court as to the peripheral scope of this constitutional right. . . . But its basic contours, which are identical in state and federal contexts, . . . are too well established to require extensive elaboration here. Whatever else it may mean, the right to counsel granted by the Sixth and Fourteenth Amendments means at least that a person is entitled to the help of a lawyer at or after the time that judicial proceedings have been initiated against him—"whether by way of formal charge, preliminary hearing, indictment, information, or arraignment." *Kirby* v. *Illinois*. . . .

There can be no doubt in the present case that judicial proceedings had been initiated against Williams before the start of the automobile ride from Davenport to Des Moines. A warrant had been issued for his arrest, he had been arraigned on that warrant before a judge in a Davenport courtroom, and he had been committed by the court to confinement in jail. The state does not contend otherwise.

There can be no serious doubt, either, that Detective Leaming deliberately and designedly set out to elicit information from Williams just as surely as—and perhaps more effectively than—if he had formally interrogated him. Detective Leaming was fully aware before departing for Des Moines that Williams was being represented in Davenport by Kelly and in Des Moines by McKnight. Yet he purposely sought during Williams' isolation from his lawyers to obtain as much incriminating information as possible. Indeed, Detective Leaming conceded as much when he testified at Williams' trial:

"Q. In fact, captain, whether he was a mental patient or not, you were trying to get all the information you could before he got to his lawyer, weren't you?

"A. I was sure hoping to find out where that little girl was, yes, sir. . . .

"Q. Well, I'll put it this way: You was hoping to get all the information you could before Williams got back to McKnight, weren't you?

"A. Yes, sir."

The state courts clearly proceeded upon the hypothesis that Detective Leaming's "Christian burial speech" had been tantamount to interrogation. Both courts recognized that Williams had been entitled to the assistance of counsel at the time he made the incriminating statements. Yet no such constitutional protection would have come into play if there had been no interrogation. . . .

The Iowa courts recognized that Williams had been denied the constitutional right to the assistance of counsel. They held, however, that he had waived that right during the course of the automobile trip from Davenport to Des Moines. The state trial court explained its determination of waiver as follows:

> "The time element involved on the trip, the general circumstances of it, and more importantly the absence on the defendant's part of any assertion of his right or desire not to give information absent the presence of his attorney, are the main foundations for the Court's conclusion that he voluntarily waived such right."

In its lengthy opinion affirming this determination, the Iowa Supreme Court applied "the totality-of-circumstances test for a showing of waiver of constitutionally-protected rights in the absence of an express waiver," and concluded "that evidence of the time element involved on the trip, the general circumstances of it, and the absence of any request or expressed desire for the aid of counsel before or at the time of giving information, were sufficient to sustain a conclusion that defendant did waive his constitutional rights as alleged.". . .

Despite Williams' express and implicit assertions of his right to counsel, Detective Leaming proceeded to elicit incriminating statements from Williams. Leaming did not preface this effort by telling Williams that he had a right to the presence of a lawyer, and made no effort at all to ascertain whether Williams wished to relinquish that right. The circumstances of record in this case thus provide no reasonable basis for finding that Williams waived his right to the assistance of counsel.

The Court of Appeals did not hold, nor do we, that under the circumstances of this case Williams *could not*, without notice to counsel, have waived his rights under the Sixth and Fourteenth Amendments. It only held, as do we, that he did not.

The crime of which Williams was convicted was senseless and brutal, calling for swift and energetic action by the police to apprehend the perpetrator and gather evidence with which he could be convicted. No mission of law enforcement officials is more important. Yet "[d]isinterested zeal for the public good does not assure either wisdom or right in the methods it pursues." *Haley* v. *Ohio*... (Frankfurter, J., concurring in the judgment). Although we do not lightly affirm the issuance of a writ of *habeas corpus* in this case, so clear a violation of the Sixth and Fourteenth Amendments as here occurred cannot be condoned. The pressures on state executive and judicial officers charged with the administration of the criminal law are great, especially when the crime is murder and the victim a small child. But it is precisely the predictability of those pressures that makes imperative a resolute loyalty to the guarantees that the Constitution extends to us all.

The judgment of the Court of Appeals is affirmed.

Chief Justice Burger dissenting:

The result reached by the Court in this case ought to be intolerable in any society which purports to call itself an organized society. It continues the Court—by the narrowest margin—on the much criticized course of punishing the public for the mistakes and misdeeds of law enforcement officers, instead of punishing the officer directly, if in fact he is guilty of wrongdoing. It mechanically and blindly keeps reliable evidence from juries whether the claimed constitutional violation involves gross police misconduct or honest human error. Williams is guilty of the savage murder of a small child; no member of the Court contends he is not. While in custody, and after no fewer than *five* warnings of his rights to silence and to counsel, he led police to the place where he had buried the body of his victim. The Court now holds the jury must not be told how the police found the body.

The Court concedes Williams was not threatened or coerced and that he acted voluntarily and with full awareness of his constitutional rights when he guided police to the body. In the face of all this, the Court now holds that because Williams was prompted by the detective's statement—not interrogation but a statement—his disclosure cannot be given to the jury.

The effect of this is to fulfill Justice Cardozo's grim prophecy that someday some court might carry the exclusionary rule to the absurd extent that its operative effect would exclude evidence relating to the body of a murder victim because of the means by which it was found. In so doing the Court regresses to playing a grisly game of "hide and seek," once more exalting the sporting theory of criminal justice which has been experiencing a decline in our jurisprudence. With Justices White and Blackmun, I categorically reject the remarkable notion that the police in this case were guilty of unconstitutional misconduct, or any conduct justifying the bizarre result reached by the Court. Apart from a brief comment on the merits, however, I wish to focus on the irrationality of applying the increasingly discredited exclusionary rule to this case.

Under well-settled precedents which the Court freely acknowledges, it is very clear that Williams had made a valid waiver of his Fifth Amendment right to silence and his Sixth Amendment right to counsel when he led police to the child's body. Indeed, even under the Court's analysis I do not understand how a contrary conclusion is possible.

The Court purports to apply as the appropriate constitutional waiver standard the familiar "intentional relinquishment or abandonment of a known right or privilege" test of *Johnson* v. *Zerbst*...(1938). ... The Court assumes, without deciding, that Williams' conduct and statements were voluntary. ... It concedes, as it must,...that Williams had been informed of and fully understood his constitutional rights and the consequences of their waiver. Then, having either assumed, or found every element necessary to make out a valid waiver under its own test, the Court reaches the astonishing conclusion that no valid waiver has been demonstrated. ...

The evidence is uncontradicted that Williams had abundant knowledge of his right to have counsel present and of his right to silence. Since the Court does not question WIlliams' mental competence, it boggles the mind to suggest that he could not understand that leading police to the child's body would have other than the most serious consequences. All of the elements necessary to make out a valid waiver are shown by the record and, paradoxically, acknowledged by the Court; we thus are left to guess how the Court reached its holding.

One plausible but unarticulated basis for the result reached is that once a suspect has asserted his right not to talk without the presence of an attorney, it becomes legally impossible to waive that right until the suspect has seen an attorney. But constitutional rights are *personal*, and an otherwise valid waiver should not be brushed aside by judges simply because an attorney was not present. The Court's holding operates to "imprison a man in his privileges," *Adams* v. *United States ex rel. McCann*... (1942); it conclusively presumes a suspect is legally incompetent to change his mind and tell the truth until an attorney is present. It denigrates an individual to some sort of nonperson whose free will has become hostage to a lawyer so that until a lawyer consents, the suspect is deprived of any legal right or power to decide for himself that he wishes to make a disclosure. It denies that the rights to counsel and silence are *personal*, nondelegable, and subject to a waiver only by that individual. The opinions in support of the Court's judgment do not enlighten us as to why police conduct—whether good or bad—should operate to suspend Williams' right to change his mind and "tell all" at once rather than waiting until he reached Des Moines.

In his concurring opinion Mr. Justice Powell suggests that the result in this case turns on whether Detective Leaming's remarks constituted "interrogation," as he views them, or whether they were "statements" intended to prick the conscience of the accused. I find it most remarkable that a murder case should turn on judicial interpretation that a statement becomes a question simply because it is followed by an incriminating disclosure from the suspect. The Court seems to be saying that since Williams said he would "tell the whole story" at Des Moines, the police should have been content and waited; of course, that would have been the wiser course, especially in light of the nuances of constitutional jurisprudence applied by the Court, but a murder case ought not turn on such tenuous strands.

In any case, the Court assures us,...this is not at all what it intends, and that a valid waiver was *possible* in these circumstances, but was not quite made. Here of course Williams did not confess to the murder in so many words; it was his conduct in guiding police to the body, not his words, which incriminated him. And the record is replete with evidence that Williams knew precisely what he was doing when he guided police to the body. The human urge to confess wrongdoing is, of course, normal in all save hardened, professional criminals, as psychiatrists and analysts have demonstrated. T. Reik, *The Compulsion to Confess.* ...

The bizarre result reached by the Court today recalls Mr. Justice Black's strong dissent in *Kaufman* v. *United States*... (1969). There, too, a defendant sought release after his conviction had been affirmed on appeal. There, as here, the defendant's guilt was manifest, and was not called into question by the constitutional claims presented. This Court granted relief because it thought reliable evidence had been unconstitutionally obtained. Mr. Justice Black's reaction, foreshadowing our long overdue holding in *Stone* v. *Powell*, serves as a fitting conclusion to the views I have expressed:

"It is seemingly becoming more and more difficult to gain acceptance for the proposition that punishment of the guilty is desirable, other things being equal. One commentator, who attempted in vain to dissuade this Court from today's holding, thought it necessary to point out that there is 'a strong public interest in convicting the guilty.'...

"...I would not let any criminal conviction become invulnerable to collateral attack where there is left remaining the probability or possibility that constitutional commands related to the integrity of the fact-finding process have been violated. In such situations society has failed to perform its obligation to prove beyond a reasonable doubt that the defendant committed the crime. But it is quite a different thing to permit collateral attack on a conviction after a trial according to due process when the defendant clearly is, by the proof and by his own admission, guilty of the crime charged. ... In collateral attacks whether by *habeas corpus* or by §2255 proceedings, I would always require that the convicted defendant raise the kind of constitutional claim that casts some shadow of a doubt on his guilt. This defendant is permitted to attack his conviction collaterally although he conceded at the trial and does not now deny that he had robbed the savings and loan association and although the evidence makes absolutely clear that he knew what he was doing. Thus, his guilt being certain, surely he does not have a constitutional right to get a new trial. I cannot possibly agree with the Court."...

Like Mr. Justice Black in *Kaufman*, I cannot possibly agree with the Court.

Justice White dissenting:

The respondent in this case killed a 10-year-old child. The majority sets aside his conviction, holding that certain statements of unquestioned reliability were unconstitutionally obtained from him, and under the circumstances probably makes it impossible to retry him. Because there is nothing in the Constitution or in our previous cases which requires the Court's action, I dissent. ...

The consequence of the majority's decision is, as the majority recognizes, extremely serious. A mentally disturbed killer whose guilt is not in question may be released. Why? Apparently, the answer is that the majority believes that the law enforcement officers acted in a way which involves some risk of injury to society and that such conduct should be deterred. However, the officers' conduct did not, and was not likely to, jeopardize the fairness of respondent's trial or in any way risk the conviction of an innocent man—the risk against which the Sixth Amendment guaranty of assistance of counsel is designed to protect.

Justice Blackmun dissenting, joined by Justices White and Rehnquist:

The State of Iowa, and 21 states and others. . . strongly urge that this Court's procedural (as distinguished from constitutional) ruling in *Miranda* v. *Arizona*. . . be re-examined and overruled. I, however, agree with the Court. . . that this is not now the case in which that issue need be considered.

What the Court chooses to do here, and with which I disagree, is to hold that respondent Williams' situation was in the mold of *Massiah* v. *United States*. . . (1964), that is, that it was dominated by a denial to Williams of his Sixth Amendment right to counsel after criminal proceedings had been instituted against him. The Court rules that the Sixth Amendment was violated because Detective Leaming "purposely sought during Williams' isolation from his lawyers to obtain as much incriminating information as possible.". . . I cannot regard that as unconstitutional *per se*.

First, the police did not deliberately seek to isolate Williams from his lawyers so as to deprive him of the assistance of counsel. . . . The isolation in this case was a necessary incident of transporting Williams to the county where the crime was committed.

Second, Leaming's purpose was not solely to obtain incriminating evidence. The victim had been missing for only two days, and the police could not be certain that she was dead. Leaming, of course, and in accord with his duty, was "hoping to find out where that little girl was,". . . , but such motivation does not equate with an intention to evade the Sixth Amendment. Moreover, the Court seems to me to place an undue emphasis. . . and aspersion on what it and the lower courts have chosen to call the "Christian burial speech," and on Williams' "deeply religious" convictions.

Third, not every attempt to elicit information should be regarded as "tantamount to interrogation.".... I am not persuaded that Leaming's observations and comments, made as the police car traversed the snowy and slippery miles between Davenport and Des Moines that winter afternoon, were an interrogation, direct or subtle, of Williams. Contrary to this Court's statement...the Iowa Supreme Court appears to me to have thought and held otherwise..., and I agree. Williams, after all, was counseled by lawyers, and warned by the arraigning judge in Davenport and by the police, and yet it was he who started the travel conversations and brought up the subject of the criminal investigation. Without further reviewing the circumstances of the trip, I would say it is clear there was no interrogation. ...

In summary, it seems to me that the Court is holding that *Massiah* is violated whenever police engage in any conduct, in the absence of counsel, with the subjective desire to obtain information from a suspect after arraignment. Such a rule is far too broad. Persons in custody frequently volunteer statements in response to stimuli other than interrogation. ... When there is no interrogation, such statements should be admissible as long as they are truly voluntary.

The *Massiah* point thus being of no consequence, I would vacate the judgment of the Court of Appeals and remand the case for consideration of the issue of voluntariness, in the constitutional sense, of Williams' statements, an issue the Court of Appeals did not reach when the case was before it.

One final word: I can understand the discomfiture the Court obviously suffers and expresses in...its opinion...and the like discomfiture expressed by Justice (now United States District Judge) Stuart of the Iowa court in the dissent he felt compelled to make by this Court's precedents. ... This was a brutal, tragic, and heinous crime inflicted upon a young girl on the afternoon of the day before Christmas. With the exclusionary rule operating as the Court effectuates it, the decision today probably means that, as a practical matter, no new trial will be possible at this date eight years after the crime, and that this respondent necessarily will go free. That, of course, is not the standard by which a case of this kind strictly is to be judged. But, as Judge Webster in dissent below observed..., placing the case in sensible and proper perspective: "The evidence of Williams' guilt was overwhelming. No challenge is made to the reliability of the fact-finding process." I am in full agreement with that observation.

The Fourth Amendment—
The Exclusionary Rule

Another of the major areas of disagreement between the Warren and Burger Courts involves the Constitution's Fourth Amendment, which reads: "The right of the people to be secure in their persons, houses, papers, and effects, against unreasonable searches and seizures, shall not be violated, and no Warrants shall issue, but upon probable cause, supported by Oath or affirmation, and particularly describing the place to be searched, and the persons or things to be seized."

Some authorities consider the Fourth Amendment the most important provision of the Bill of Rights. According to Prof. Monrad Paulsen, "the other freedoms, freedom of speech, of assembly, of religion, of political action, presuppose that arbitrary and capricious police action has been restrained. Security in one's home and person is the fundamental right without which there can be no liberty."

The Fourth Amendment seeks to guard against "unreasonable searches and seizures" by requiring government agents to obtain search warrants. In general, in order to obtain a warrant the police must present to a magistrate sufficient evidence to demonstrate "probable cause" that a crime was or is about to be committed.* A warrant under the Fourth

---

*The Supreme Court permits the search of an auto if there is probable cause to believe that it contains contraband or that it is being used to violate the

Amendment, moreover, must be specific "in particularly describing the place to be searched and the persons or things to be seized." A warrant that does not meet this requirement is referred to as a general warrant. The Fourth Amendment's ban on general warrants relates directly to the use of such warrants by the British prior to the American Revolution.

The major question involved in interpreting the Fourth Amendment is this: Can evidence obtained in violation of the Fourth Amendment be used as evidence in court? A ban on the use of such evidence in court is referred to as the "exclusionary rule."

Two theories have been advanced in support of the exclusionary rule. One holds that the prestige and moral authority of the government is undermined when the government uses evidence that, although valid, has been obtained by unconstitutional methods. Expressing this position, Justice Louis Brandeis said: "Our government is potent, the omnipresent teacher. For good or for ill, it teaches the whole people by its example. Crime is contagious. If the government becomes a law breaker, it breeds contempt for law."

Others see the exclusionary rule primarily as a means of regulating the police. This view was set forth by Supreme Court Justice Frank Murphy in 1949. According to Murphy: "Only by exclusion can we impress upon the zealous prosecutor that violation of the Constitution will do him no good. And only when that point is driven home can the prosecutor be expected to emphasize the importance of observing constitutional demands in his instructions to the police." The difficulty of this position was described by Justice Benjamin Cardozo: "The criminal is to go free because the constable has blundered. . . . A room is searched against the law, and the body of a murdered man is found. . . . The privacy of the home has been infringed, and the murderer goes free."

---

law. Another exception to the general rule requiring search warrants permits the police to search a person placed under arrest.

The ability of the exclusionary rule to deter unconstitutional police behavior has been questioned by a number of authorities. In some 80% of all felony cases there is no trial from which evidence can be excluded because the defendant chooses to plead guilty in the hope of receiving a lesser sentence. Also, as Chief Justice Warren Earl Burger pointed out in 1971: "The prosecutor who loses his case because of police misconduct is not an official of the police department. . . . He does not have control or direction over police procedures or police action that lead to the exclusion of evidence."

To some critics, the most unsatisfactory aspect of the exclusionary rule is its heavy-handedness. An honest, relatively insignificant error on the part of a policeman can lead to the exclusion of valuable evidence just as does deliberate, wholesale violation of a defendant's rights.

Defenders of the exclusionary rule, while acknowledging its defects, argue that police practices have improved throughout the country in recent years as a result of the exclusionary rule and that the Supreme Court was forced to seek to control police behavior because of the failure of state and local governments to discharge this responsibility.

Use of Illegally Seized Evidence

The Supreme Court in *Weeks v. United States* held in 1914 that evidence produced by illegal searches could not be used in federal trials. Since the Bill of Rights had not been applied to the states at that time, the question of whether such evidence could be introduced in state trials did not arise.

In *Wolf v. Colorado*, the Supreme Court held in 1949 that the Fourth Amendment was binding on the states. In requiring the states to adhere to the Fourth Amendment, the court, however, refused to prohibit the use of unconstitutionally seized evidence in state trials. Justice Felix Frankfurter noted in the majority opinion that such evidence could be used in most English-speaking countries and that in the U.S. only 17 states followed the federal practice of barring the use in court of illegally obtained evidence.

In one of the most controversial rulings in Supreme Court history, the Warren Court overturned that precedent June 19, 1961 in barring the use of evidence obtained in violation of the Fourth Amendment in state trials. The 5-4 decision was rendered in the case of *Mapp v. Ohio*. As stated by the majority: "There is no war between the Constitution and common sense. Presently, a federal prosecutor may make no use of evidence illegally seized, but a state's attorney across the street may, although he supposedly is operating under the enforcement prohibitions of the same amendment. Thus the state, by admitting evidence unlawfully seized, serves to encourage disobedience to the federal Constitution which it is bound to uphold."

In conceding the truth of Justice Benjamin Cardozo's remark that under the exclusionary rule the "criminal is to go free because the constable has blundered," the majority asserted that the integrity of the judicial process demanded such a course. "Nothing can destroy a government more quickly than its failure to observe its own laws, or worse, its disregard of the charter of its own existence," it said.

Almost immediately on being appointed to the Supreme Court in 1969, Chief Justice Burger made clear his opposition to the exclusionary rule. His attitude suggested that the exclusionary rule might ultimately be abandoned or seriously undermined by a new majority.

Chief Justice Burger's dislike of the exclusionary rule was first set forth in his dissenting opinion in *Bivens v. Six Unknown Agents*, decided June 21, 1971. The issue before the Court was whether an individual can bring an action in federal court to sue for violation of his Fourth Amendment rights.

Webster Bivens, an ex-convict and narcotics dealer, had sought to bring suit in federal court after six agents of the Federal Bureau of Narcotics entered his apartment at 6:30 one morning and arrested him for alleged narcotics violations. The agents had neither an arrest nor a search warrant. They handcuffed Bivens in front of his wife and children, threatened to arrest the entire family and searched the apartment. Bivens was then taken to a federal courthouse, where he was interrogated and booked. Thereafter, Bivens sought to sue each agent for $15,000 for what he described as great humiliation, embarrassment and mental suffering as a result of the agents' conduct.

The majority ruled that Bivens' suit could be brought to court. Chief Justice Burger, in dissent, accused the majority of constructing a "remedy of its own" to compensate for the failure of the exclusionary rule to deter such unconstitutional police behavior. Rather than encouraging damage suits against law officers, Burger suggested that Congress establish a special tribunal to award damages "to the completely innocent persons who are sometimes the victims of illegal police conduct." Such a proposal, he said, by compensating victims of unconstitutional searches, would negate the need for an exclusionary rule as a check on police misconduct while permitting redress to innocent victims of police misconduct.

Justices Warn vs. Abandoning Exclusionary Rule

In a dissenting opinion in *U.S. v. Peltier*, decided June 25, 1975, Justice Brennan, joined by Justice Marshall, took strong exception to what they considered the court's emerging view that the exclusionary rule should not be applied in instances of good faith police violations of the Fourth Amendment.

The case centered on whether *Almeida-Sanchez v. U.S.*, a 1973 decision, should be applied retroactively. That case held that random warrantless automobile searches conducted some 25 miles from the Mexican border by border-patrol agents violated the Fourth Amendment. Four months before that decision, Peltier had been stopped in his car by roving border-patrol officials acting without a warrant near the Mexican border. Evidence of unlawful possession of marijuana was found in the car trunk. Attorneys for Peltier argued that the conviction should be overturned on the ground that *Almeida-Sanchez* should be retroactively applied.

By a 5-4 vote, the Court ruled that *Almeida-Sanchez* should not be applied to searches preceding its announcement. Justice Rehnquist, in the majority opinion, reasoned that the exclusionary rule is designed to serve to deter Fourth Amendment violations and to preserve judicial integrity by refusing to sanction willful unconstitutional practices. Neither of these purposes, he said, would be served by applying *Almeida-Sanchez* retroactively.

Thus, reasoned the majority, "If the purpose of the exclusionary rule is do deter unlawful police conduct, then evidence obtained from a search should be suppressed only if it can be said that the law enforcement officer had knowledge, or may properly be charged with knowledge, that the search was unconstitutional under the Fourth Amendment."

The Brennan-Marshall dissent argued that the logic of this proposition could be applied with equal force to all Fourth Amendment violations in stating their belief that the good-faith violation exception used in this case would, "when a suitable opportunity arises," be held "applicable to all search and seizure cases."

Contrary to the majority, they stated, the exclusionary rule is not based on the deterrence rationale. Rather, they said, it focuses "upon general, not specific deterrence" and depends "not upon threatening a sanction for lack of compliance but upon removing an inducement to violate Fourth Amendment rights." The rule, they said, is aimed at all law enforcement officers and society at large.

According to the dissenters, were the exclusionary rule limited to deliberate Fourth Amendment violations, as suggested by the majority, the courts would be faced with the difficult task of determining the state of mind of the police officers involved in each Fourth Amendment case in deciding whether to admit certain evidence into court.

Burger Further Denounces Exclusionary Rule

In 1976, Chief Justice Burger further discussed what he considered the drawbacks of the exclusionary rule. The case involved was *Stone v. Powell*. The issue before the Court was whether a person convicted in state courts could appeal in federal court on the basis of an alleged violation of the Fourth Amendment following a full and fair review of the Fourth Amendment claim in state court. The majority in a 6-3 decision held that such claims could not be raised in federal court. Burger, in a concurring opinion, enlarged on his views concerning the exclusionary rule as previously stated in *Bivens*. Justice White, in a separate opinion, stated that he would join four or more justices in "substantially limiting the reach of the exclusionary rule as presently administered under the Fourth Amendent in federal and state criminal trials."

Burger, in opposition to the exclusionary rule, claimed that time had shown the need to modify the exclusionary rule, "even if it is retained for a small and limited category of cases." He described the function of the exclusionary rule as "simple—the exclusion of truth from the fact-finding process."

The operation of the rule under the Fourth Amendment is unlike the exclusion of unconstitutionally obtained confessions, he said. "A confession produced after intimidating or coercive interrogation is inherently dubious," he asserted. The Fourth Amendment exclusionary rule, on the other hand, he continued, "is based on the hope that events in the courtroom or appellate chambers, long after the crucial acts took place, will somehow modify the way in which policemen conduct themselves. A more clumsy, less direct means of imposing sanctions is difficult to imagine, particularly since the issue whether the policeman did indeed run afoul of the Fourth Amendment is not resolved until years after the event."

According to the Chief Justice, "[n]otwithstanding Herculean efforts, no empirical study has been able to demonstrate that the rule does in fact have any deterrent effect." Therefore, he said, "The burden rightly rests upon those who ask society to ignore trustworthy evidence of guilt, at the expense of setting obviously guilty criminals free to ply their trade."

Burger noted that in his *Bivens* dissent five years earlier he had suggested that the exclusionary rule need not be totally abandoned until some meaningful alternative to protect innocent persons from police misconduct had been adopted. But now, he said, he was persuaded that continued court approval of the exclusionary rule was a barrier to such legislative reform since the legislatures had no assurance that the adoption of such a remedy would cause the courts to drop the exclusionary rule.

In urging his fellow justices to overturn the exclusionary rule, or to limit its scope to "egregious, bad-faith conduct," Burger predicted that such action "would inspire a surge of activity toward providing some kind of statutory remedy for persons injured by police mistakes or misconduct."

Justice White, in agreeing with Burger concerning the workings of the exclusionary rule, stated that *Mapp* should not be overruled but rather should be "substantially modified so as to prevent its application in those many circumstances where the evidence at issue was seized by an officer acting in the good-faith belief that his conduct comported with existing law and having reasonable grounds for this belief."

On the issue of whether the use of such unconstitutionally obtained evidence in court would taint the judicial process, White claimed that "[a]dmitting the evidence in such circumstances does not render judges participants in Fourth Amendment violations. The violation, if there was one, has already occurred and the evidence is at hand. Furthermore, there has been only mistaken, but unintentional and faultless conduct by enforcement officers. Exclusion of the evidence does not cure the invasion of the defendant's rights which he has already suffered."

ABRIDGMENTS OF DECISIONS ON FOURTH AMEND-MENT & EXCLUSIONARY RULE

Bivens v. Six Unknown Agents (403 U.S. 388 June 21, 1971)

Chief Justice Burger dissenting:

I dissent from today's holding which judicially creates a damage remedy not provided for by the Constitution and not enacted by Congress. We would more surely preserve the important values of the doctrine of separation of powers—and perhaps get a better result—by recommending a solution to the Congress as the branch of government in which the Constitution has vested the legislative power. Legislation is the business of the Congress, and it has the facilities and competence for that task—as we do not. . . .

This case has significance far beyond its facts and its holding. For more than 55 years this court has enforced a rule under which evidence of undoubted reliability and probative value had been suppressed and excluded from criminal cases whenever it was obtained in violation of the Fourth Amendment. *Weeks v. United States*. . . (1914). . . . This rule was extended to the States in *Mapp v. Ohio*. . . . The rule has rested on a theory that suppression of evidence in these circumstances was imperative to deter law enforcement authorities from using improper methods to obtain evidence.

The deterrence theory underlying the suppression doctrine, or exclusionary rule, has a certain appeal in spite of the high price society pays for such a drastic remedy. Notwithstanding its plausibility many judges and lawyers and some of our most distinguished legal scholars have never quite been able to escape the force of Cardozo's statement of the doctrine's anomalous result: "The criminal is to go free because the constable has blundered. . . . A room is searched against the law, and the body of a murdered man is found. . . . The privacy of the home has been infringed, and the murderer goes free." *People v. DeFore*. . . .

The plurality opinion in *Irvine v. California*. . . (1954) catalogued the doctrine's defects: "Rejection of the evidence does nothing to punish the wrongdoing official, while it may, and likely will, release the wrongdoing defendant. It deprives society of its remedy against one lawbreaker because he has been pursued by another. It protects one against whom incriminating evidence is discovered, but does nothing to protect innocent persons who are the victims of illegal but fruitless searches.''

From time to time members of the Court, recognizing the validity of these protests, have articulated varying alternative justifications for the suppression of important evidence in a criminal trial. Under one of these alternative theories the rule's foundation is shifted to the "sporting contest" thesis that the government must "play the game fairly" and cannot be allowed to profit from its own illegal acts. *Olmstead v. United States*...(1928) (dissenting opinions). ... But the exclusionary rule does not ineluctably flow from a desire to ensure that government plays the "game" according to the rules. If an effective alternative remedy is available, concern for official observance of the law does not require adherence to the exclusionary rule. Nor is it easy to understand how a court can be thought to endorse a violation of the Fourth Amendment by allowing illegally seized evidence to be introduced against a defendant if an effective remedy is provided against the government.

The exclusionary rule has also been justified on the theory that the relationship between the self-incrimination clause of the Fifth Amendment and the Fourth Amendment requires the suppression of evidence seized in violation of the latter. ...

Even ignoring, however, the decisions of this Court which have held that the Fifth Amendment applies only to "testimonial" disclosures, *United States v. Wade*...(1967); *Schmerber v. California* ...(1966), it seems clear that the self-incrimination clause does not protect a person from the seizure of evidence that is incriminating. It protects a person only from being the conduit by which the police acquire evidence. Mr. Justice Holmes once put it succinctly, "A party is privileged from producing the evidence but not from its production." *Johnson v. United States*...(1913).

It is clear, however, that neither of these theories undergirds the decided cases in this Court. Rather the exclusionary rule has rested on the deterrent rationale—the hope that law enforcement officials would be deterred from unlawful searches and seizures if the illegally seized, albeit trustworthy, evidence was suppressed often enough and the courts persistently enough deprived them of any benefits they might have gained from their illegal conduct.

This evidentiary rule is unique to American jurisprudence. Although the English and Canadian legal systems are highly regarded, neither has adopted our rule.

I do not question the need for some remedy to give meaning and teeth to the constitutional guarantees against unlawful conduct by government officials. . . . But the hope that this objective could be accomplished by the exclusion of reliable evidence from criminal trials was hardly more than a wistful dream. Although I would hesitate to abandon it until some meaningful substitute is developed, the history of the suppression doctrine demonstrates that it is both conceptually sterile and practically ineffective in accomplishing its stated objective. This is illustrated by the paradox that an unlawful act against a totally innocent person—such as petitioner claims to be—has been left without an effective remedy, and hence the court finds it necessary now—55 years later—to construct a remedy of its own.

Some clear demonstration of the benefits and effectiveness of the exclusionary rule is required to justify it in view of the high price it extracts from society—the release of countless guilty criminals. . . . But there is no empirical evidence to support the claim that the rule actually deters illegal conduct of law enforcement officials. . . .

There are several reasons for this failure. The rule does not apply any direct sanction to the individual official whose illegal conduct results in the exclusion of evidence in a criminal trial. With rare exceptions law enforcement agencies do not impose direct sanctions on the individual officer responsible for a particular judicial application of the suppression doctrine. . . . Thus there is virtually nothing done to bring about a change in his practices. The immediate sanction triggered by the application of the rule is visited upon the presecutor whose case against a criminal is either weakened or destroyed. The doctrine deprives the police in no real sense. . . .

The suppression doctrine vaguely assumes that law enforcement is a monolithic governmental enterprise. For example, the dissenters in *Wolfe v. Colorado*. . . argued that "Only by exclusion can we impress upon the zealous *prosecutor* that violation of the Constitution will do him no good. And only when that point is driven home can the *prosecutor* be expected to emphasize the importance of observing the constitutional demands in *his instructions to the police.*" (Emphasis added.)

But the prosecutor who loses his case because of police misconduct is not an official in the police department; he can rarely set in motion any corrective action or administrative penalties. Moreover, he does not have control or direction over police procedures of police action that lead to the exclusion of evidence. . . .

Whatever educational effect the rule conceivably might have in theory is greatly diminished in fact by the realities of law enforcement work. Policemen do not have the time, inclination or training to read and grasp the nuances of the appellate opinions that ultimately define the standards of conduct they are to follow. ...

The presumed educational effect of judicial opinions is also reduced by the long time lapse—often several years—between the original police action and its final judicial evaluation. Given a policeman's pressing responsibilities, it would be surprising if he ever becomes aware of the final result after such a delay. Finally the exclusionary rule's deterrent impact is diluted by the fact that there are large areas of police activity which do not result in criminal prosecutions—hence the rule has virtually no applicability and no effect in such situations. ...

Today's holding seeks to fill one of the gaps of the suppression doctrine—at the price of impinging on the legislative and policy functions which the Constitution vests in Congress. Nevertheless, the holding serves the useful purpose of exposing the fundamental weaknesses of the suppression doctrine. Suppressing unchallenged truth has set guilty criminals free but demonstrably has neither deterred deliberate violations of the Fourth Amendment nor decreased those errors in judgment which will inevitably occur given the pressures inherent in police work having to do with serious crimes.

Although unfortunately ineffective, the exclusionary rule has increasingly been characterized by a single, monolithic and drastic judicial response to all official violations of legal norms. Inadvertent errors of judgment that do not work any grave injustice will inevitably occur under the pressure of police work. These honest mistakes have been treated in the same way as deliberate and flagrant *Irvine*-type violations of the Fourth Amendment. For example, in *Miller v. United States*...(1958), reliable evidence was suppressed because of a police officer's failure to say a "few more words" during the arrest and search of a known narcotics peddler.

This court's decision announced today in *Coolidge v. New Hampshire* dramatically illustrates the extent to which the doctrine represents a mechanically inflexible response to widely varying degrees of police error and the resulting high price which society pays. I dissented in *Coolidge* primarily because I do not believe the Fourth Amendment had been violated. Even on the court's contrary premise, however, whatever violation occurred was surely insufficient in nature and extent to justify the drastic result dictated by the suppression doctrine. A fair trial by jury has resolved doubts as to Coolidge's guilt. But now his conviction on retrial is placed in serious question by the remand for a new trial—years after the crime—in which evidence which the New Hampshire courts found relevant and reliable will be withheld from the jury's consideration. . . .

Freeing either a tiger or a mouse in a schoolroom is an illegal act, but no rational person would suggest that these acts should be punished in the same way. From time to time judges have occasion to pass on regulations governing police procedures. I wonder what would be the judicial response to a police order authorizing "shoot-to-kill" with respect to every fugitive. It is easy to predict our collective wrath and outrage. We, in common with all rational minds, would say that the police response must relate to the gravity and need; that a "shoot" order might conceivably be tolerable to prevent the escape of a convicted killer but surely not for a car thief, a pickpocket or a shoplifter.

I submit that society has at least as much right to expect rationally graded responses from judges in place of the universal "capital punishment" we inflict on all evidence when police error is shown in its acquisition. . . . Yet for over 55 years, and with increasing scope and intensity as today's *Coolidge* holding shows, our legal system has treated vastly dissimilar cases as if they were the same. . . .

Instead of continuing to enforce the suppression doctrine, inflexibly, rigidly, and mechanically, we should view it as one of the experimental steps in the great tradition of the common law and acknowledge its shortcomings. But in the same spirit we should be prepared to discontinue what the experience of over half a century has shown neither deters errant officers nor affords a remedy to the totally innocent victims of official misconduct.

I do not propose, however, that we abandon the suppression doctrine until some meaningful alternative can be developed. In a sense our legal system has become the captive of its own creation. To overrule *Weeks* and *Mapp*, even assuming the court was not prepared to take that step, could raise yet new problems. Obviously the public interest would be poorly served if law enforcement officials were suddenly to gain the impression, however erroneous, that all constitutional restraints on police had somehow been removed—that an open season on "criminals" had been declared.

Reasonable and effective substitutes [for the suppression doctrine] can be formulated if Congress would take the lead. . . . I see no insuperable obstacle to the elimination of the suppression doctrine if Congress would provide some meaningful and effective remedy against unlawful conduct by government officials.

The problems of both error and deliberate misconduct by law enforcement officials call for a workable remedy. Private damage actions against individual police officers concededly have not adequately met this requirement, and it would be fallacious to assume today's work of the court in creating a remedy will really accomplish its stated objective. There is some validity to the claims that juries will not return verdicts against individual officers except in those unusual cases where the violation has been flagrant or where the error has been complete, as in the arrest of the wrong person or the search of the wrong house. . . . Jurors may well refuse to penalize a police officer at the behest of a person they believe to be a "criminal" and probably will not punish an officer for honest errors of judgment. . . .

I conclude, therefore, that an entirely different remedy is necessary but it is one that in my view is as much beyond judicial power as the step the court takes today. Congress should develop an administrative or quasi-judicial remedy against the government itself to afford compensation and restitution for persons whose Fourth Amendment rights have been violated. . . .

A simple structure would suffice. For example, Congress could enact a statute along the following lines: (a) a waiver of sovereign immunity as to the illegal acts of law enforcement officials committed in the performance of assigned duties; (b) the creation of a cause of action for damages sustained by any person aggrieved by conduct of governmental agents in violation of the Fourth Amendment or statutes regulating official conduct; (c) the creation of a tribunal. . .to adjudicate all claims under the statute; (d) a provision that this statutory remedy is in lieu of the exclusion of evidence securled for use in criminal cases in violation of the Fourth Amendment; and (e) a provision directing that no evidence, otherwise admissible, shall be excluded from any criminal proceeding because of violation of the Fourth Amendment.

. . .Finally, appellate judicial review could be made available on much the same basis that it is now provided as to district courts and regulatory agencies. This would leave to the courts the ultimate responsibility for determining and articulating standards.

Once the constitutional validity of such a statute is established, it can reasonably be assumed that the states would develop their own remedial systems on the federal model. Indeed there is nothing to prevent a state from enacting a comparable statutory scheme without waiting on the Congress. Steps along these lines would move our system toward more responsible law enforcement on the one hand and away from the irrational and drastic results of the suppression doctrine on the other. Independent of the alternative embraced in this dissenting opinion, I believe the time has come to re-examine the scope of the exclusionary rule and consider at least some narrowing of its thrust so as to eliminate the anomalies it has produced.

...I can only hope now that the Congress will manifest a willingness to view realistically the hard evidence of the half-century history of the suppression doctrine revealing thousands of cases in which the criminal was set free because of the constable blundered and virtually no evidence that innocent victims of police error... have been afforded meaningful redress.

U.S. v. Peltier 422 U.S. 531 (June 25, 1975)

Justice Brennan dissenting, joined by Justice Marshall:

...The Court's opinion depends upon an entirely new understandng of the exclusionary rule in Fourth Amendment cases, one which, if the vague contours outlined today are filled in as I fear they will be, forecasts the complete demise of the exclusionary rule as fashioned by this Court in over 61 years of Fourth Amendment jurisprudence. See *Weeks* v. *United States*...(1914). An analysis of the Court's unsuccessfully veiled reformulation demonstrates that its apparent rush to discard 61 years of constitutional development has produced a formula difficult to comprehend and, on any understanding of its meaning, impossible to justify.

The Court signals its new approach in these words: "If the purpose of the exclusionary rule is to deter unlawful police conduct, then evidence obtained from a search should be suppressed only if it can be said that the law enforcement officer had knowledge, or may properly be charged with knowledge, that the search was unconstitutional under the Fourth Amendment."...True, the Court does not state in so many words that this formulation of the exclusionary rule is to be applied beyond the present retroactivity context. But the proposition is stated generally and, particularly in view of the concomitant expansion of prospectivity announced today,...I have no confidence that the new formulation is to be confined to putative retroactivity cases. Rather, I suspect that when a suitable opportunity arises, today's revision of the exclusionary rule will be pronounced applicable to all search-and-seizure cases. I therefore register my strong disagreement now.

The new formulation obviously removes the very foundation of the exclusionary rule as it has been expressed in countless decisions. Until now the rule in federal criminal cases decided on direct review has been that suppression is necessarily the sanction to be applied when it is determined that the evidence was in fact illegally acquired. The revision unveiled today suggests that instead of that single inquiry, district judges may also have to probe the subjective knowledge of the official who orders the search, and the inferences from existing law that official should have drawn. The decision whether or not to order suppression would then turn upon whether based on that expanded inquiry, suppression would comport with either the deterrence rationale of the exclusionary rule or "the imperative of judicial integrity.". . .

Other defects of today's new formulation are also patent. First, this new doctrine could stop dead in its tracks judicial development of Fourth Amendment rights. For if evidence is to be admitted in criminal trials in the absence of clear precedent declaring the search in question unconstitutional, the first duty of a court will be to deny the accused's motion to suppress if he cannot cite a case invalidating a search of seizure on identical facts. Yet, even its opponents concede that the great service of the exclusionary rule has been its usefulness in forcing judges to enlighten our understanding of Fourth Amendment guarantees. "It is. . .imperative to have a practical procedure by which courts can review alleged violations of constitutional rights and articulate the meaning of those rights. The advantage of the exclusionary rule—entirely apart from any direct deterrent effect—is that it provides an occasion for judicial review, and it gives credibility to the constitutional guarantees. By demonstrating that society will attach serious consequences to the violation of constitutional rights, the exclusionary rule invokes and magnifies the moral and educative force of the law. Over the long term this may integrate some fourth amendment ideals into the value system or norms of behavior of law enforcement agencies." Oaks, Studying the Exclusionary Rule in Search and Seizure, 37 *U. Chi. L. Rev.* 665, 756 (1970). . . . While distinguished authority has suggested that an effective affirmative remedy could equally serve that function, see Oaks,. . .and *Bivens* v. *Six Unknown Federal*

Narcotics Agents...(1971) (Burger, C. J., dissenting), no equally effective alternative has yet been devised.

Second, contrary to the Court's assumption, the exclusionary rule does not depend in its deterrence rationale on the punishment of individual law enforcement officials. Indeed, one general fallacy in the reasoning of critics of the exclusionary rule is the belief that the rule is meant to deter official wrongdoers by punishment or threat of punishment. It is also the fallacy of the Court's attempt today to outline a revision in the exclusionary rule.

Deterrence can operate in several ways. The simplest is special or specific deterrence—punishing an individual so that *he* will not repeat the same behavior. But "[t]he exclusionary rule is not aimed at special deterrence since it does not impose any direct punishment on a law enforcement official who has broken the rule. ... The exclusionary rule is aimed at affecting the wider audience of all law enforcement officials and society at large. It is meant to discourage violations by individuals who have never experienced any sanction for them." Oaks....

Thus, the exclusionary rule, focused upon general, not specific, deterrence, depends not upon threatening a sanction for lack of compliance but upon removing an *inducement* to violate Fourth Amendment rights. *Elkins v. United States...*(1960), clearly explained that the exclusionary rule's "purpose is to deter—to compel respect for the constitutional guaranty in the only effectively available way—*by removing the incentive to disregard it.*" (Emphasis added.) "A criminal court system functioning without an exclusionary rule...is the equivalent of a government purchasing agent paying premium prices for evidence branded with the stamp of unconstitutionality.... If [the government] receives the products of [illegal] searches and seizures...and uses them as the means of convicting people whom the officer conceives it to be his job to get convicted, it is not merely tolerating but *inducing* unconstitutional searches and seizures." Amsterdam.... Perspectives on the 4th amendment, 58 *Minn. L. Rev. (1974)*...(Emphasis supplied.)

Today's formulation extended to all search-and-seizure cases would inevitably introduce the same uncertainty, by adding a new layer of factfinding in deciding motions to suppress in the already heavily burdened federal courts. The district courts would have to determine, and the appellate courts to review, subjective states of mind of numerous people...and reasonable objective extrapolations of existing law, on each of the thousands of suppression motions presented each year. Nice questions will have to be faced, such as whether to exclude evidence obtained in a search which officers believed to be unconstitutional but which in fact was not, and whether to exclude evidence obtained in a search in fact unconstitutional and believed to be unconstitutional, but which the ordinary, reasonable police officer might well have believed was constitutional. One criticism of the present formulation of the exclusionary rule is that it may deflect the inquiry in a criminal trial from the guilt of the defendant to the culpability of the police. The formulation suggested today would vastly exacerbate this possibility, heavily burden the lower courts, and worst of all, erode irretrievably the efficacy of the exclusion principle. Indeed, "no [federal] court could know what it should rule in order to keep its processes on solid constitutional ground.". . . Because of the superficial and summary way that the Court treats the question the formulation will, I am certain, be unsatisfactory even to those convinced, as I am not, that the exclusionary rule must be drastically overhauled.

If a majority of my colleagues are determined to discard the exclusionary rule in Fourth Amendment cases, they should forthrightly do so, and be done with it. This business of slow strangulation of the rule, with no opportunity afforded parties most concerned to be heard, would be indefensible in any circumstances. But to attempt covertly the erosion of an important principle over 61 years in the making as applied in federal courts clearly demeans the adjudicatory function, and the institutional integrity of this Court.

Stone v. Powell (July 6, 1976)

Chief Justice Burger concurring:

I concur in the Court's opinion. By way of dictum, and somewhat hesitantly, the Court notes that the holding in this case leaves undisturbed the exclusionary rule as applied to criminal trials. For reasons stated in my dissent in *Bivens v. Six Unknown Named Federal Agents*. . .(1971), it seems clear to me that the exclusionary rule has been operative long enough to demonstrate its flaws. The time has come to modify its reach, even if it is retained for a small and limited category of cases.

Over the years, the strains imposed by reality, in terms of the costs to society and the bizarre miscarriages of justice that have been experienced because of the exclusion of reliable evidence when the "constable blunders," have led the Court to vacillate as to the rationale for deliberate exclusion of truth from the factfinding process. The rhetoric has varied with the rationale to the point where the rule has become a doctrinaire result in search of validating reasons.

In evaluating the exclusionary rule, it is important to bear in mind exactly what the rule accomplishes. Its function is simple—the exclusion of truth from the factfindng process.... The operation of the rule is therefore unlike that of the Fifth Amendment's protection against compelled self-incrimination. A confession produced after intimidating or coercive interrogation is inherently dubious. If a suspect's will has been overborne, a cloud hangs over his custodial admissions; the exclusion of such statements is based essentially on their lack of reliability. This is not the case as to *reliable* evidence—a pistol, a packet of heroin, counterfeit money, or the body of a murder victim—which may be judicially declared to be the result of an "unreasonable" search. The reliability of such evidence is beyond question; its probative value is certain.

This remarkable situation—one unknown to the common-iaw tradition—had its genesis in a case calling for the protection of private papers against governmental intrusions. *Boyd v. United States*. . . (1886). See also *Weeks v. United States*. . . (1914). In *Boyd*, the Court held that private papers were inadmissible because of the government's violation of the Fourth and Fifth Amendments. In Weeks, the Court excluded private letters seized from the accused's home by a federal official acting without a warrant. In both cases, the Court had a clear vision of what it was seeking to protect. What the Court said in *Boyd* shows how far we have strayed from the original path:

> "The search for and seizure of stolen or forfeited goods, or goods liable to duties and concealed to avoid the payment thereof, *are totally different things from a search for and seizure of a man's private books and papers* for the purpose of obtaining information therein contained, or of using them as evidence against him. The two things differ *toto coelo*." . . . (Emphasis added.)

'In *Weeks*, the Court emphasized that the Goverment, under settled principles of common law, had no right to keep a person's *private papers.* The Court noted that the case did not involve "burglar's tools or other *proofs of guilt....*" (Emphasis added.)

From this origin, the exclusionary rule has been changed in focus entirely. It is now used almost exclusively to exclude from evidence articles which are unlawful to be possessed or tools and instruments of crime. Unless it can be rationally thought that the Framers considered it essential to protect the liberties of the people to hold that which it is unlawful to possess, then it becomes clear that our constitutional course has taken a most bizarre tack.

The drastically changed nature of judicial concern—from the protection of personal papers or effects in one's private quarters, to the exclusion of that which the accused had no right to possess—is only one of the more recent anamolies of the rule. The original incongruity was the rule's inconsistency with the general proposition that "our legal system does not attempt to do justice incidentally and to enforce penalties by indirect means." 8 Wigmore, *Evidence* § 2181, at 6 (McNaughten rev ed 1961). The rule is based on the hope that events in the courtroom or appellate chambers, long after the crucial acts took place, will somehow modify the way in which policemen conduct themselves. A more clumsy, less direct means of imposing sanctions is difficult to imagine, particularly since the issue whether the policeman did indeed run afoul of the Fourth Amendment is often not resolved until years after the events....

Despite this anamoly, the exclusionary rule now rests upon its purported tendency to deter police misconduct,...although, as we know, the rule has long been applied to wholly good-faith mistakes and to purely technical deficiencies in warrants. Other rhetorical generalizations, including the "imperative of judicial integrity," have not withstood analysis as more and more critical appraisals of the rule's operation have appeared. See, *e.g.,* Oaks, Studying the Exclusionary Rule in Search and Seizure, 37 *U Chi L Rev* 665 (1970). Indeed, settled rules demonstrate that the "judicial integrity" rationalization is fatally flawed. First, the Court has refused to entertain claims that evidence was unlawfully seized unless the claimant could demonstrate that he had standing to press the contention. ... Second, as one scholar has correctly observed:

"[I]t is difficult to accept the proposition that the exclusion of improperly obtained evidence is necessary for 'judicial integrity' when no such rule is observed in other common law jurisdictions such as England and Canada, whose courts are otherwise regarded as models of judicial decorum and fairness." Oaks.

Despite its avowed deterrent objective, proof is lacking that the exclusionary rule, a purely judge-created device based on "hard cases," serves the purpose of deterrence. Notwithstanding Herculean efforts, no empirical study has been able to demonstrate that the rule does in fact have any deterrent effect. In the face of dwindling support for the rule some would go so far as to extend it to civil cases. *United States v. Janis*. . . [1976]

To vindicate the continued existence of this judge-made rule, it is incumbent upon those who seek its retention—and surely its *extension*—to demonstrate that it serves its declared deterrent purpose and to show that the results outweigh the rule's heavy costs to rational enforcement of the criminal law. . . . The burden rightly rests upon those who ask society to ignore trustworthy evidence of guilt, at the expense of setting obviously guilty criminals free to ply their trade.

In my view, it is an abdication of judicial responsibility to exact such exorbitant costs from society purely on the basis of speculative and unsubstantiated assumptions. Judge Henry Friendly has observed:

> "[T]he same authority that empowered the Court to supplement the [Fourth] Amendment by the exclusionary rule a hundred and twenty-five years after its adoption, likewise allows it to modify that rule as the 'lessons of experience' may teach." Friendly, The Bill of Rights as a Code of Criminal Procedure, 53 *Cal L Rev* 929, 952-953 (1965).

In *Bivens,* I suggested that, despite its grave shortcomings, the rule need not be totally abandoned until some meaningful alternative could be developed to protect innocent persons aggrieved by police misconduct. With the passage of time, it now appears that the continued existence of the rule, as presently implemented, inhibits the development of rational alternatives. The reason is quite simple: incentives for developing new procedures or remedies will remain minimal or nonexistent so long as the exclusionary rule is retained in its present form.

It can no longer be assumed that other branches of government will act while judges cling to this Draconian, descredited device in its present absolutist form. Legislatures are unlikely to create statutory alternatives, or impose direct sanctions on errant police officers or on the public treasury by way of tort actions, so long as persons who commit serious crimes continue to reap the enormous and undeserved benefits of the exclusionary rule. And of course, by definition the direct beneficiaries of this rule can be none but persons guilty of crimes. With this extraordinary "remedy" for Fourth Amendment violations, however slight, inadvertent or technical, legislatures might assume that nothing more should be done, even though a grave defect of the exclusionary rule is that it offers no relief whatever to victims of overzealous police work who never appear in court. . . . And even if legislatures were inclined to experiment with alternative remedies, they have no assurance that the judicially created rule will be abolished or even modified in response to such legislative innovations. The unhappy result, as I see it, is that alternatives will inevitably by stymied by rigid adherence on our part to the exclusionary rule. I venture to predict that overruling this judicially contrived doctrine—or limiting its scope to egregious, bad-faith conduct—would inspire a surge of activity toward providing some kind of statutory remedy for persons injured by police mistakes or misconduct.

The Court's opinion today eloquently reflects something of the dismal social costs occasioned by the rule. . . . As Mr. Justice White correctly observes today in his dissent, the exclusionary rule constitutes a "senseless obstacle to arriving at the truth in many criminal trials." . . . He also suggests that the rule be substantially modified "so as to prevent its application in those many circumstances where the evidence at issue was seized by an officer acting in the good faith belief that his conduct comported with existing law and having reasonable grounds for this belief." . . .

From its genesis in the desire to protect private papers, the exclusionary rule has now been carried to the point of potentially excluding from evidence the traditional *corpus delicti* in a murder or kidnapping case. . . . Expansion of the reach of the exclusionary rule has brought Cardozo's grim prophecy in *People v. Defore*, . . . (1926), nearer to fulfillment:

> "A room is searched against the law, and the body of a murdered man is found. If the place of discovery may not be proved, the other circumstances may be insufficient to connect the defendant with the crime. The privacy of the home has been infringed, and the murderer goes free. . . . We may not subject society to these dangers until the Legislature has spoken with a clearer voice."

The Need for Search Warrants

The Supreme Court under Chief Justice Warren Burger has paid considerable attention to the issue of when a Fourth Amendment search warrant is required. The Court has long held that the need for a search warrant can be waived under only the most limited of circumstances. In general, the Court has held that an exception to the requirement for a search warrant is permissable only in the case of a search incidental to a lawful arrest. Under such circumstances, the police are authorized to search the person placed under arrest and the area within the suspect's immediate control. The reason for those exceptions is to allow for an immediate search for weapons and to prevent the suspect from seizing and destroying evidence at the time of his arrest. The need for a search warrant can always be waived, if the suspect grants the police permission to conduct a search.

A number of issues remain, however. Must, for example, the police advise a person of his right to refuse a search prior to seeking his permission to do so? In the case of *Schneckloth v. Bustamonte* (1973), the Burger Court answered that question in the negative.

Another leading Burger Court Fourth Amendment ruling *U.S. v. Robinson* (1973), holds that the police may search small items on the possession of a suspect at the time of his arrest even though they are not thought to contain a weapon or evidence relating to the crime for which the suspect is arrested. In 1977, the court, over the objections of the U.S. Justice Department, ruled that the need for a search warrant is not limited to searches of persons, homes, offices, and communications in stipulating the need for a search warrant prior to searching the luggage of a person placed under arrest (*U.S. v. Chadwick*).

Consent to Search

In a 6-3 decision in *Schneckloth v. Bustamonte* May 29, 1973, the Supreme Court held that the prosecution need not prove that a person was aware of his right to refuse to consent to a search and that evidence obtained from such searches could be used as evidence. The majority opinion by Justice Stewart held that it would be totally "impractical" for the police to be required to advise persons of their right to refuse a police search. The issue, according to the court, is not whether a warning has been given, but only if the consent was obtained voluntarily or on the basis of coercion.

Justice Brennan, in dissent, argued that "[i]t wholly escapes me how our citizens can meaningfully be said to have waived something as precious as a constitutional guarantee without even being aware of its existence."

Searches of Arrested Persons

In a key decision handed down Dec. 11, 1973, the Supreme Court approved, 6-3, a police search of a cigarette package found to contain heroin in the possession of a person arrested for a traffic violation. The circumstances involved in the case, *U.S. v. Robinson*, are these. Robinson was arrested by a Washington D.C. police officer for driving an automobile without a license. In arresting Robinson, the officer, as part of a routine arrest procedure, "frisked" Robinson by running his hands over the outside of Robinson's clothing. In so doing, he felt an object in Robinson's breast pocket. The officer then removed the unidentified object from the pocket, found it to be a crumpled cigarette package and opened it. Inside were 14 capsules of heroin.

The Court of Appeals, in overturning the conviction, held that a police officer, after placing a person under arrest, may not ordinarily proceed to fully search the prisoner. Rather, according to the Appeals Court, the officer should only conduct a limited frisk of the outer clothing of the suspect and remove such weapons that may be discovered as a result of that frisk. A full search under this formula would be permitted, however, to secure further evidence of the crime. Since Robinson was arrested for driving without a license, a search for evidence was not permissable within this framework.

Justice Rehnquist, in speaking for the Supreme Court, refused to accept the lower court's reasoning in holding that it was not unreasonable, under the Fourth Amendment, for the police to conduct a full search of a person lawfully arrested. A "police officer's determination as to how and where to search the person of a suspect whom he has arrested is necessarily a quick *ad hoc* judgment that the Fourth Amendment does not require to be broken down into an analysis of each step of the search," he declared.

Justice Marshall, in a dissenting opinion joined by Justices Brennan and Douglas, argued that assuming even that it was permissable for the police officer in this instance to have removed the cigarette package from Robinson's pocket, there was no basis for the officer to have opened it since it clearly could not have contained evidence relating to Robinson's crime. Moreover, once the package was in the possession of the officer, they said, there was no danger of it containing a tiny concealed weapon that could be employed by Robinson. The dissenters claimed that the majority ruling would permit that police under similar circumstances to inspect the wallet or a sealed letter of a person placed under arrest.

Therefore, according to Marshall, ''[t]he search conducted by Officer Jencks in this case went far beyond what was reasonably necessary to protect him or to ensure that respondent would not effect an escape from custody. In my view, it therefore fell outside the scope of a properly drawn 'search incident to an arrest' exception to the Fourth Amendment warrant requirement.''

In a companion case decided the same day, the Court in *Gustafson v. Florida*, upheld the conviction of a person convicted of illegal possession of marijuana cigarettes that were seized in the course of an arrest for driving while not having his driver's license in his possession.

Court Again Limits Warrant Requirement

In *U.S. v. Edwards*, decided March 26, 1974, the Court approved the warrantless search of the clothing of a person ten hours after he had been jailed. In this instance, Edwards had been arrested and jailed for breaking into a post office. Access to the building had been obtained by opening a window with a prybar.

The day following his arrest, Edwards' clothing was taken from him and found to contain paint chips that matched those from the post office window. All of the justices agreed that the police acted in good faith and that a warrant to search Edward's clothing could have been obtained. On this basis, the majority, in a 5-4 ruling, upheld on the conviction on the basis that the search was reasonable.

The dissenting justices, while agreeing that the search *per se* was reasonable, sought to overturn the conviction on the ground that the issue was not whether the search was reasonable, but whether it was reasonable to proceed without a search warrant. Since there was no reasonable basis for not obtaining a warrant, the minority did not approve the search. ''The intrusion here was hardly a shocking one, and it cannot be said that the police acted in bad faith,'' Justice Stewart wrote in dissent. ''The Fourth Amendment, however,'' he said, "was not designed to apply only to situations when the intrusion is massive and the violation of privacy shockingly flagrant." Stewart sought to buttress this contention by quoting an oft cited 1964 Supreme Court admonition:

It may be that it is the obnoxious thing in its mildest and most repulsive form; but illegitimate and unconsitutional practices get their first footing in that way, namely by silent approaches and slight deviations from legal modes of procedure. This can only be obviated by adhering to the rule that constitutional provisions for the security of person and property should be liberally construed. (*U.S. v. Boyd*)

Court Extends Warrant Requirement

In a 7-2 decision, *U.S. v. Chadwick*, decided June 21, 1977, the Supreme Court rejected the U.S. Justice Department view that the Fourth Amendment search warrant requirement extends only to homes, offices and communications. In so doing, the court held the Fourth Amendment to require police officials to obtain a search warrant prior to searching the luggage of a person placed under arrest.

Absent an arrest, there is no question that the police in such cases are required to obtain a search warrant based on a showing of probable cause to believe evidence of criminal conduct is present. This decision, however, turned on the issue of whether that requirement is necessary when a person is placed under arrest.

The case involved a situation in which Amtrak railroad officials in San Diego observed two persons loading a footlocker on a Boston-bound train. Their suspicions were aroused when they noticed that the trunk was unusually heavy for its size, and that it was leaking talcum powder, often used to mask the odor of marijuana. Because one of the men matched a profile used to spot drug traffickers, the officials reported the matter to federal agents, who met the train in Boston with a dog trained to detect marijuana.

After the dog indicated the presence of marijuana, agents followed the two men to a waiting automobile and arrested them and the driver. The trunk was taken to the federal building in Boston and searched without consent. The search disclosed a large quantity of marijuana and the suspects were convicted of possession of marijuana and the intent to distribute it.

Speaking for the majority, Chief Justice Burger ruled out the search on the grounds that the Fourth Amendment is intended to safeguard the right of privacy outside of one's home and one's person and that the fact of the arrest did not eliminate the need for a search warrant since there was ample opportunity to have obtained one. (Given the circumstances of the case, it is reasonable to assume that a valid search warrant would have been issued.)

In so doing, the Court rejected the government's contention that the Fourth Amendment protects only dwellings and other specifically designated locales. The Court restated its previously enunciated position that the Fourth Amendment "protects people, not places."

Justices Blackman and Rehnquist, in dissent, argued that property seized in conjunction with a valid arrest in a public place should be subject to a search without a warrant. The dissenters argued that the majority had permitted "fortuitous circumstances" to control the case. Had the police searched the footlocker at the train station, the search would have been constitutional, they claimed, since the police under *Chimel v. California* (1969) are authorized to conduct on-the-spot searchs of the area within the "immediate control" of an arrested person. Were the police, moreover, to have waited until the defendants started to drive away with the footlocker, there similarly would have been no question as to the legitimacy of the search, they said, in view of the "automobile search" exception to the Fourth Amendment that permits the warrantless search of automobiles because of their inherent mobility. "It is decisions of the kind made by the Court today that make criminal law a trap for the unwary policeman and detract from the important activities of detecting criminal activity and protecting the public safety," the minority concluded.

Justice Brennan, in concurring with the majority, said that it was "deeply distressing that the Department of Justice whose mission is to protect the constitutional liberties of the people of the United States, should even appear to be seeking to subvert them by the extreme and dubious legal arguments" used in the case.

ABRIDGMENT OF SEARCH WARRANT DECISIONS

Schneckloth v. Bustamonte (412 U.S. 218, May 29, 1973)

Justice Stewart delivering the opinion of the Court:

It is well settled under the Fourth and Fourteenth Amendments that a search conducted without a warrant issued upon probable cause is *"per se* unreasonable. . . subject only to a few specifically established and well-delineated exceptions.''. . . It is equally well settled that one of the specifically established exceptions to the requirements of both a warrant and probable cause is a search that is conducted pursuant to consent. . . . The constitutional question in the present case concerns the definition of "consent" in this Fourth and Fourteenth Amendment context.

The respondent was brought to trial in a California court upon a charge of possessing a check with intent to defraud. He moved to suppress the introduction of certain material as evidence against him on the ground that the material had been acquired through an unconstitutional search and seizure. In response to the motion, the trial judge conducted an evidentiary hearing where it was established that the material in question had been acquired by the state under the following circumstances:

While on routine patrol in Sunnyvale, California, at approximately 2:40 in the morning, Police Officer James Rand stopped an automobile when he observed that one headlight and its license plate light were burned out. Six men were in the vehicle. Joe Alcala and the respondent, Robert Bustamonte, were in the front seat with Joe Gonzales, the driver. Three older men were seated in the rear. When, in response to the policeman's question, Gonzales could not produce a driver's license, Officer Rand asked if any of the other five had any evidence of identification. Only Alcala produced a license, and he explained that the car was his brother's. After the six occupants had stepped out of the car at the officer's request and after two additional policemen had arrived, Officer Rand asked Alcala if he could search the car. Alcala replied, "Sure, go ahead." Prior to the search no one was threatened with arrest and, according to Officer Rand's uncontradicted testimony, it "was all very congenial at this time." Gonzales testified that Alcala actually helped in the search of the car, by opening the trunk and glove compartment. In Gonzales' words: "[T]he police officer asked Joe [Alcala], he goes, 'Does the trunk open?' And Joe said, 'Yes.' He went to the car and got the keys and opened up the trunk." Wadded up under the left rear seat, the police officers found three checks that had previously been stolen from a car wash.

The trial judge denied the motion to suppress, and the checks in question were admitted in evidence at Bustamonte's trial. On the basis of this and other evidence he was convicted. . . .

It is important to make it clear at the outset what is not involved in this case. The respondent concedes that a search conducted pursuant to a valid consent is constitutionally permissible. In *Katz v. United States*, . . . and more recently in *Vale v. Louisiana*, . . . we recognized that a search authorized by consent is wholly valid. . . . And similarly the state concedes that "[w]hen a prosecutor seeks to rely upon consent to justify the lawfulness of a search, he has the burden of proving that the consent was, in fact, freely and voluntarily given." . . .

The precise question in this case, then, is what must the prosecution prove to demonstrate that a consent was "voluntarily" given. And upon that question there is a square conflict of views between the state and federal courts that have reviewed the search involved in the case before us. The Court of Appeals for the Ninth Circuit concluded that it is an essential part of the state's initial burden to prove that a person knows he has a right to refuse consent. The California courts have followed the rule that voluntariness is a question of fact to be determined from the totality of all the circumstances, and that the state of a defendant's knowledge is only one factor to be taken into account in asseessing the voluntariness of a consent. . . .

This Court's decisions reflect a frank recognition that the Constitution requires the sacrifice of neither security nor liberty. The due process clause does not mandate that the police forgo all questioning, or that they be given *carte blanche* to extract what they can from a suspect. "The ultimate test remains that which has been the only clearly established test in Anglo-American courts for two hundred years: the test of voluntariness. Is the confession the product of an essentially free and unconstrained choice by its maker? If it is, if he has willed to confess, it may be used against him. If it is not, if his will has been overborne and his capacity for self-determination critically impaired, the use of his confession offends due process." *Culombe v. Connecticut.* . . .

In determining whether a defendant's will was overborne in a particular case, the Court has assessed the totality of all the surrounding circumstances—both the characteristics of the accused and the details of the interrogation. Some of the factors taken into account have included the youth of the accused,...his lack of education,... or his low intelligence,... the lack of any advice to the accused of his constitutional rights,... the length of detention,...the repeated and prolonged nature of the questioning,... and the use of physical punishment such as the deprivation of food or sleep.... In all of these cases, the Court determined the factual circumstances surrounding the confession, assessed the psychological impact on the accused, and evaluated the legal significance of how the accused reacted....

The significant fact about all of these decisions is that none of them turned on the presence or absence of a single controlling criterion; each reflected a careful scrutiny of all the surrounding circumstances. See *Miranda v. Arizona*,...(Harlan, J., dissenting); ...(White, J., dissenting). In none of them did the Court rule that the due process clause required the prosecution to prove as part of its initial burden that the defendant knew he had a right to refuse to answer the questions that were put. While the state of the accused's mind, and the failure of the police to advise the accused of his rights, were certainly factors to be evaluated in assessing the "voluntariness" of an accused's responses, they were not in and of themselves determinative....

Similar considerations lead us to agree with the courts of California that the question whether a consent to a search was in fact "voluntary" or was the product of duress or coercion, express or implied, is a question of fact to be determined from the totality of all the circumstances. While knowledge of the right to refuse consent is one factor to be taken into account, the government need not establish such knowledge as the *sine qua non* of an effective consent. As with police questioning, two competing concerns must be accommodated in determining the meaning of a "voluntary" consent—the legitimate need for such searches and the equally important requirement of assuring the absence of coercion.

In situations where the police have some evidence of illicit activity, but lack probable cause to arrest or search, a search authorized by a valid consent may be the only means of obtaining important and reliable evidence. In the present case for example, while the police had reason to stop the car for traffic violations, the state does not contend that there was probable cause to search the vehicle or that the search was incident to a valid arrest of any of the occupants. Yet, the search yielded tangible evidence that served as a basis for prosecution, and provided some assurance that others, wholly innocent of the crime, were not mistakenly brought to trial. And in those cases where there is probable cause to arrest or search, but where the police lack a warrant, a consent search may still be valuable. If the search is conducted and proves fruitless, that in itself may convince the police that an arrest with its possible stigma and embarrassment is unnecessary, or that a far more extensive search pursuant to a warrant is not justified. In short, a search pursuant to consent may result in considerably less inconvenience for the subject of the search, and, properly conducted, is a constitutionally permissible and wholly legitimate aspect of effective police activity.

But the Fourth and Fourteenth Amendments require that a consent not be coerced, by explicit or implicit means, by implied threat or covert force. For, no matter how subtly the coercion was applied, the resulting "consent" would be no more than a pretext for the unjustified police intrusion against which the Fourth Amendment is directed. In the words of the classic admonition in *Boyd v. United States...*:

> "It may be that it is the obnoxious thing in its mildest and least repulsive form; but illegitimate and unconstitutional practices get their first footing in that way, namely, by silent approaches and slight deviations from legal modes of procedure. This can only be obviated by adhering to the rule that constitutional provisions for the security of person and property should be liberally construed. A close and literal construction deprives them of half their efficacy, and leads to gradual depreciation of the right, as if it consisted more in sound than in substance. It is the duty of courts to be watchful for the constitutional rights of the citizen, and against any stealthy encroachments thereon."

The problem of reconciling the recognized legitimacy of consent searches with the requirement that they be free from any aspect of official coercion cannot be resolved by any infallible touchstone. To approve such searches without the most careful scrutiny would sanction the possibility of official coercion; to place artificial restrictions upon such searches would jeopardize their basic validity. Just as was true with confessions, the requirement of a "voluntary" consent reflects a fair accommodation of the constitutional requirements involved. In examining all the surrounding circumstances to determine if in fact the consent to search was coerced, account must be taken of subtly coercive police questions, as well as the possible vulnerable subjective state of the person who consents. Those searches that are the product of police coercion can thus be filtered out without undermining the continuing validity of consent searches. In sum, there is no reason for us to depart in the area of consent searches, from the traditional definition of "voluntariness.". . .

One alternative that would go far toward proving that the subject of a search did know he had a right to refuse consent would be to advise him of that right before eliciting his consent. That, however, is a suggestion that has been almost universally repudiated by both federal and state courts, and, we think, rightly so. For it would be thoroughly impractical to impose on the normal consent search the detailed requirements of an effective warning. Consent searches are part of the standard investigatory techniques of law enforcement agencies. They normally occur on the highway, or in a person's home or office, and under informal and unstructured conditions. The circumstances that prompt the initial request to search may develop quickly or be a logical extension of investigative police questioning. The police may seek to investigate further suspicious circumstances or to follow up leads developed in questioning persons at the scene of a crime. These situations are a far cry from the structured atmosphere of a trial where, assisted by counsel if he chooses, a defendant is informed of his trial rights.... And, while surely a closer question, these situations are still immeasurably far removed from "custodial interrogation" where, in *Miranda v. Arizona*...we found that the Constitution required certain now familiar warnings as a prerequisite to police interrogation. Indeed, in language applicable to the typical consent search, we refused to extend the need for warnings:

> "Our decision is not intended to hamper the traditional function of police officers in investigating crime.... When an individual is in custody on probable cause, the police may, of course, seek out evidence in the field to be used at trial against him. Such investigation may include inquiry of persons not under restraint. General on-the-scene questioning as to facts surrounding a crime or other general questioning of citizens in the fact-finding process is not affected by our holding. It is an

act of responsible citizenship for individuals to give whatever information they may have to aid in law enforcement."...

Consequently, we cannot accept the position of the Court of Appeals in this case that proof of knowledge of the right to refuse consent is a necessary prerequisite to demonstrating a "voluntary" consent. Rather, it is only by analyzing all the circumstances of an individual consent that it can be ascertained whether in fact it was voluntary or coerced. It is this careful sifting of the unique facts and circumstances of each case that is evidenced in our prior decisions involving consent searches....

In short, neither this Court's prior cases, nor the traditional definition of "voluntariness" requires proof of knowledge of a right to refuse as the *sine qua non* of an effective consent to a search....

Much of what has already been said disposes of the argument that the Court's decision in the *Miranda* case requires the conclusion that knowledge of a right to refuse is an indispensable element of a valid consent. The considerations that informed the Court's holding in *Miranda* are simply inapplicable in the present case. In *Miranda* the Court found that the techniques of police questioning and the nature of custodial surroundings produce an inherently coercive situation. The Court concluded that "[U]nless adequate protective devices are employed to dispel the compulsion inherent in custodial surround-ings, no statement obtained from the defendant can truly be the product of his free choice."... And at another point the Court noted that "without proper safeguards the process of in-custody interrogation of persons suspected or accused of crime contains inherently compelling pressures which work to undermine the individual's will to resist and to compel him to speak where he would not otherwise do so freely."...

In this case, there is no evidence of any inherently coercive tactics—either from the nature of the police questioning or the environment in which it took place. Indeed, since consent searches will normally occur on a person's own familiar territory, the specter of incommunicado police interrogation in some remote station house in simple inapposite. There is no reason to believe, under circumstances such as are present here, that the response to a policeman's question is presumptively coerced; and there is, therefore, no reason to reject the traditional test for determining the voluntariness of a person's response. *Miranda*, of course, did not reach investigative questioning of a person not in custody, which is most directly analogous to the situation of a consent search, and it assuredly did not indicate that such questioning ought to be deemed inherently coercive. . . .

It is also argued that the failure to require the government to establish knowledge as a prerequisite to a valid consent, will relegate the Fourth Amendment to the special province of "the sophisticated, the knowledgeable and the privileged." We cannot agree. The traditional definition of voluntariness we accept today has always taken into account evidence of minimal schooling, low intelligence, and the lack of any effective warnings to a person of his rights; and the voluntariness of any statement taken under those conditions has been carefully scrutinized to determine whether it was in fact voluntarily given.

Our decision today is a narrow one. We hold only that when the subject of a search is not in custody and the state attempts to justify a search on the basis of his consent, the Fourth and Fourteenth Amendments require that it demonstrate that the consent was in fact voluntarily given, and not the result of duress or coercion, express or implied. Voluntariness is a question of fact to be determined from all the circumstances, and while the subject's knowledge of a right to refuse is a factor to be taken into account, the prosecution is not required to demonstrate such knowledge as a prerequisite to establishing a voluntary consent. . . .

Justice Brennan dissenting:

The Fourth Amendment specifically guarantees "[t]he right of the people to be secure in their persons, houses, papers, and effects, against unreasonable searches and seizures. . . ." We have consistently held that governmental searches conducted pursuant to a validly obtained warrant or reasonably incident to a valid arrest do not violate this guarantee. Here, however, as the Court itself recognizes, no search warrant was obtained and the State does not even suggest "that there was probable cause to search the vehicle or that the search was incident to a valid arrest of any of the occupants." . . . As a result, the search of the vehicle can be justified soley on the ground that the owner's brother gave his consent—that is, that he waived his Fourth Amendment right "to be secure" against an otherwise "unreasonable" search. The Court holds today that an individual can effectively waive this right even though he is totally ignorant of the fact that in the absence of his consent, such invasions of his privacy would be constitutionally prohibited. It wholly escapes me how our citizens can meaningfully be said to have waived something as precious as a constitutional guarantee without ever being aware of its existence. In my view, the Court's conclusion is supported neither by "linguistics," nor by "epistemology," nor, indeed, by "common sense." I respectfully dissent.

U.S. v. Robinson (414 U.S. 219, Dec. 11, 1973)

Justice Rehnquist delivering the opinion of the Court:

Respondent Robinson was convicted in United States District Court for the District of Columbia of the possession and facilitation of concealment of heroin. . . . He was sentenced to concurrent terms of imprisonment for these offenses. . . .

On April 23, 1968, at approximately 11 p. m., Officer Richard Jenks, a 15-year veteran of the District of Columbia Metropolitan Police Department, observed the respondent driving a 1965 Cadillac near the intersection of 8th and C Streets, N.E., in the District of Columbia. Jenks, as a result of previous investigation following a check of respondent's operator permit four days earlier, determined there was reason to believe that respondent was operating a motor vehicle after the revocation of his operator's permit. This is an offense defined by statue in the District of Columbia which carries a mandatory minimum jail term, a mandatory minimum fine, or both. . . .

Jenks signaled respondent to stop the automobile, which respondent did, and all three of the occupants emerged from the car. At that point Jenks informed respondent that he was under arrest for "operating after revocation and obtaining a permit by misrepresentation." It was assumed by the Court of Appeals, and is conceded by the respondent here, that Jenks has probable cause to arrest respondent, and that he effected a full-custody arrest.

In accordance with procedures prescribed in police department instructions, Jenks then began to search respondent. He explained at a subsequent hearing that he was "face-to-face" with the respondent, and "placed [his] hands on [the respondent], my right-hand to his left breast like this (demonstrating) and proceeded to pat him down thus [with the right hand]." During this patdown, Jenks felt an object in the left breast pocket of the heavy coat respondent was wearing, but testified that he "couldn't tell what it was" and also that he "couldn't actually tell the size of it." Jenks then reached into the pocket and pulled out the object, which turned out to be a "crumpled up cigarette package." Jenks testified that at this point he still did not know what was in the package:

> "As I felt the package I could feel objects in the package but I I couldn't tell what they were.... I knew they weren't cigarettes."

The officer then opened the cigarette pack and found 14 gelatin capsules of white powder which he thought to be, and which later analysis proved to be, heroin. Jenks then continued his search of respondent to completion, feeling around his waist and trouser legs, and examining the remaining pockets. The heroin seized from the respondent was admitted into evidence at the trial which resulted in his conviction in the District Court....

...We conclude that the search conducted by Jenks in this case did not offend the limits imposed by the Fourth Amendment, and we therefore reverse the judgment of the Court of Appeals....

The justification or reason for the authority to search incident to a lawful arrest rests quite as much on the need to disarm the suspect in order to take him into custody as it does on the need to preserve evidence on his person for later use at trial....

Nor are we inclined, on the basis of what seems to us to be a rather speculative judgment, to qualify the breadth of the general authority to search incident to a lawful custodial arrest on an assumption that persons arrested for the offense of driving while their licenses have been revoked are less likely to possess dangerous weapons than are those arrested for other crimes....

But quite apart from these distinctions, our more fundamental disagreement with the Court of Appeals arises from its suggestion that there must be litigated in each case the issue of whether or not there was present one of the reasons supporting the authority for a search of the person incident to a lawful arrest. We do not think the long line of authorities of this Court dating back to *Weeks*, or what we can glean from the history of practice in this country and in England, requires such a case-by-case adjudication. A police officer's determination as to how and where to search the person of a suspect whom he has arrested is necessarily a quick *ad hoc* judgment which the Fourth Amendment does not require to be broken down in each instance into an analysis of each step in the search. The authority to search the person incident to a lawful custodial arrest, while based upon the need to disarm and to discover evidence, does not depend on what a court may later decide was the probability in a particular arrest situation that weapons or evidence would in fact be found upon the person of the suspect. A custodial arrest of a suspect based on probable cause; is a reasonable intrusion under the Fourth Amendment; that intrusion being lawful, a search incident to the arrest requires no additional justification. It is the fact of the lawful arrest which establishes the authority to search, and we hold that in the case of a lawful custodial arrest a full search of the person is not only an exception to the warrant requirement of the Fourth Amendment, but is also a "reasonable" search under that Amendment.

The search of respondent's person conducted by Officer Jenks in this case and the seizure from him of the heroin, were permissible under established Fourth Amendment law. While thorough, the search partook of none of the extreme or patently abusive characteristics which were held to violate the due process clause of the Fourteenth Amendment in *Rochin* v. *California*...(1952). Since it is the fact of custodial arrest which gives rise to the authority to search, it is of no moment that Jenks did not indicate any subjective fear of the respondent or that he did not himself suspect that respondent was armed. Having in the course of a lawful search come upon the crumpled package of cigarettes, he was entitled to inspect it; and when his inspection revealed the heroin capsules, he was entitled to seize them as "fruits, instrumentalities, or contraband" probative of criminal conduct. ...

Justice Marshall, joined by Justices Douglas and Brennan, dissenting:

Certain fundamental principles have characterized this Court's Fourth Amendment jurisprudence over the years. Perhaps the most basic of these was expressed by Mr. Justice Butler, speaking for a unanimous Court in *Go-Bart Co.* v. *United States*...(1931): "There is no formula for the determination of reasonableness. Each case is to be decided on its own facts and circumstances." ... As we recently held: "The constitutional validity of a warrantless search is preeminently the sort of question which can only be decided in the concrete factual context of the individual case." *Sibron* v. *New York*...(1968). And the intensive, at times painstaking, case-by-case analysis characteristic of our Fourth Amendment decisions bespeaks our "jealous regard for maintaining the integrity of individual rights." *Mapp* v. *Ohio*...

In the present case, however, the majority turns its back on these principles, holding that "the fact of the lawful arrest" always establishes the authority to conduct a full search of the arrestee's person, regardless of whether in a particular case "there was present one of the reasons supporting the authority for a search of the person incident to a lawful arrest." ... The majority's approach represents a clear and marked departure from our long tradition of case-by-case adjudication of the reasonableness of searches and seizures under the Fourth Amendment. I continue to believe that "[t]he scheme of the Fourth Amendment becomes meaningful only when it is assured that at some point the conduct of those charged with enforcing the laws can be subjected to the more detached, neutral scrutiny of a judge who must evaluate the reasonableness of a particular search or seizure in light of the particular circumstances." ... *Terry* v. *Ohio* (1968). Because I find the majority's reasoning to be at odds with these fundamental principles, I must respectfully dissent. ...

The majority's attempt to avoid case-by-case adjudication of Fourth Amendment issues is not only misguided as a matter of principle, but is also doomed to fail as a matter of practical application. As the majority itself is well aware,...the powers granted the police in this case are strong ones, subject to potential abuse. Although, in this particular case, Officer Jenks was required by police department regulations to make an in-custody arrest rather than to issue a citation, in most jurisdictions and for most traffic offenses the determination of whether to issue a citation or effect a full arrest is discretionary with the officer. There is always the possibility that a police officer, lacking probable cause to obtain a search warrant, will use a traffic arrest as a pretext to conduct a search. ... I suggest this possiblity not to impugn the integrity of our police, but merely to point out that case-by-case adjudication will always be necessary to determine whether a full arrest was effected for purely legitimate reasons or, rather, as a pretext for searching the arrestee. "An arrest may not be used as a pretext to search for evidence." *United States* v. *Lefkowitz*...(1932). ...

The majority states that "[a] police officer's determination as to how and where to search the person of a suspect whom he has arrested is necessarily a quick *ad hoc* judgment which the Fourth

Amendment does not require to be broken down in each instance into an analysis of each step in the search." . . . No precedent is cited for this broad assertion—not surprisingly, since there is none. Indeed, we only recently rejected such "a rigid all-or-nothing model of justification and regulation under the Amendment, [for] it obscures the utility of limitations upon the scope, as well as the initiation, of police action as a means of constitutional regulation. This Court has held in the past that a search which is reasonable at its inception may violate the Fourth Amendment by virtue of its intolerable intensity and scope." *Terry* v. *Ohio*. . . . As we there concluded, "in determining whether the seizure and search were 'unreasonable' our inquiry is a dual one—whether the officer's action was justified at its inception, and whether it was reasonably related in scope to the circumstances which justified the interference in the first place." . . .

The majority opinion fails to recognize that the search conducted by Officer Jenks did not merely involve a search of respondent's person. It also included a separate search of effects found on his person. And even were we to assume, *arguendo*, that it was reasonable for Jenks to remove the object he felt in respondent's pocket, clearly there was no justification consistent with the Fourth Amendment which would authorize his opening the package and looking inside.

To begin with, after Jenks had the cigarette package in his hands, there is no indication that he had reason to believe or did in fact believe that the package contained a weapon. More importantly, even if the crumpled-up cigarette package had in fact contained some sort of small weapon, it would have been impossible for respondent to have used it once the package was in the officer's hands. Opening the package, therefore, did not further the protective purpose of the search. Even the dissenting opinion in the Court of Appeals conceded that "since the package was now in the officer's possession, any risk of the prisoner's use of a weapon in this package had been eliminated." . . .

It is suggested, however, that since the custodial arrest itself represents a significant intrusion into the privacy of the person, any additional intrusion by way of opening or examining effects found on the person is not worthy of constitutional protection. But such an approach was expressly rejected by the Court in *Chimel*. There it was suggested that since the police had lawfully entered petitioner's house to effect an arrest, the additional invasion of privacy stemming from an accompanying search of the entire house was inconsequential. The Court answered: "[W]e can see no reason why, simply because some interference with an individual's privacy and freedom of movement has lawfully taken place, further intrusions should automatically be allowed despite the absence of a warrant that the Fourth Amendment would otherwise require." ...

The Fourth Amendment preserves the right of "the people to be secure in their persons, houses, papers, and effects, against unreasonable searches and seizures...." *Chimel* established the principle that the lawful right of the police to interfere with the security of the person did not, standing alone, automatically confer the right to interfere with the security and privacy of his house. Hence, the mere fact of an arrest should be no justification, in and of itself, for invading the privacy of the individual's personal effects. The government argues that it is difficult to see what constitutionally protected "expectation of privacy" a prisoner has in the interior of a cigarette pack. One wonders if the result in this case would have been the same were respondent a businessman who was lawfully taken into custody for driving without a license and whose wallet was taken from him by the police. Would it be reasonalbe for the police officer, because of the possibility that a razor blade was hidden somewhere in the wallet, to open it, remove all the contents, and examine each item carefully? Or suppose a lawyer lawfully arrested for a traffic offense is found to have a sealed envelope on his person. Would it be permissible for the arresting officer to tear open the envelope in order to make sure that it did not contain a clandestine weapon— perhaps a pin or a razor blade? ... Would it not be more consonant with the purpose of the Fourth Amendment and the legitimate needs of the police to require the officer, if he has any question whatsoever about what the wallet or letter contains, to hold on to it until the arrestee is brought to the precinct station?

I, for one, cannot characterize any of these intrusions into the privacy of an individual's papers and effects as being negligible incidents to the more serious intrusion into the individual's privacy stemming from the arrest itself. Nor can any principled distinction be drawn between the hypothetical searches I have posed and the search of the cigarette package in this case. The only reasoned distinction is between warrantless searches which serve legitimate protective and evidentiary functions and those that do not. ...

The search conducted by Officer Jenks in this case went far beyond what was reasonably necessary to protect him from harm or to ensure that respondent would not effect an escape from custody. In my view, it therefore fell outside the scope of a properly drawn "search incident to arrest" exception to the Fourth Amendment's warrant requirement. I would affirm the judgment of the Court of Appeals holding that the fruits of the search should have been suppressed at respondent's trial.

U.S. v. Edwards (415 U.S. 800, March 26, 1974)

Justice White delivering the opinion of the Court:

The question here is whether the Fourth Amendment should be extended to exclude from evidence certain clothing taken from respondent Edwards while he was in custody at the city jail approximately 10 hours after his arrest.

Shortly after 11 p. m. on May 31, 1970, respondent Edwards was lawfully arrested on the streets of Lebanon, Ohio, and charged with attempting to break into that city's Post Office. He was taken to the local jail and placed in a cell. Contemporaneously or shortly thereafter, investigation at the scene revealed that the attempted entry had been made through a wooden window which apparently had been pried up with a pry bar, leaving paint chips on the window sill and wire mesh screen. The next morning, trousers and a T-shirt were purchased for Edwards to substitute for the clothing which he had been wearing at the time of and since his arrest. His clothing was then taken from him and held as evidence. Examination of the clothing revealed paint chips matching the samples that had been taken from the window. This evidence and his clothing were received at trial over Edwards' objection that neither the clothing nor the results of its examination were admissible because the warrantless seizure of his clothing was invalid under the Fourth Amendment.

. . .

The prevailing rule under the Fourth Amendment that searches and seizures may not be made without a warrant is subject to various exceptions. One of them permits warrantless searches incident to custodial arrest, *United States* v. *Robinson*. . .(1973); *Chimel* v. *California*. . .(1969); *Weeks* v. *United States*. . .(1914), and has traditionally been justified by the reasonableness of searching for weapons, instruments of escape, and evidence of crime when a person is taken into offical custody and lawfully detained. . . .

It is also plain that searches and seizures that could be made on the spot at the time of arrest may legally be conducted later when the accused arrives at the place of detention. If need be, *Abel* v. *United States*...(1960), settled this question. There the defendant was arrested at this hotel, but the belongings taken with him to the place of detention were searched there. In sustaining the search, the Court noted that a valid search of the property could have been made at the place of arrest and perceived little difference

> "when the accused decides to take the property with him, for search of it to occur instead at the first place of detention when the accused arrives there, especially as the search of property carried by an accused to the place of detention had additional justifications, similar to those which justify a search of the person of one who is arrested." ...

The courts of appeals have followed this same rule, holding that both the person and the property in his immediate possession may be searched at the station house after the arrest has occurred at another place and if evidence of crime is discovered, it may be seized and admitted in evidence. Nor is there any doubt that clothing or other belongings may be seized upon arrival of the accused at the place of detention and later subjected to laboratory analysis or that the test results are admissble at trial.

Conceding all this, the Court of Appeals in this case nevertheless held that a warrant is required where the search occurs after the administrative mechanics of arrest have been completed and the prisoner is incarcerated. But even on these terms, it seems to us that the normal processes incident to arrest and custody had not been completed when Edwards was placed in his cell on the night of May 31. With or without probable cause, the authorities were entitled at that point not only to search Edwards' clothing but also to take it from him and keep it in offical custody. There was testimony that this was the standard practice in this city. The police were also entitled to take from Edwards any evidence of the crime in his immediate possession, including his clothing. And the Court of Appeals acknowledged that contemporaneously with or shortly after the time Edwards went to his cell, the police had probable cause to believe that the articles of clothing he wore were themselves material evidence of the crime for which he had been arrested. ...
But it was late at night; no substitute clothing was then available for Edwards to wear, and it would certainly have been unreasonable for

the police to have stripped respondent of this clothing and left him exposed in his cell throughout the night. . . . When the substitutes were purchased the next morning, the clothing he had been wearing at the time of arrest was taken from him and subjected to laboratory analysis. This was no more than taking from respondent the effects in his immediate possession that constituted evidence of crime. This was and is a normal incident of a custodial arrest, and reasonable delay in effectuating it does not change the fact that Edwards was no more imposed upon than he could have been at the time and place of the arrest or immediately upon arrival at the place of detention. The police did no more on June 1 than they were entitled to do incident to the usual custodial arrest and incarceration.

Other closely related considerations sustain the examination of the clothing in this case. It must be remembered that on both May 31 and June 1 the police had lawful custody of Edwards and necessarily of the clothing he wore. When it became apparent that the articles of clothing were evidence of the crime for which Edwards was being held, the police were entitled to take, examine, and preserve them for use as evidence, just as they are normally permitted to seize evidence of crime when it is lawfully encountered. . . . Surely, the clothes could have been brushed down and vacuumed while Edwards had them on in the cell, and it was similarly reasonable to take and examine them as the police did, paritcularly in view of the existence of probable cause linking the clothes to the crime. Indeed, it is difficult to perceive what is unreasonable about the police's examining and holding as evidence those personal effects of the accused that they already have in their lawful custody as the result of a lawful arrest. . . .

Justice Stewart, joined by Justices Douglas, Brennan and Marshall, dissenting:

The Court says that the question before us "is whether the Fourth Amendment should be extended" to prohibit the warrantless seizure to Edwards' clothing. I think, on the contrary, that the real question in this case is whether the Fourth Amendment is to be ignored. For in my view the judgment of the Court of Appeals can be reversed only by disregarding established Fourth Amendment principles firmly embodied in many previous decisions of this Court.

As the Court has repeatedly emphasized in the past, "the most basic constitutional rule in this area is that 'searches conducted outside the judicial process, without prior approval by judge or magistrate, are *per se* unreasonable under the Fourth Amendment— subject only to a few specifically established and well-delineated exceptions.' " *Coolidge* v. *New Hampshire,...Katz* v. *United States....* Since it is conceded here that the seizure of Edwards' clothing was not made pursuant to a warrant, the question becomes whether the government has met its burden of showing that the circumstances of this seizure brought it within one of the "jealously and carefully drawn" exceptions to the warrant requirement.

The Court finds a warrant unnecessary in this case because of the custodial arrest of the respondent. It is, of course, well settled that the Fourth Amendment permits a warrantless search or seizure incident to a constitutionally valid custodial arrest.... But the mere fact of an arrest does not allow the police to engage in warrantless searches of unlimited geographic or temporal scope. Rather, the search must be spatially limited to the person of the arrestee and the area within his reach, *Chimel* v. *California*...and must, as to time, be "substantially contemporaneous with the arrest," *Stoner* v. *California*...; *Preston* v. *United States.*

Under the facts of this case, I am unable to agree with the Court's holding that the search was "incident" to Edwards' custodial arrest. The search here occurred fully 10 hours after he was arrested, at a time when the administrative processing and mechanics of arrest had long since come to an end. His clothes were not seized as part of an "inventory" of a prisoner's effects, nor were they taken pursuant to a routine exchange of civilian clothes for jail garb. And the considerations that typically justify a warrantless search incident to a lawful arrest were wholly absent here. As Mr. Justice Black stated for a unanimous Court in *Preston* v. *United States...:*

> "The rule allowing contemporaneous searches is justified, for example, by the need to seize weapons and other things which might be used to assalt an officer or effect an escape, as well as by the need to prevent the destruction of evidence of the crime— things which might easily happen where the weapon or evidence is on the accused's person or under his immediate control. But these justifications are absent where a search is remote in time or place from the arrest."

Accordingly, I see no justification for dispensing with the warrant requirement here. The police had ample time to seek a warrant, and no exigent circumstances were present to excuse their failure to do so. Unless the exceptions to the warrant requirement are to be "enthroned into the rule," *United States* v. *Rabinowitz*...(Frankfurter, J., dissenting), this is precisely the sort of situation where the Fourth Amendment requires a magistrate's prior approval for a search.

The Court says that the relevant question is "not whether it was reasonable to procure a search warrant, but whether the search itself was reasonable."... Precisely such a view, however, was explicitly rejected in *Chimel* v. *California*..., where the Court characterized the argument as "founded on little more than a subjective view regarding the acceptability of certain sorts of police conduct, and not on considerations relevant to Fourth amendment interests." As they were in *Chimel,* the words of Mr. Justice Frankfurter are again most relevant here:

> "To say that the search must be reasonable is to require some criterion of reason. It is no guide at all either for a jury or for district judges or the police to say that an 'unreasonable search' is forbidden—that the search must be reasonable. What is the test of reason which makes a search reasonable? The test is the reason underlying and expressed by the Fourth Amendment: the history and the experience which it embodies and the safeguards afforded by it against the evils to which it was a response. There must be a warrant to permit search, barring only inherent limitations upon that requirement when there is a good excuse for not getting a search warrant...." *United States* v. *Rabinowitz* (dissenting opinion).

The intrusion here was hardly a shocking one, and it cannot be said that the police acted in bad faith. The Fourth Amendment, however, was not designed to apply only to situations where the intrusion is massive and the violation of privacy shockingly flagrant. Rather, as the Court's classic admonition in *Boyd* v. *United States*...put the matter:

> "It may be that it is the obnoxious thing in its mildest and least repulsive form; but illegitimate and unconstitutional practices get their first footing in that way, namely, by silent approaches and slight deviations from legal modes of procedure. This can only be obviated by adhering to the rule that constitutional provisions for the security of person and property should be liberally construed. A close and literal construction deprives them of

half their efficacy, and leads to gradual depreciation of the right, as if it consisted more in sound than in substance. It is the duty of courts to be watchful for the constitutional rights of the citizen, and against any stealthy encroachments thereon."

Because I believe that the Court today unjustifiably departs from well-settled constitutional principles, I respectfully dissent.

U.S. v. Chadwick (June 21, 1977)

Chief Justice Burger in delivering the opinion of the Court:

We granted *certiorari* in this case to decide whether a search warrant is required before federal agents may open a locked footlocker which they have lawfully seized at the time of the arrest of its owners, when there is probable cause to believe the footlocker contains contraband....

In this Court the government again contends that the Fourth Amendment warrant clause protects only interests traditionally identified with the home. Recalling the colonial writs of assistance, which were often executed in searches of private dwellings, the government claims that the warrant clause was adopted primarily, if not exclusively, in response to unjustified intrusions into private homes on the authority of general warrants. The government argues there is no evidence that the Framers of the Fourth Amendment intended to disturb the established practice of permitting warrantless searches outside the home, or to modify the initial clause of the Fourth Amendment by making warrantless searches supported by probable cause *per se* unreasonable.

Drawing on its reading of history, the government argues that only homes, offices and private communications implicate interests which lie at the core of the Fourth Amendment. Accordingly, it is only in these contexts that the determination whether a search or seizure is reasonable should turn on whether a warrant has been obtained. In all other situations, the government contends, less significant privacy values are at stake, and the reasonableness of a government intrusion should depend solely on whether there is probable cause to believe evidence of criminal conduct is present. Where personal effects are lawfully seized outside the home on probable cause, the government would thus regard searches without a warrant as not "unreasonable."

We do not agree that the warrant clause protects only dwellings and other specifically designated locales. As we have noted before, the Fourth Amendment "protects people, not places," *Katz* v. *United States*...(1967); more particularly, it protects people from unreasonable government intrusions into their legitimate expectations of privacy. In this case, the warrant clause makes a significant contribution to that protection. The question, then, is whether a warrantless search in these circumstances was unreasonable....

In this case, important Fourth Amendment privacy interests were at stake. By placing personal effects inside a double-locked footlocker, respondents manifested an expectation that the contents would remain free from public examination. No less than one who locks the doors of his home against intruders, one who safeguards his personal possessions in this manner is due the protection of the Fourth Amendment warrant clause. There being no exigency, it was unreasonable for the government to conduct this search without the safeguards a judicial warrant provides.

The government does not contend that the footlocker's brief contact with Chadwick's car makes this an automobile search, but it is argued that the rationale of our automobile search cases demonstrates the reasonableness of permitting warrantless searches of luggage; the government views such luggage as analogous to motor vehicles for Fourth Amendment purposes. It is true that, like the footlocker in issue here, automobiles are "effects" under the Fourth Amendment, and searches and seizures of automobiles are therefore subject to the constitutional standard of reasonableness. But this Court has recognized significant differences between motor vehicles and other property which permit warrantless searches of automobiles in circumstances in which warrantless searches would not be reasonable in other contexts....

...[T]he government urges that the Constitution permits the warrantless search of any property in the possession of a person arrested in public, so long as there is probable cause to believe that the property contains contraband or evidence of crime. Although recognizing that the footlocker was not within respondents' immediate control, the government insists that the search was reasonable bacause the footlocker was seized contemporaneously with respondents' arrests and was searched as soon thereafter as was practicable. The reasons justifying search in a custodial arrest are quite different. Then a custodial arrest is made, there is always some danger that the person arrested may seek to use a weapon, or that evidence may be concealed or destroyed. To safeguard himself and others, and to prevent the loss of evidence, it has been held reasonable for the arresting officer to conduct a prompt, warrantless "search of the arrestee's person and the area 'within his immediate control'—construing that phrase to mean the area from within which he might gain possession of a weapon or destructible evidence." *Chimel* v. *California....* See also *Terry* v. *Ohio...* (1968).

Such searches may be conducted without a warrant, and they may also be made whether or not there is probable cause to believe that the person arrested may have a weapon or is about to destroy evidence. The potential dangers lurking in all custodial arrests make warrantless searches of items within the "immediate control" area reasonable without requiring the arresting officer to calculate the probability that weapons or destructibe evidence may be involved. *United States* v. *Robinson...*(1973); *Terry* v. *Ohio....* However, warrantless searches of luggage or other property seized at the time of an arrest cannot be justified as incident to that arrest either if the "search is remote in time or place from the arrest." *Preston* v. *United States...*, or no exigency exists. Once law enforcement officers have reduced luggage or other personal property not immediately associated with the person of the arrestee to their exclusive control, and there is no longer any danger that the arrestee might gain access to the property to seize a weapon or destroy evidence, a search of that property is no longer an incident of the arrest.

Here the search was conducted more than an hour after federal agents had gained exclusive control of the footlocker and long after respondents were securely in custody; the search therefore cannot be viewed as incidental to the arrest or as justified by any other exigency. Even though on this record the issuance of a warrant by a judicial officer was reasonably predictable, a line must be drawn. In our view, when no exigency is shown to support the need for an immediate search, the warrant clause places the line at the point where the property to be searched comes under the exclusive dominion of police authority. Respondents were therefore entitled to the protection of the warrant clause with the evaluation of a neutral magistrate, before their privacy interests in the contents of the footlocker were invaded.

Justice Blackmun, joined by Justice Rehnquist, dissenting:

[S]ince the suspect's expectations of privacy are properly abated by the fact of arrest itself, it would be better, in my view, to adopt a clear-cut rule permitting property seized in conjunction with a valid arrest in a public place to be searched without a warrant. Such an approach would simplify the constitutional law of criminal procedure without seriously derogating from the values protected by the Fourth Amendment's prohibition of unreasonable searches and seizures.

The approach taken by the Court has the perverse result of allowing fortuitous circumstances to control the outcome of the present case. The agents probably could have avoided having the footlocker search held unconstitutional either by delaying the arrest for a few minutes or by conducting the search on the spot rather than back at their office. Probable cause for the arrest was present from the time respondents Machado and Leary were seated on the footlocker inside Boston's South Station and the agents' dog signalled the presence of marihunan. Rather than make an arrest at this moment, the agents commendably sought to determine the possible involvement of others in the illegal scheme. They waited a short time until respondent Chadwick arrived and the footlocker had been loaded into the trunk of his car, and then made the arrest. But if the agents had postponed the arrest just a few minutes longer until the respondents started to drive away, then the car could have been seized, taken to the agents' office, and all its contents—including the footlocker—searched without a warrant.

Alternatively, the agents could have made a search of the footlocker at the time and place of the arrests. Machado and Leary were standing next to an open automobile trunk containing the footlocker, and thus it was within the area of their "immediate control." And certainly the footlocker would have been properly subject to search at the time if the arrest had occurred a few minutes earlier while Machado and Leary were seated on it.

In many cases, of course, small variations in the facts are determinative of the legal outcome. Criminal law necessarily involves some line drawing. But I see no way that these alternative courses of conduct, which likely would have been held constitutional under the Fourth Amendment, would have been any more solicitous of the privacy or well-being of the respondents. Indeed, as Judge Thomsen observed in dissenting from this aspect of the Court of Appeals' decision that is today affirmed, the course of conduct followed by the agents in this case was good police procedure. It is decisions of the kind made by the Court today that make criminal law a trap for the unwary policeman and detract from the important activities of detecting criminal activity and protecting the public safety.

Eyewitness Identification

In an effort to lessen the chances of a mistaken identification at police lineups, the Warren Court June 12, 1967 overturned two convictions on the grounds that the defendants were not granted the opportunity to have their attorneys witness a lineup in which they were forced to participate. The right to counsel during a police lineup was imposed on federal and state authorities in the companion cases of *U.S. v. Wade* and *Gilbert v. California*.

In issuing those rulings, the Warren Court majority held that the history of criminal law was "rife" with instances of mistaken identifications. The integrity of a lineup can be compromised by many factors, as for example, if a black-haired suspect is placed in a lineup among a group of light-haired persons, of if a suspect is required to wear distinctive clothing similar to that worn by the perpetrator of the crime. Eyewitnesses are also more apt to focus on a particular suspect if they have seen him in the custody of the police prior to the lineup. If done intentionally, such tactics result in what the police sometimes call an "Oklahoma show-up."

The purpose of having an attorney present during a lineup is to report any irregularities to the trial judge.

A defendant's right to an attorney during a lineup was sharply limited by the Burger Court in *Kirby v. Illinois*,

171

decided June 7, 1972. Kirby was the first case in which President Nixon's four appointees to the Court, Chief Justice Warren Earl Burger and Justices Harry A. Blackmun, Lewis F. Powell, Jr. and William H. Rehnquist, had an opportunity to review a leading Warren Court criminal law decision. Justice Potter Stewart, who had dissented in the court's 1967 rulings that extended the right of counsel to lineups, joined the newer justices to form a five-man majority. They held that the right of counsel did not extend to lineups conducted *prior* to the placing of formal charges against the defendant.

The result of the decision was to permit the police to conduct lineups in the absence of defense counsel prior to bringing formal charges against the suspect. In effect, this eliminated the requirement of defense counsel at virtually all lineups since the police could postpone indictment until after the lineup. The decision, however, eliminated the potential problem of an innocent suspect, who, under the old requirements, might have been required to spend several hours in a police station waiting for a lawyer before he could be shown to eyewitnesses and cleared.

According to the majority, the right of counsel did not commence until the suspect was formally charged, "for it is only then that the government has committed itself to prosecute, and only then that the adverse positions of the government and defendant have solidified." The majority, therefore, said it refused "to import into a routine police investigation" the Sixth Amendment right of counsel. The majority acknowledged, however, the right of the defense to have excluded from evidence identifications obtained from any lineup shown to have been conducted unfairly.

Justice Brennan, joined by Douglas and Marshall, asserted in a minority opinion that the need for a lawyer was consistent throughout the entire criminal procedure. In permitting the police to conduct lineups in the absence of defense counsel in the interval between an arrest and the bringing of formal charges, Brennan asserted that the majority had resorted to "mere formalism." Justice White, in a one-sentence dissent, stated that the court's previous rulings on the subject extended to all lineups.

Identification by Photographs

In *U.S.* v. *Ash*, June 21, 1973, the Burger Court held that the Sixth Amendment right to an attorney does not grant the accused the right to have counsel present when the government shows witnesses photographs of the accused and other persons in seeking to obtain an eyewitness identification of the offender.

The issue, thus, was the same as in previous decisions in which the Court held that the defendant has the right to have an attorney present during a post-indictment lineup. A difference was only that in this instance the case concerned a photographic display used in lieu of an actual lineup.

In ruling against the right to an attorney under these circumstances, the majority opinion by Justice Blackmun held that the historical background of the Sixth Amendment right to counsel suggests that the Amendment was designed to assure the assistance of counsel during the actual trial when the accused was confronted with the intricacies of the law and the advocacy of the public prosecutor. The purpose of extending the right to counsel to lineups, the court said, was in keeping with this notion of preventing the prosecutor from taking advantage of the accused. Thus, the majority said, the test used for determining the scope of the right to counsel requires an examination of the event to "determine whether the accused required aid in coping with legal problems or assistance in meeting his adversary."

As concerns photographic identifications, the majority held that the right to counsel is not called for since the accused himself is not present at the time of the display and no possibility arises that the accused might be mislead by his lack of familiarity with the law or overpowered by the prosecution. Regarding the danger from the use of unfair photographic displays, the majority held that the danger here was no greater than in other areas. "Evidence favorable to the accused may be withheld; testimony of witnesses may be manipulated; the results of laboratory tests may be contrived," the court noted. "The primary safeguard against abuses of this kind," the court said, "is the ethical responsibility of the prosecutor."

Failing here, the court said, instances of abuses can always be introduced at the trial.

The three dissenting Justices—Brennan, Douglas and Marshall—viewed the decision as "another step towards the complete evisceration of the fundamental constitutional principles" established by the Warren Court six years earlier in *Wade*.

According to the dissent, the dangers of mistaken identification are more acute in the case of photographic lineups than in "live" ones and the ability of the police to shape an eyewitness' response in such situations is also greater. In what it called "a triumph of form over substance," the dissenting opinion sharply criticized the logic of the majority contention that the need for counsel is limited to situations in which the accused is personally confronted with the prosecuting attorney at a "trial-like confrontation."

ABRIDGMENTS OF EYEWITNESS IDENTIFICATION DECISIONS

Kirby v. Illinois (406 U.S. 682, June 7, 1972)

Justice Stewart, whom Chief Justice Burger and Justices Blackmun and Rehnquist joined, delivering the judgment of the Court:

In *United States* v. *Wade*...and *Gilbert* v. *California*...this court held "that a post-indictment pretrial lineup at which the accused is exhibited to identifying witnesses is a critical stage of the criminal prosecution; that police conduct of such a lineup without notice to and in the absence of his counsel denies the accused his Sixth [and Fourteenth] Amendment right to counsel and calls in question the admissibility at trial of the in-court identifications of the accused by witnesses who attended the lineup."... Those cases further held that no "in-court identifications" are admissible in evidence if their "source" is a lineup conducted in violation of this constitutional standard. "Only a *per se* exclusionary rule as to such testimony can be an effective sanction," the court said, "to assure that law enforcement officers will respect the accused's constitutional right to the presence of his counsel at the critical lineup."... In the present case we are asked to extend the *Wade-Gilbert per se* exclusionary rule to identification testimony based upon a police station showup that took place *before* the defendant had been indicted or otherwise formally charged with any criminal offense.

On Feb. 21, 1968, a man named Willie Shard reported to the Chicago police that the previous day two men had robbed him on a Chicago street of a wallet containing, among other things, travellers checks and a Social Security card. On Feb. 22, two police officers stopped the petitioner and a companion, Ralph Bean, on West Madison Street in Chicago. When asked for identification, the petitioner produced a wallet that contained three travellers checks and a Social Security card, all bearing the name of Willie Shard. Papers with Shard's name on them were also found in Bean's possession. When asked to explain his possession of Shard's property, the petitioner first said that the travellers checks were "play money" and then told the officers that he had won them in a crap game. The officers then arrested the petitioner and Bean and took them to a police station.

Only after arriving at the police station, and checking the records there, did the arresting officers learn of the Shard robbery. A police car was then dispatched to Shard's place of employment, where it picked up Shard and brought him to the police station. Immediately upon entering the room in the police station where the petitioner and Bean were seated at a table, Shard positively identified them as the men who had robbed him two days earlier. No lawyer was present in the room, and neither the petitioner nor Bean had asked for legal assistance or been advised of any right to the presence of counsel.

More than six weeks later, the petitioner and Bean were indicted for the robbery of Willie Shard. Upon arraignment, counsel was appointed to represent them, and they pleaded not guilty. A pretrial motion to suppress Shard's identification testimony was denied, and at the trial Shard testified as a witness for the prosecution. In his testimony he described his identification of the two men at the police station on Feb. 22 and identified them again in the courtroom as the men who had robbed him on Feb. 20. He was cross-examined at length regarding the circumstances of his identification of the two defendants.... The jury found both defendants guilty, and the petitioner's conviction was affirmed on appeal....

We note at the outset that the constitutional privilege against compulsory self-incrimination is in no way implicated here....

...[T]he doctrine of *Miranda* v. *Arizona*...has no applicability whatever to the issue before us. For the *Miranda* decision was based exclusively upon the Fifth and Fourteenth Amendment privilege against compulsory self-incrimination, upon the theory that custodial *interrogation* is inherently coercive.

The *Wade-Gilbert* exclusionary rule, by contrast, stems from a quite different constitutional guarantee—the guarantee of the right to counsel contained in the Sixth and Fourteenth Amendments. Unless all semblance of principled constitutional adjudication is to be abandoned, therefore, it is to the decisions construing that guarantee that we must look in determining the present controversy.

In a line of constitutional cases in this court stemming back to the court's landmark opinion in *Powell* v. *Alabama* [1932]..., it has been firmly established that a person's Sixth and Fourteenth Amendment right to counsel attaches only at or after the time that adversary judicial proceedings have been initiated against him....

This is not to say that a defendant in a criminal case has a constitutional right to counsel only at the trial itself. The *Powell* case makes clear that the right attaches at the time of arraignment, and the court has recently held that it exists also at the time of a

preliminary hearing. *Coleman* v. *Alabama* [1970]. . . . But the point
is that, while members of the court have differed as to existence of
the right to counsel in the contexts of some of the above cases, *all* of
those cases have involved points of time at or after the initiation of
adversary judicial criminal proceedings—whether by way of formal
charge, preliminary hearing, indictment, information, or arraignment. . . .

The initiation of judicial criminal proceedings is far from a mere
formalism. It is the starting point of our whole system of adversary
criminal justice. For it is only then that the government has
committed itself to prosecute, and only then that the adverse
positions of government and defendant have solidified. It is then
that a defendant finds himself faced with the prosecutorial forces of
organized society, and immersed in the intricacies of substantive and
procedural criminal law. It is this point, therefore, that marks the
commencement of the "criminal prosecutions" to which alone the
explicit guarantees of the Sixth Amendment are applicable. . . .

In this case we are asked to import into a routine police
investigation an absolute constitutional guarantee historically and
rationally applicable only after the onset of formal prosecutorial
proceedings. We decline to do so. Less than a year after *Wade* and
Gilbert were decided, the court explained the rule of those decisions
as follows: "The rationale of those cases was that an accused is
entitled to counsel at any 'critical stage of the *prosecution*,' and that
a post-indictment lineup is such a 'critical stage.' " (Emphasis
supplied). *Simmons* v. *United States.* . . . We decline to depart from
that rationale today by imposing a *per se* exclusionary rule upon
testimony concerning an identification that took place long before
the commencement of any prosecution whatever.

. . . What has been said is not to suggest that there may not be
occasions during the course of a criminal investigation when the
police do abuse identification procedures. Such abuses are not
beyond the reach of the Constitution. As the court pointed out in
Wade itself, it is always necessary to "scrutinize *any* pretrial
confrontation. . . ." . . . The due process clause of the Fifth and
Fourteenth Amendments forbids a lineup that is unnecessarily
suggestive and conducive to irreparable mistaken identification.
Stovall v. *Denno* (1967). . . . When a person has not been formally
charged with a criminal offense, *Stovall* strikes the appropriate
constitutional balance between the right of a suspect to be protected
from prejudicial procedures and the interest of society in the prompt
and purposeful investigation of an unsolved crime.

Justice Brennan, whom Douglas and Marshall joined, dissenting:

...In *Wade*, after concluding that the lineup conducted in that case did not violate the accused's right against self-incrimination,...the court addressed the argument "that the assistance of counsel at the lineup was indispensable to protect Wade's most basic right as a criminal defendant—his right to a fair trial at which the witnesses against him might be meaningfully cross-examined."...
The court began by emphasizing that the Sixth Amendment guarantee "encompasses counsel's assistance whenever necessary to assure a meaningful 'defence.' "...

It was that constitutional principle that the court applied in *Wade* to pretrial confrontations for identification purposes. The court first met the government's contention that a confrontation for identification is " a mere preparatory step in the gathering of the prosecution's evidence," much like the scientific examination of fingerprints and blood samples. The court responded that in the latter instances "the accused has the opportunity for a meaningful confrontation of the government's case at trial through the ordinary processes of cross-examination of the government's expert witnesses and the presentation of the evidence of his own experts." The accused thus has no right to have counsel present at such examinations: "they are not critical stages since there is minimal risk that his counsel's absence at such stages might derogate from his right to a fair trial."...

In contrast, the court said, "the confrontation compelled by the state between the accused and the victim or witnesses to a crime to elicit identification evidence is peculiarly riddled with innumerable dangers and variable factors which might seriously, even crucially, derogate from a fair trial."... Most importantly, "the accused's inability effectively to reconstruct at trial any unfairness that occurred at the lineup may deprive him of his only opportunity meaningfully to attack the credibility of the witness' courtroom identification."...

In view of *Wade*, it is plain, and the plurality today does not attempt to dispute it, that there inhere in a confrontation for identification conducted after arrest the identical hazards to a fair trial that inhere in such a confrontation conducted "after the onset of formal prosecutorial proceedings."... The plurality apparently considers an arrest, which for present purposes we must assume to be based upon probable cause, to be nothing more than part of "a routine police investigation"... and thus not "the starting point of our whole system of adversary criminal justice." ... An arrest, according to the plurality, does not face the accused "with the prosecutorial forces of organized society," nor immerse him "in the intricacies of substantive and procedural criminal law." Those consequences ensue, says the plurality, only with "[t]he initiation of judicial criminal proceedings," "[f]or it is only then that the government has committed itself to prosecute, and only then that the adverse positions of government and defendant have solidified." ... If these propositions do not amount to "mere formalism,"... it is difficult to know how to characterize them. An arrest evidences the belief of the police that the perpetrator of a crime has been caught. A post-arrest confrontation for identification is not "a mere preparatory step in the gathering of the prosecution's evidence." *Wade*.... A primary, and frequently, sole, purpose of the confrontation for identification at that stage is to accumulate proof to buttress the conclusion of the police that they have the offender in hand. The plurality offers no reason ... for concluding that a post-arrest confrontation for identification, unlike a post-charge confrontation, is not among those "critical confrontations of the accused by the prosecution at pretrial proceedings where the results might well settle the accused's fate and reduce the trial itself to a mere formality." ...

The highly suggestive form of confrontation employed in this case underscores the point. This showup was particulary fraught with the peril of mistaken identification. In the setting of a police station squad room where all present except petitioner and Bean were police officers, the danger was quite real that Shard's understandable resentment might lead him too readily to agree with the police that the pair under arrest, and the only persons exhibited to him, were indeed the robbers. "It is hard to imagine a situation more clearly conveying the suggestion to the witness that the one presented is believed guilty by the police." *Id*. ... The state had no case without Shard's identification testimony,* and safeguards against that consequence were therefore of critical importance. Shard's testimony itself demonstrates the necessity for such safeguards. On direct examination, Shard identified petitioner and Bean not as the alleged robbers on trial in the courtroom but as the pair he saw at the

---

*Bean took the stand and testified that he and petitioner found Shard's travellers checks and Social Security card two hours before their arrest strewn upon the ground in an alley.

police station. His testimony thus lends strong support to the observation, quoted by the court in *Wade*, . . . that "[i]t is a matter of common experience that, once a witness has picked out the accused at the line-up, he is not likely to go back on his word later on, so that in practice the issue of identity may (in the absence of other relevant evidence) for all practical purposes be determined there and then, before the trial." . . .

Wade and *Gilbert*, of course, happened to involve post-indictment confrontations. Yet even a cursory perusal of the opinions in those cases reveals that nothing at all turned upon that particular circumstance. In short, it is fair to conclude that rather than "declin[ing] to depart from [the] rationale" of *Wade* and *Gilbert*, . . . the plurality today, albeit purporting to be engaged in "principled constitutional adjudication," . . . refuses even to recognize that "rationale." For my part, I do not agree that we "extend" *Wade* and *Gilbert* . . . by holding that the principles of those cases apply to confrontations for identification conducted after arrest. Because Shard testified at trial about his identification of petitioner at the police station showup, the exclusionary rule of *Gilbert* . . . requires reversal.

Justice White dissenting:

United States v. *Wade* . . . and *Gilbert* v. *California* . . . govern this case and compel reversal of the judgment of the Illinois Supreme Court.

U.S. v. Ash (413 U.S. 300, June 21, 1973)

Justice Blackmun delivering the opinion of the Court:

In this case the Court is called upon to decide whether the Sixth Amendment grants an accused the right to have counsel present whenever the government conducts a post-indictment photographic display, containing a picture of the accused, for the purpose of allowing a witness to attempt an identification of the offender. . . .

On the morning of Aug. 26, 1965, a man with a stocking mask entered a bank in Washington, D. C., and began waving a pistol. He ordered an employee to hang up the telephone and instructed all others present not to move. Seconds later a second man, also wearing a stocking mask, entered the bank, scooped up money from teller's drawers into a bag, and left. The gunman followed, and both men escaped through an alley. The robbery lasted three or four minutes.

A government informer, Clarence McFarland, told authorities that he had discussed the robbery with Charles J. Ash, Jr., the respondent here. Acting on this information, an FBI agent, in February 1966, showed five black-and-white mug shots of Negro males of generally the same age, height, and weight, one of which was of Ash, to four witnesses. All four made uncertain identifications of Ash's picture. At this time Ash was not in custody and had not been charged. On April 1, 1966, an indictment was returned charging Ash and a codefendant, John L. Bailey, in five counts. . . .

Trial was finally set for May 1968, almost three years after the crime. In preparing for trial, the prosecutor decided to use a photographic display to determine whether the witnesses he planned to call would be able to make in-court identifications. Shortly before the trial, an FBI agent and the prosecutor showed five color photographs to the four witnesses who previously had tentatively identified the black-and-white photograph of Ash. Three of the witnesses selected the picture of Ash, but one was unable to make any selection. None of the witnesses selected the picture of Bailey which was in the group. This post-indictment identification provides the basis for respondent Ash's claim that he was denied the right to counsel at a "critical stage" of the prosecution. . . .

At trial, the three witnesses who had been inside the bank identified Ash as the gunman, but they were unwilling to state that they were certain of their identifications. None of these made an in-court identification of Bailey. The fourth witness, who had been in a car outside the bank and who had seen the fleeing robbers after they had removed their masks, made positive in-court identifications of both Ash and Bailey. Bailey's counsel then sought to impeach this in-court identification by calling the FBI agent who had shown the color photographs to the witnesses immediately before trial. Bailey's counsel demonstrated that the witness who had identified Bailey in court had failed to identify a color photograph of Bailey. During the course of the examination, Bailey's counsel also, before the jury, brought out the fact that this witness had selected another man as one of the robbers. At this point the prosecutor became concerned that the jury might believe that the witness had selected a third person when, in fact, the witness had selected a photograph of Ash. After a conference at the bench, the trial judge ruled that all five color photographs would be admitted into evidence. The Court of Appeals held that this constituted the introduction of a post-indictment identification at the prosecutor's request and over the objection of defense counsel.

McFarland testified as a government witness. He said he had discussed plans for the robbery with Ash before the event and, later, had discussed the results of the robbery with Ash in the presence of Bailey. McFarland was shown to possess an extensive criminal record and a history as an informer.

The jury convicted Ash on all counts. It was unable to reach a verdict on the charges against Bailey, and his motion for acquittal was granted. Ash received concurrent sentences on the several counts, the two longest being 80 months to 12 years.

The five-member majority of the Court of Appeals held that Ash's right to counsel, guaranteed by the Sixth Amendment, was violated when his attorney was not given the opportunity to be present at the photographic displays conducted in May 1968 before the trial. The majority relied on this Court's lineup cases, *United States* v. *Wade*...(1967), and *Gilbert* v. *California*, (1967), and on *Stovall* v. *Denno*...(1967). ...

This review of the history and expansion of the Sixth Amendment counsel guarantee demonstrates that the test utilized by the Court has called for examination of the event in order to determine whether the accused required aid in coping with legal problems or assistance in meeting his adversary. Against the background of this traditional test, we now consider the opinion of the Court of Appeals.

Although the Court of Appeals' majority recognized the argument that "a major purpose behind the right to counsel is to protect the defendant from errors that he himself might make if he appeared in court alone," the court concluded that "other forms of prejudice," mentioned and recognized in Wade, could also give rise to a right to counsel. ... These forms of prejudice were felt by the court to flow from the possibilities for mistaken identification inherent in the photographic display.

We conclude that the dangers of mistaken identfication, mentioned in *Wade*, were removed from context by the Court of Appeals and were incorrectly utilized as a sufficient basis for requiring counsel. Although *Wade* did discuss possibilities for suggestion and the difficulty for reconstructing suggestivity, this discussion occurred only after the Court had concluded that the lineup constituted a trial-like confrontation, requiring the "Assistance of Counsel" to preserve the adversary process by compensating for advantages of the prosecuting authorities.

The above discussion of *Wade* has shown that the traditional Sixth Amendment test easily allowed extension of counsel to a lineup. The similarity to trial was apparent, and counsel was needed to render "Assistance" in counterbalancing any "overreaching" by the prosecution.

After the Court in *Wade* held that a lineup constituted a trial-like confrontation requiring counsel, a more difficult issue remained in the case for consideration. The same changes in law enforcement that led to lineups and pretrial hearings also generated other events at which the accused was confronted by the prosecution. The government had argued in *Wade* that if counsel was required at a lineup, the same forceful considerations would mandate counsel at other preparatory steps in the "gathering of the prosecution's evidence," such as, for particular example, the taking of finger-prints or blood samples. . . .

The Court concluded that there were differences. Rather than distinguishing these situations from the lineup in terms of the need for counsel to assure an equal confrontation at the time, the Court recognized that there were times when the subsequent trial would cure a one-sided confrontation between prosecuting authorities and the uncounseled defendant. In other words, such stages were not "critical." Referring to fingerprints, hair, clothing, and other blood samples, the Court explained:

"Knowledge of the techniques of science and technology is sufficiently available, and the variables in techniques few enough, that the accused has the opportunity for a meaningful confrontation of the government's case at trial through the ordinary processes of cross-examination of the government's expert witnesses and the presentation of the evidence of his own experts." . . .

The structure of *Wade*, viewed in light of the careful limitation of the Court's language to "confrontations," makes it clear that lack of scientific precision and inability to reconstruct an event are not the tests for requiring counsel in the first instance. These are, instead, the tests to determine whether confrontation with counsel at trial can serve as a substitute for counsel at the pretrial confronta-tion. If accurate reconstruction is possible, the risks inherent in any confrontation still remain, but the opportunity to cure defects at trial causes the confrontation to cease to be "critical." The opinion of the Court even indicated that changes in procedure might cause a lineup to cease to be a "critical" confrontation. . . .

"Legislative or other regulations, such as those of local police departments, which eliminate the risks of abuse and unintentional suggestion at lineup proceedings and the impediments to meaningful confrontation at trial may also remove the basis for regarding the stage as 'critical.' " . . .

The Court of Appeals considered its analysis complete after it decided that a photographic display lacks scientific precision and ease of accurate reconstruction at trial. That analysis, under *Wade*, however, merely carries one to the point where one must establish that the trial itself can provide no substitute for counsel if a pretrial confrontation is conducted in the absence of counsel. . . .

A substantial departure from the historical test would be necessary if the Sixth Amendment were interpreted to give Ash a right to counsel at the photographic identification in this case. Since the accused himself is not present at the time of the photographic display, and asserts no right to be present, . . . no possibility arises that the accused might be misled by his lack of familiarity with the law or overpowered by his professional adversary. Similarly, the counsel guarantee would not be used to produce equality in a trial-like adversary confrontation. Rather, the guarantee was used by the Court of Appeals to produce confrontation at an event that previously was not analogous to an adversary trial.

Even if we were willing to view the counsel guarantee in broad terms as a generalized protection of the adversary process, we would be unwilling to go so far as to extend the right to a portion of the prosecutor's trial-preparation interviews with witnesses. Although photography is relatively new, the interviewing of witnesses before trial is a procedure that predates the Sixth Amendment. In England in the 16th and 17th centuries counsel regularly interviewed witnesses before trial. . . . The traditional counterbalance in the American adversary system for these interviews arises from the equal ability of defense counsel to seek and interview witnesses himself.

That adversary mechanism remains as effective for a photographic display as for other parts of pretrial interviews. No greater limitations are placed on defense counsel in constructing displays, seeking witnesses, and conducting photographic identifications than those applicable to the prosecution. Selection of the picture of a person other than the accused, or the inability of a witness to make any selection, will be useful to the defense in precisely the same manner that the selection of a picture of the defendant would be useful to the prosecution. . . .

Pretrial photographic identifications, however, are hardly unique in offering possibilities for the actions of the prosecutor unfairly to prejudice the accused. Evidence favorable to the accused may be withheld; testimony of witnesses may be manipulated; the results of laboratory tests may be contrived. In many ways the prosecutor, by accident or by design, may improperly subvert the trial. The primary safeguard against abuses of this kind is the ethical responsibility of the prosecutor, who, as often has been said, may "strike hard blows" but not "foul ones." *Berger* v. *United States*...(1935)...If that safeguard fails, review remains available under due process standards. ... These same safeguards apply to misuse of photographs. ...

We are not persuaded that the risks inherent in the use of photographic displays are so pernicious that an extraordinary system of safeguards is required.

We hold, then, that the Sixth Amendment does not grant the right to counsel at photographic displays conducted by the government for the purpose of allowing a witness to attempt an identification of the offender. This holding requires reversal of the judgment of the Court of Appeals. ...

Justice Brennan, joined by Justices Douglas and Marshall, dissenting:

The Court holds today that a pretrial display of photographs to the witnesses of a crime for the purpose of identifying the accused, unlike a lineup, does not constitute a "critical stage" of the prosecution at which the accused is constitutionally entitled to the presence of counsel. In my view, today's decision is wholly unsupportable in terms of such considerations as logic, consistency, and, indeed, fairness. As a result, I must reluctantly conclude that today's decision marks simply another step towards the complete evisceration of the fundamental constitutional principles established by this Court, only six years ago, in *United States* v. *Wade*...(1967); *Gilbert* v. *California*...(1967); and *Stovall* v. *Denno*...(1967). I dissent. ...

As the Court of Appeals recognized, "the dangers of mistaken identification...set forth in *Wade* are applicable in large measure to photographic as well as corporeal identifications." ... To the extent that misidentification may be attributable to a witness' faulty memory or perception, or inadequate opportunity for detailed observation during the crime, the risks are obviously as great at a photographic display as at a lineup. But "[b]ecause of the inherent limitations of photography, which presents its subject in two dimensions rather than the three dimensions of reality,...a photographic identification, even when properly obtained, is clearly inferior to a properly obtained corporeal identification." P. Wall, *Eye-Witness Indentification in Criminal Cases* 70 (1965). Indeed, noting "the hazards of initial identification by photograph," we have expressly recognized that "a corporeal identification...is normally more accurate" than a photographic identification. *Simmons* v. *United States*...(1968). Thus, in this sense at least, the dangers of misidentification are even greater at a photographic display than at a lineup.

Moreover, as in the lineup situation, the possibilities for impermissible suggestion in the context of a photographic display are manifold. ... Such suggestion, intentional or unintentional, may derive from three possible sources. First, the photographs themselves might tend to suggest which of the pictures is that of the suspect. For example, differences in age, pose, or other physical characteristics of the persons represented, and variations in the mounting, background, lighting, or markings of the photographs all might have the effect of singling out the accused.

Second, impermissible suggestion may inhere in the manner in which the photographs are displayed to the witness. The danger of misidentification is, of course, "increased if the police display to the witness...the pictures of several persons among which the photograph of a single such individual recurs or is in some way emphasized." ... And, if the photographs are arranged in an asymmetrical pattern, or if they are displayed in a time sequence that tends to emphasize a particular photograph, "any identification of the photograph which stands out from the rest is no more reliable than an identification of a single photograph, exhibited alone." P. Wall, *supra*. ...

Third, gestures or comments of the prosecutor at the time of the display may lead an otherwise uncertain witness to select the "correct" photograph. For example, the prosecutor might "indicate to the witness that [he has] other evidence that one of the persons pictured committed the crime," and might even point to a particular photograph and ask whether the person pictured "looks familiar." More subtly, the prosecutor's inflection, facial expressions, physical motions, and myriad other almost imperceptible means of communication might tend, intentionally or unintentionally, to compromise the witness' objectivity. Thus, as is the case with lineups, "[i]mproper photographic identification procedures, . . . by exerting a suggestive influence upon the witnesses, can often lead to an erroneous identification. . . ." P. Wall, *supra*. . . . And "[r]egardless of how the initial misidentification comes about, the witness thereafter is apt to retain in his memory the image of the photograph rather than of the person actually seen. . . ." *Simmons* v. *United States*. . . .

Moreover, as with lineups, the defense can "seldom reconstruct" at trial the mode and manner of photographic identification. It is true, of course, that the photographs used at the pretrial display might be preserved for examination at trial. But "it may also be said that a photograph can preserve the record of a lineup; yet this does not justify a lineup without counsel." . . . Indeed, in reality, preservation of the photographs affords little protection to the unrepresented accused. For, although retention of the photographs may mitigate the dangers of misidentification due to the suggestiveness of the photgraphs themselves, it cannot in any sense reveal to defense counsel the more subtle, and therefore more dangerous, suggestiveness that might derive from the manner in which the photographs were displayed or any accompanying comments or gestures. Moreover, the accused cannot rely upon the witnesses themselves to expose these latter sources of suggestion, for the witnesses are not "apt to be alert for conditions prejudicial to the suspect. And if they were, it would likely be of scant benefit to the suspect" since the witnesses are hardly "likely to be schooled in the detection of suggestive influences." . . .

Finally, and *unlike* the lineup situation, the accused himself is not even present at the photographic identification, thereby reducing the likelihood that irregularities in the procedures will ever come to light. Indeed, in *Wade*, the government itself observed:

"When the defendant is present—as he is during a lineup—he may personally observe the circumstances, report them to his attorney, and (if he chooses to take the stand) testify about them at trial. . . . [I]n the absence of an accused, on the other hand, there is no one present to verify the fairness of the interview or to report any irregularities. If the prosecution were tempted to engage in 'sloppy or biased or fraudulent' conduct. . ., it would be far more likely to do so when the accused is absent than when he himself is being 'used.' "

Thus, the difficulties of reconstructing at trial an uncounseled photographic display are at least equal to, and possibly greater than, those involved in reconstructing an uncounseled lineup. . . .

Ironically, the Court does not seriously challenge the proposition that presence of counsel at a pretrial photographic display is essential to preserve the accused's right to a fair trial on the issue of identification. Rather, in what I can only characterize a triumph of form over substance, the Court seeks to justify its result by engrafting a wholly unprecedented—and wholly unsupportable—limitation on the Sixth Amendment right of "the accused. . . to have the Assistance of Counsel for his defence." Although apparently conceding that the right to counsel attaches, not only at the trial itself, but at all "critical stages" of the prosecution, . . . the Court holds today that, in order to be deemed "critical," the particular "stage of the prosecution" under consideration must, at the very least, involve the physical "presence of the accused," at a "trial-like confrontation" with the government, at which the accused requires the "guiding hand of counsel." According to the Court a pretrial photographic identification does not, of course, meet these criteria. . . .

The fundamental premise underlying *all* of this Court's decisions holding the right to counsel applicable at "critical" pretrial proceedings, is that a "stage" of the prosecution must be deemed "critical" for the purposes of the Sixth Amendment if it is one at which the presence of counsel is necessary "to protect the fairness of *the trial itself.*" *Schneckloth* v. *Bustamonte.* . .(1973) (emphasis added). . . .

This established conception of the Sixth Amendment guarantee is, of course, in no sense dependent upon the physical "presence of the accused," at a "trial-like confrontation" with the government, at which the accused requires the "guiding hand of counsel." On the contrary, in *Powell* v. *Alabama.* . .(1932), the seminal decision in this area, we explicitly held the right to counsel applicable at a stage of the pretrial proceedings involving *none* of the three criteria set forth by the Court today. In *Powell*, the defendants in a state felony prosecution were not appointed counsel until the very eve of trial. This Court held, in no uncertain terms, that such an appointment could not satisfy the demands of the Sixth Amendment, for " '[i]t is vain. . .to guarantee [the accused] counsel without giving the latter any opportunity to acquaint himself with the facts or law of the case.' ". . . In other words, *Powell* made clear that, in order to preserve the accused's right to a fair trial and to "effective and substantial" assistance of counsel at that trial, the Sixth Amendment guarantee necessarily encompasses a reasonable period of time before trial during which counsel might prepare the defense. Yet it can hardly be said that this preparatory period of research and investigation involves the physical "presence of the accused," at a "trial-like confrontation" with the government, at which the accused requires the "guiding hand of counsel." . . .

Thus, contrary to the suggestion of the Court, the conclusion in *Wade* that a pretrial lineup is a "critical stage" of the prosecution did not in any sense turn on the fact that a lineup involves the physical "presence of the accused" at a "trial-like confrontation" with the government. And that conclusion most certainly did not turn on the notion that presence of counsel was necessary so that counsel could offer legal advice or "guidance" to the accused at the lineup. On the contrary, *Wade* envisioned counsel's function at the lineup to be primarily that of a trained observer, able to detect the existence of any suggestive influences and capable of understanding the legal implications of the events that transpire. Having witnessed the proceedings, counsel would then be in a position effectively to reconstruct at trial any unfairness that occurred at the lineup, thereby preserving the accused's fundamental right to a fair trial on the issue of identification.

There is something ironic about the Court's conclusion today that a pretrial lineup identification is a "critical stage" of the prosecution because counsel's presence can help to compensate for the accused's deficiencies as an observer, but that a pretrial photographic identification is not a "critical stage" of the prosecution because the accused is not able to observe at all. In my view, there simply is no meaningful difference, in terms of the need for attendance of counsel, between corporeal and photographic identifications. And applying established and well-reasoned Sixth Amendment principles, I can only conclude that a pretrial photographic display, like a pretrial lineup, is a "critical stage" of the prosecution at which the accused is constitutionally entitled to the presence of counsel.

Habeas Corpus & Ramifications

U.S. Experience With Habeas Corpus

The Burger Court has also become involved in disagreement over the right of habeas corpus, a constitutional guarantee whose implications for political freedom perhaps even transcend the guarantee's utility in criminal justice. Two recent Burger Court decisions have been criticized as restricting the historical right of habeas corpus. Sen. Gaylord Nelson (D, Wis.), urging legislation to reinforce habeas corpus, inserted in the Congressional Record April 20, 1977 a statement summarizing U.S. judicial experience with the writ. An abridgment of his statement (including his critical comments on the Burger Court's decisions) follows:

... [T]wo Supreme Court decisions last year... departed radically from longstanding precedent and seriously curtailed the rights of those in custody to petition the federal courts for a writ of *habeas corpus.* ...

In *Francis* v. *Henderson,* . . . the Supreme Court held that a state prisoner who failed to make a timely challenge to the composition of the grand jury that indicted him could not, after his conviction, bring that challenge in a federal *habeas corpus* proceeding. In

191

reaching this decision, the Court rejected the existing law that, absent a deliberate bypass of state procedures, a procedural default by a state prisoner will not foreclose him from making a constitutional challenge through a *habeas* petition. The Court had reached a similar conclusion three years earlier for federal prisoners, holding that constitutional claims might be waived for the purpose of 28 U.S.C. section 2255, which is analogous to *habeas corpus*, if the prisoners had not raised them within the time limits spelled out by the Federal Rules of Criminal Procedure. *Davis* v. *United States*...(1973).

In *Stone* v. *Powell*...(1976), the Court held that when a state has provided an opportunity for a full and fair litigation of a Fourth Amendment claim of illegal search and seizure, a state prisoner may not be granted *habeas* relief on the ground that evidence illegally seized from him was used against him at trial. In reaching this decision, the Court reached the umprecendented conclusion that certain constitutional rights cannot be vindicated through a *habeas corpus* petition. ...

The legislation I am proposing...would overrule *Francis* and *Stone*. ...

Legislation overruling Supreme Court decisions is a major step which should be taken only after careful consideration and under narrow circumstances. In support of the legislation there are four points which the Senate should consider:

First, *habeas corpus* is one of our most cherished constitutional rights. Its diminution reduces the freedom of all Americans.

Second, *habeas corpus* in this country has been liberally granted and construed, by Congress and the courts, particularly in the last 50 years. The *Francis* and *Stone* decisions reverse that historical trend, without justification, and without a willingness to acknowledge the scope of the departure.

Third, these decisions represent a significant incursion on the constitutional power and obligation of Congress, under article III of the Constitution, to define the jurisdiction of the federal courts.

Finally, these decisions convey the impression of being justified, at least in part, by the Supreme Court's desire to cope with the increased caseload of the federal courts. However serious this problem may be, the remedy must come from Congress, and not from the Court in the guise of decisions on the merits. ...

... As Justice Brennan wrote, dissenting in *Stone against Powell*, the decision was "in keeping with the regrettable recent trend of barring the federal courthouse door to individuals with meritorious claims."

Most of these troubling decisions have involved restrictive interpretations of title 42, United States Code, section 1983, the Civil Rights Act of 1871, the principal statute which permits aggrieved individuals to challenge government actions which they believe to be violative of their constitutional rights. . . .

The "province" of *habeas corpus*, "shaped to guarantee the most fundamental of all rights, is to provide an effective and speedy instrument by which judicial inquiry may be had into the legality of the detention of a person. It allows restraints contrary to our fundamental law, the constitution, to be challenged, even when the conviction has been imposed by a court of competent jurisdiction." *Carafas* v. *LaVallee*...(1968). As Justice Holmes once wrote, "*Habeas corpus* cuts through all forms and goes to the very tissue of the structure. It comes in from the outside, not in subordination to the proceedings," *Frank* v. *Mangum*...(1915).

Title 28, United States Code, secion 2241 *et seq.* is the federal law governing petitions for *habeas corpus*: 2241(a) provides that "writs of *habeas corpus* may be granted by the Supreme Court, any Justice thereof, the district courts and any circuit judge within their respective jurisdictions." Section 2254 sets forth the grounds for a motion for *habeas* by a state prisoner: section 2255 is the counterpart for federal prisoners. Although the federal prisoner has wider grounds on which to base a motion, the crucial aspect of both sections is that a state or federal prisoner can seek *habeas* or post-conviction relief on the grounds that the prisoner is "in custody in violation of the Constitution or laws or treaties of the United States."

Throughout our history, *habeas corpus* has been known as the Great Writ, a cornerstone of individual freedom. It is "the most celebrated writ in the English law." 3 *Blackstone Commentaries* 129. It is "a writ antecedent to statute, and throwing its root deep into the genius of our common law. It is perhaps the most important writ known to the constitutional law of England, affording as it does an imperative remedy in all cases of illegal restraint and confinement. . . . *Secretary of the State for Home Affairs* v. *O'Brien*, (1923). . . .

In the United States, *habeas corpus* was received into our law during the colonial period, explicitly recognized in article I, section 9, clause 2 of the Constitution and incorporated into the first grant of federal court jurisdiction, act of Sept. 24, 1789. . . . Chief Justice John Marshall recognized *habeas corpus* to be a "great constitutional privilege.". . . Nearly 150 years later, the Supreme Court reaffirmed the importance of *habeas corpus*, writing:

> We repeat what has been so truly said of the federal writ: "There is no higher duty than to maintain it unimpaired." *Boman* v. *Johnston*, . . .(1939) and unsuspended, save only in the cases specified in our Constitution. *Smith* v. *Bennett*. . . (1968). *Fay* v. *Noia*. . .(1963).

Although no body of law developed over 150 years can ever be completely consistent, it is fair to say that the Supreme Court has accorded great respect to the writ of *habeas corpus*. Moreover, in the past half century, the Court in a series of decisions has greatly expanded the concept of *habeas corpus*. The early concept of *habeas* was that it guaranteed only that proper legal processes had been followed. The stated doctrine was that the writ would issue only if the court which committed the prisoner had lacked jurisdiction to do so. However, in *Moore* v. *Dempsey*. . .(1923), the court held that a prisoner could attack his conviction by *habeas corpus*, even if the court proceedings were formally proper, if those proceedings were under the sway of a mob, making the trial a mere sham. In *Mooney* v. *Holohan*. . .(1935), the court extended *habeas* to a prisoner whose conviction rested on perjured testimony; in *Johnson* v. *Zerbst*. . . (1938), the court concluded *habeas* was appropriate because although the trial court originally had "jurisdiction," it relinquished it by not providing the petitioner with counsel. Finally in 1942, the court completely discarded the jurisdictional fiction and stated that—

> The use of the writ in federal courts to test the constitutional validity of a conviction for crime is not restricted to those cases where the judgment of conviction is void for want of jurisdiction of the trial court to render it. It extends also to those exceptional cases where the conviction has been in disregard of the Constitutional rights of the accused, and where the writ is the only effective means of preserving his rights. *Waley* v. *Johnston* . . .(1942).

In 1963, the Court decided *Fay* v. *Noia*. . . . The issue before the Court was whether federal *habeas corpus* relief could be granted to a state prisoner who had been denied state post-conviction remedies, because a coerced confession claim had been decided against him and the prisoner had allowed the time for a direct appeal to lapse without seeking state appellate review. In a painstaking review of the history of the Great Writ, the majority of the Court, *per* Justice Brennan, concluded that the lower federal courts had erred in denying the writ. The essence of the court's conclusion was that the Great Writ was the remedy for incarcerations in violation of fundamental rights. Therefore, if Noia was in prison in violation of his constitutional rights, federal *habeas corpus* was an available remedy for him to challenge that incarceration, despite his procedural default. In reaching that decision, the Court considered at great length its effect on the relationship between state and federal courts, but concluded that the state's interest would be adequately protected by a deliberate bypass standard, and that no stricter standard could be accepted given the overriding importance of *habeas corpus*:

We fully grant . . . that the exigencies of federalism warrant a limitation whereby the federal judge has the discretion to deny relief to one who has deliberately sought to subvert or evade the the orderly adjudication of his federal defense in the state courts. Surely no stricter rule is a realistic necessity. . . . [I]f because of inadvertence or neglect he runs afoul of a state procedural requirement, and thereby forfeits his state remedies, appellate and collateral, as well as direct review thereof in this Court, those consequences should be sufficient to vindicate the state's valid interest in orderly procedure. Whatever residuum of state interest there may be under such circumstances in manifestly insufficient in the face of the federal policy, drawn from the ancient principles of the writ of *habeas corpus*, embodied both in the federal Constitution and in the *habeas corpus* provisions of the Judicial Code, and consistently upheld by this Court, of affording an effective remedy for restraints contrary to the Constitution.

Although we hold that the jurisdiction of the federal courts on *habeas corpus* is not affected by procedural defaults incurred by the applicant during the state court proceedings, we recognize a limited discretion in the federal judge to deny relief to an applicant under certain circumstances . . . narrowly circumscribed, in conformity to the historic role of the writ of *habeas corpus* as an effective and imperative remedy for detentions contrary to fundamental law, the principle is unexceptionable. We therefore hold that the federal *habeas* judge may in his discretion deny relief to an applicant who has deliberately by-passed the orderly procedure of the state courts and in so doing has forfeited his state court remedies.

But we wish to make very clear that this grant of discretion is not to be interpreted as a permission to introduce legal fictions into federal *habeas corpus*. The classic definition of waiver enunciated in *Johnson* v. *Zerbst...*—"an intentional relinquishment or abandonment of a known right or privilege"— furnishes the controlling standard. If a *habeas* applicant, after consultation with competent counsel or otherwise, understandingly and knowingly forewent the privilege of seeking to vindicate his federal claims in the state courts, whether for strategic, tactical, or any other reasons that can fairly be described as the deliberate by-passing of state procedures, then it is open to the federal courts on *habeas* to deny him all relief if the state courts refused to entertain his federal claims on the merits—though of course only after the federal court has satisfied itself, by holding a hearing or by some other means, of the facts bearing upon the applicant's default. ...

In my view, this statement reflects a profound understanding of priorities in a free society dedicated to constitutional rights. The Court decided that the states' interest in orderly procedure could not prevail over the constitutional rights of a person wrongfully incarcerated. Until this term, the Supreme Court had repeatedly reaffirmed the holding of *Fay*. ...

At the same time, a series of court decisions has established that the notion of being "in custody" should be construed liberally. Originally *habeas* was appropriate only in those cases in which petitioner's claim, if upheld, would result in an immediate release from prison. *McNally* v. *Hill...*(1934). Subsequently, the Court concluded that a person on parole was "in custody" for the purpose of raising a *habeas* claim. *Jones* v. *Cunningham...*(1963). Similarly, later court decisions established that *habeas* claims could be raised by individuals at large on their own recognizance, but subject to several conditions pending execution of sentence. *Hensley* v. *Municipal Court...*(1973) and those released on bail after conviction pending final disposition of their cases *Lefkowitz* v. *Newsome* ...(1975). These decisions underscore the view that *habeas* "is not now and never had been a static, narrow, formalistic remedy; its scope has grown to achieve its grand purpose—the protection of individuals against erosion of their right to be free from wrongful restraints upon their liberty. Besides physical imprisonment, there are other restraints on a man's liberty, restraints not shared by the public generally, which have been thought sufficient in the English-speaking world to support the issuance of *habeas corpus.*" *Hammond* v. *Lenfest*, (2d Cir. 1968), quoting *Jones* v. *Cunningham* ... (1963).

Against this background, *Francis* v. *Henderson* ... was a startling, regrettable departure. In *Davis* v. *United States* ... (1973), the Court had held that a federal prisoner who had failed to make a timely challenge to the allegedly unconstitutional composition of the grand jury which indicted him could not subsequently attack his conviction under 28 U.S.C. 2255. In *Francis*, the Court extended the *Davis* ruling to bar a state prisoner from a *habeas* challenge to the allegedly unconstitutional composition of the grand jury which indicted him. The majority of the court concluded that since *Davis* held that the federal courts must give effect to the legitimate rules and time limitations imposed by F.R. Crim. P. 12(b) (2):

> Then surely considerations of comity and federalism require that they give no less effect to the same clear interests when asked to overturn state criminal proceedings." *Francis* v. *Henderson.* ...

The Court concluded that applying the *Davis* rule with "equal force" meant that petitioner must show not only "cause" for the untimely challenge, but also actual prejudice resulting from the failure to comply.

This holding obviously departs sharply from *Fay against Noia.* After summarizing the holding of *Fay*, Mr. Justice Brennan wrote in his dissent:

> Yet the Court, invoking "comity and federalism," would now essentially preclude federal *habeas* relief for state defendants deprived on their constitutional rights, so long as the state required that they assert those rights within a certain time period; this absolute and automatic "waiver" of the underlying constitutional claim would apparently take effect whether or not the defendant knew of his rights, whether or not the "untimely" challenge was nevertheless made at a time when no legitimate state interest would be upset by an adjudication of the claim on the merits, and whether or not mere inadvertence or actual incompetence of counsel accounted for the untimely challenge. *Francis* v. *Henderson* ... (dissenting opinion of Brennan).

The dissent was particularly critical of the Court's willingness to undercut *Fay against Noia* without confronting the case's precedential impact:

It is particularly distressing... [that]...the Court exposes its hostility towards and makes substantial inroads into the precedential force of *Fay* without directly confronting its underlying premises, continuing validity, or the possibility of distinguishing the failure to raise different constitutional rights in a timely manner in the state courts. Such "oversights" are especially ironical in light of the Court's recent admonition that "[o]ur institutional duty is to follow until changed the law as it now is, not as some members of the Court might wish it to be." *Hudgens* v. *NLRB*...(1976)....

Underlying both *Francis* and *Davis* is apparently the view that defendants must be deterred from raising procedural claims after the Court, witnesses, and the parties have gone to the burden and expense of a trial. However, as the Court recognized in *Fay*, deterrence is only an effective policy for prisoners who act knowingly and intentionally. Prisoners who because of inexperience, poor counsel, or other reasons are unaware of their rights will not be deterred by the Court's new standard; they will simply be trapped in "an airtight system of forefeitures." (*Fay* v. *Noia*. ...) In *Davis* and *Francis* the Court has thereby elevated the state and federal interests in efficiency above the rights of individuals to have their constitutional claims heard. ...

The holding of *Stone against Powell* was equally disturbing, and the reasoning no more compelling. Powell had been convicted of murder in state court because of crucial testimony concerning a revolver which had been taken from him when he was arrested for violating a vagrancy statute. On appeal, the state courts rejected Powell's claim that the vagrancy statute was unconstitutional and, therefore, the resulting search was invalid. The federal Court of Appeals, however, concluded that the statute was unconstitutional and the search unlawful. The Supreme Court reversed, holding that when the state has provided an opportunity for full and fair litigation of a Fourth Amendment claim, a state prisoner may not be granted *habeas corpus* relief on the ground that evidence obtained through an unconstitutional search and seizure was introduced at trial. In reaching the decision, the Court distinguished away *Kaufman* v. *United States*...(1969), which held squarely that a federal prisoner could raise search and seizure claims in a motion to vacate sentence based on 28 U.S.C. section 2255.

The Court's majority reached its result by arguing first, that the exclusionary rule, made applicable to the states in *Mapp* v. *Ohio*...(1960) was not constitutionally required, but a "judicially created remedy designed to safeguard Fourth Amendment rights generally through its deterrent effect. ..." The Court went on to note that the exclusionary rule did not establish an absolute bar against the use of illegally seized evidence; such evidence can be used in a grand jury proceeding, *United States* v. *Calandra*...(1974), or in a trial court to impeach a defendant, *Walder* v. *United States*...(1954). Since the purpose of the rule is deterrence and the extension of the rule to *habeas corpus* would not greatly add to its deterrent effect below, the Court chose not to extend it to *habeas corpus*. The Court buttressed its holding by distinguishing the exclusionary rule which "deflects the truth-finding process and often frees the guilty" from others constitutional rights, such as the Fifth Amendment right to be free from self-incrimination, the violation of which could distort the search for guilt or innocence, *Stone* v. *Powell*. ...

The dissent's scorn for this reasoning was stated plainly. *Mapp* was obviously constitutionally based "or there would be no basis for applying the exclusionary rule in state criminal proceedings." Cases like *Walder* and *Calandra* cut back on the substance of the exclusionary rule, but they were constitutional decisions, rather than judicial interpretations of the *habeas* statute to foreclose the prisoner from seeking *habeas*. Most important, 28 U.S.C. section 2254 provides that *habeas corpus* will be granted if a prisoner "is in custody in violation of the Constitution." There is nothing in the statute or its legislative history leading to the conclusion that some constitutional rights are subordinate to others.

The effect of these decisions is a severe curtailment of the right of *habeas corpus*. Moreover, in Justice Brennan's words, the premises underlying the decisions, particularly *Stone*, mark the cases "as a harbinger of future eviserations of the *habeas* statutes..." *Stone*. ... For a major premise in the court's decision is reflected in the observation that—

> Resort to *habeas corpus*, especially for purposes other than to assure that no innocent person suffers an unconstitutional loss of liberty, results in serious intrusions on values important to our system of government. They include (i) the most effective

utilization of limited judicial resources, (ii) the necessity of finality in criminal trials, (iii) the minimization of friction between our federal and state systems of justice and (iv) the maintenance of the constitutional balance upon which the doctrine of federalism is founded. *Stone.* . . .

These considerations will be no less important in future *habeas* cases. They will inevitably be balanced against the right to *habeas*, to which the court majority does not accord the exalted position that history does. In the eyes of the court, *habeas* has been reduced to the level of just another appeal. As Justice Rehnquist, writing for the court in *Davis*, noted—

> We find it difficult to conceptualize the application of one waiver rule for purposes of federal appeal and another for purposes of federal *habeas corpus*. . . .

Yet this reasoning disregards two centuries of history concerning the Great Writ. The Court was more accurate in *Townsend* v. *Sain* . . . (1963) writing:

> The whole history of the writ—its unique developments— refutes a construction of the federal courts' *habeas corpus* powers that would assimilate their tasks to that of courts of appellate review. The function on *habeas* is different. It's to test by way of an original civil proceeding, independent of the normal channels of review of criminal judgments, the very gravest allegations. . . .

. . . History makes it obvious that the operation of the *habeas corpus* statutes is a proper concern of Congress. In the Judiciary Act of 1789. Congress granted the federal courts authority to issue the writs in cases of prisoners in custody of the United States. In 1867, Congress expanded the writ to state prisoners, giving relief in "all cases where any person may be restrained of his or her liberty in violation of the Constitution or any treaty or law of the United States." Act of February 5, 1867, c. 28 s. 1, Stat. 385. In that act:

> Congress was enlarging the *habeas* remedy . . . not only in extending its coverage to state prisoners, but also in making its procedures more efficient.

The Supreme Court, shortly after the passage of the act, described it in equally broad terms:

This legislation is of the most comprehensive character. It brings within the *habeas corpus* jurisdiction of every writ and of every judge every possible case of privation of liberty contrary to the National Constitution, treaties or laws. It is impossible to widen this jurisdiction. *Ex Parte McCardle* . . . (1868); *Fay v. Noia.* . . .

In *Johnson* v. *Zerbst* . . . (1938), the Court noted:

The scope of inquiry in *habeas corpus* proceedings has been broadened—not narrowed—since the adoption of the Sixth Amendment . . . Congress has expanded the rights of a petitioner for *habeas corpus.* . . . There [is] no doubt of the authority of the Congress to thus liberalize the common law procedure on habeas corpus. . . . *Walter* v. *Johnston* . . . (1941).

Evaluating the relationship between Congress and the Supreme Court on *habeas corpus*, Justice Frankfurter wrote:

Congress could have left the enforcement of federal constitutional rights governing the administration of criminal justice in the States exclusively to the state courts. These tribunals are under the same duty as the federal courts to respect rights under the United States Constitution. . . . It is not for us to determine whether this power should have been vested in the federal courts. . . . [*T*]*he wisdom of such a modification in the law is for Congress to consider,* particularly in view of the effect of the expanding concept of due process upon enforcement by the state of their criminal laws. *It is for this Court to give fair effect to the habeas corpus jurisdiction as enacted by Congress. By giving the federal courts that jurisdiction, Congress imbedded into federal legislation the historic function of habeas corpus adapted to reaching an enlarged area of claims. Brown* v. *Allen* . . . (1953) (emphasis added).

The division of responsibility is relatively straightforward: It is the responsibility of the court to define the substantive scope of constitutional rights but "it is for Congress to decide what the most efficacious method is for enforcing federal constitutional rights and asserting the primacy of Federal law." *Stone* v. *Powell*. . . (dissenting opinion of Brennan).

Once the congressional interest is clear, the need for corrective legislation becomes obvious. Section 2254 provides that—

A state prisoner can seek a writ of *habeas corpus*...on the ground that he is in custody in violation of the Constitution. ...

Since the Fourth Amendment is violated by the use of evidence illegally seized against a petitioner, it is clear that in those circumstances, petitioner would have the right to petition the district court of a writ of *habeas corpus*. To my knowledge, there is not a shred of legislative history to suggest that Congress somehow intended to exclude Fourth Amendment rights from the plain language of the *habeas* status, and the majority in *Stone* does not produce any. As Justice Brennan pointed out:

> There remains, as noted before, no basis whatsoever in the language or legislative history of the *habeas* statutes for establishing such a hierarchy of federal rights, certainly there is no constitutional warrant in this Court to override a Congressional determination respecting federal court review of decisions of state judges determining constitutional claims of state prisoners. *Stone*. ...

Francis is an equally disturbing derogative of congressional intent. Federal *habeas* for state prisoners has been a controversial subject for years, and Congress has not been oblivious to the furor. The tension created in relations between State and federal courts prompted congressional enactment of 2254 (b) and (c), a codification of the case law rule requiring that state prisoners exhaust state court remedies before applying for federal *habeas*. But the consideration of comity embodied in the exhaustion requirement dictates only that federal *habeas* can be delayed until after the state court determination, not foreclosed. In *Fay*, the court concluded that to rule otherwise would convert "a rule of timing...[into] a rule circumscribing the power of the federal courts on *habeas*, in defiance of unmistakable, congressional intent." *Fay* v. *Noia*...(1963); *Stone* v. *Powell*...(Brennan dissenting).

The "unmistakable congressional intent" perceived by the Court in *Fay* has not changed in the last 13 years. "Indeed," as Justice Brennan points out, "subsequent congressional efforts to amend those jurisdictional statutes to effectuate the result that [the Court] accomplish[es] by judicial flat have consistently proved unsuccessful." *Stone*. ... In 1968, for example, a provision in the Omnibus Crime Control & Safe Streets Act, as reported by the Senate Judiciary Committee, would have abolished federal *habeas* for state court prisoners. Despite the passions of that particular year, that section was deleted from the bill by the Senate overwhelmingly. The Senate apparently agreed with the views expressed by the minority of the Judiciary Committee that—

A hundred years of experience under the federal *habeas corpus* provisions forcefully demonstrate that absolute reliance on state courts to protect federal rights does not adequately protect those rights. To abolish this jurisdiction would roll back a century of progress in American constitutional law and restore American criminal procedure to the dark ages of the early 1900s. . . .

. . . There is a related, disturbing point. It is no secret that the federal courts are seriously clogged. . . .

Congress has responded to the burden on the federal courts slowly and incompletely. . . .

It is troubling that the federal courts are backlogged and that the Congress has responded insufficiently. But it is more disturbing that the recent series of cases cutting off access to the federal courts conveys the impression of being prompted at least as much by concern about the judicial caseload as by concern for the merits of the cases. . . .

For example, in 1971, the Court held that a person whose Fourth Amendment rights were violated by a federal agent had a cause of action for damages against that agent, grounded directly on the Fourth Amendment, even though there was no federal statute creating such a cause of action. *Bivens v. Six Unknown Named Police Agents*. . . (1971). In dissent, Justice Black argued that the creation of a new cause of action was a legislative function. He then pointed out that even if the Court viewed it as a judicial function, there were "many reasons why we should decline to create a cause of action":

The courts of the United States as well as those of the states are choked with lawsuits. . . . A majority of these cases are brought by citizens with substantial complaints—persons who are physically or economically injured by torts or frauds or governmental infringement of their rights; persons who have been unjustly deprived of their liberty or their property; and persons who have not yet received the equal opportunity in education, employment, and pursuit of happiness that was the dream of our forefathers. Unfortunately, there have also been a growing number of frivolous lawsuits, particularly actions for damages against law enforcement officers whose conduct has been judicially sanctioned by state trial and appellate courts and in many instances even by this Court. My fellow justices on this Court and our brethren throughout the federal judiciary know only too well the time-consuming task of conscientiously pouring over hundreds of thousands of pages of factual allegations of misconduct by police, judicial and corrections officials... (dissenting opinion of Black). ...

...The judicial backlog problem is particularly sensitive where *habeas corpus* is involved. There is no doubt that prisoners' petitions comprise a substantial percentage of the federal courts' docket, or that over 90% of these petitions lack merit. But this predicament is not new. ...

Yet..., the federal courts have continued to function. Some evidence suggests that while the burden on the courts is plainly serious, it is less crushing than unvarnished statistics would suggest. In a comprehensive study of *habeas corpus*, the *Harvard Law Review* observed:

> Yet it is all too easy to overstate the strain that an expanded *habeas* jurisdiction and expanded federal constitutional rights put on the judicial system. Most of the petitions were quickly dismissed: less than 500 reached the hearing state, and most of those hearings lasted less than one day. Nor was the burden on the states staggering: many petitions do not even require a response; less than 10% of the state convictions attacked had to be defended in a hearing, and so few prisoners were released that the burden of retrial must be small. ...

An empirical study of the handling and effect of *habeas* petitions in the federal district court in Massachusetts points to the same conclusion. That study termed the effect of *Fay against Noia* "slight," and concluded that more than 50% of all *habeas* petitions were disposed of within 50 days after they had been filed. ...

...[T]he problem is not new, it has been recognized and Congress has chosen not to ease the judicial caseload by making radical changes in the *habeas corpus* statute. What is different now from the past is that the Supreme Court has apparently taken matters into its own hands, alleviating the judicial backlog by striking sharply at the premises underlying *habeas* jurisdiction. The strong sense which emerges from the majority opinions in *Davis, Francis,* and *Stone* is that *habeas corpus* is not particularly important. ...

But if comprehensive reform cannot be accomplished, decisions like *Stone* and *Francis* should still be overruled swiftly and unequivocally. The assertion of constitutional rights—and the existence of a federal forum to review those claims—is vitally important for the society, as well as for the petitioner. Our willingness to use scarce judicial resources in this way reflects again the high priority this society places on constitutional liberties and individual freedom.

. . . When the Supreme Court restricts access to the lower courts, the impact falls disproportionately on the poor, minorities, and those seeking to challenge the political, economic, and social *status quo*. Most often, those who find the courthouse door closed are precisely those individuals and groups most in need of "heightened judicial solicitude," in the words of Justice Stone's famous footnote in *Carolene Products*. . . .

. . . Justice Frankfurter wrote in the landmark *habeas corpus* case, *Brown against Allen:*

The meritorious claims are few, but our procedures must ensure that those few claims are not stifled by discriminating generalities. . . For surely it is an abuse to deal too casually and too lightly with rights guaranteed by the federal Constitution, even though they invoke limitations upon state power and may be invoked by those morally unworthy.

Too often in the past, politicians have conveyed the message that full respect for the constitutional rights of those who commit crimes frustrates effective law enforcement. The inference is that we could somehow reduce the constitutional rights of "bad" people, while leaving intact the rights of law abiding Americans. Surely this is a dangerous delusion. When constitutional rights are short-changed in the name of the law and order or judicial efficiency, the rights of the innocent will be lost as surely as the rights of the guilty. . . .

Congressional Research Report

Additional background on U.S. experience with habeas corpus had been provided by the American Law Division of the Congressional Research Service July 13, 1976 in response to a request of Sen. Charles C. Mathias Jr. (R, Md.), who joined Sen. Nelson in

*the latter's legislative proposals for strengthening
the habeas corpus right. An abridgment of the Congressional Research Service's report follows:*

I. THE HISTORICAL DEVELOPMENT

The writ of *habeas corpus* that we know is considerably changed
from the common law writ known to the framers and protected from
all but a limited class of suspension by Article I, § 9, cl. 2. That writ
was the "Great Writ," the *habeas corpus ad sub-jiciendum,* by
which a court would inquire into the lawfulness of a detention of a
petitioner. The Court early adopted the common law understanding
that the writ was unavailable to one convicted of crime by a court of
competent jurisdiction. *Ex parte Watkins*...(1830). The only
exceptions to the strict jurisdictional standard were claims grounded
on illegality in sentencing, *Ex parte Lange*...(1873), and on conviction under an unconstitutional statute. *Ex parte Siebold*...(1879).
See *McNally* v. *Hill*,...(1934).[1]

Watkins and the cases following upon it interpreted the
unilluminating grant of power in the Judiciary Act of 1789...to
courts of the United States to issue writs of *habeas corpus* for
prisoners in jail under or by color of authority of the Untied States.
Thus, *federal habeas* jurisdiction over state prisoners did not exist
except to summon them as witnesses. *Ex parte Dorr*...(1845).[2] But

---

[1] Justice Brennan's opinion in *Fay* v. *Noia*...(1963) undertook a lengthy
exegis to demonstrate that the common law understanding was actually that
"restraints contrary to fundamental law, by whatever authority imposed,
could be redressed by writ of *habeas corpus.*" ... Most of the scholarly
commentary is contrary to the Brennan reading of history. E.g., Oaks,
"Legal History in the High Court—*Habeas Corpus,*" 64 Mich. L. Rev. 451
(1966); Bator, "Finality in Criminal Law and Federal *Habeas Corpus* for
State Prisoners," 76 Harv. L. Rev. 441, 465-474 (1963) (pre-*Noia*):
"Developments in the Law—Federal *Habeas Corpus,*" 83 Harv. L. Rev.
1038, 1045-1050 (1970). It is unclear why Justice Brennan undertook this
effort to establish the historicity of the broad proposition; it had been clearly
established in *Brown* v. *Allen*...(1953). ...

[2] This statement, and the cases, assume that a statute is necessary to confer
jurisdiction upon federal courts to grant the writ. *Ex parte Bollman*...
(1807). One scholar has argued that the federal courts have the power absent
statute as a direct implication of the suspension clause. Paschal, "The
Constitution and *Habeas Corpus,*" 1970 Duke L.J. 605.

by the Habeas Corpus Act of 1867,...Congress empowered the "courts of the United States...to grant writs of *habeas corpus* in all cases where any person may be restrained of his or her liberty in violation of the Constitution, or of any treaty or law of the United States. ..." Justice Brennan, in *Fay* v. *Noia*..., read this broad language as evincing a congressional intent to enlarge the *habeas* to provide a collaterial method additional to and independent of direct Supreme Court review of state court decisions for the vindication of the new constitutional guarantees incorporated in the Thirteenth and Fourteenth Amendments. Accord: *Brown* v. *Allen*, *supra*, 488 (Justice Frankfurter concurring).[3] Whatever the Act was intended to mean by Congress, the courts did not immediately begin to expand the scope of the writ, according it pretty much the scope and meaning previously given it when the 1789 Act was being construed. *In re Wood*...(1891); *In re Jugiro*...(1891); *Andrews* v. *Swartz*...(1895); *Bergemann* v. *Backer*...(1895).

The modern expansion of the writ may be said to have started with *Frank* v. *Mangum*...(1915), although as viewed from today's perspective the judgment in Frank may seem restrictive. But the law of *habeas* prior to Frank was...that "if a court of competent jurisdiction adjudicated a federal question in a criminal case, its decision of that question was final, subject only to appeal, and not subject to redetermination on *habeas corpus.*" ... The expansion that had occurred previously had consisted of enlargements of the concept of jurisdiction. The *Frank* case work a different expansion.

Frank contended that his conviction had been obtained through mob intimidation of the trial. The state appellate court had made an independent inquiry into the issue and concluded that the evidence did not support the claim. The Supreme Court affirmed a federal district court's refusal to issue a *habeas* writ, laying down as law this proposition: if it is found that the state tribunals have failed to provide corrective process (in the sense of giving a petitioner a fair opportunity to raise and litigate his constitutional claim) in the state courts, then the federal *habeas corpus* court may proceed to adjuciate the merits of that claim, but if it is found that a state court of competent jurisdiction has fully and fairly adjudicated the claim,

---

[3]Here, too, the scholarly opinion appears to be against a broad reading of the 1867 Act. E.g., Bator, *op. cit.*, 474-477; Mayers, "The *Habeas Corpus* Act of 1867: The Supreme Court as Legal Historian," 33 U. Chi. L. Rev. 31 (1865).

then that decision is immune from collateral attack and alleged error on the merits of the federal question should be reviewed by the Supreme Court on direct review. The lawfulness of the detention to be inquired into by the *habeas* court is to be determined not by whether, as in *Frank*, the conviction was procured by mob domination but whether the state's process afforded the defendant adequate opportunity to raise and have passed upon adequately the question of mob domination; mob domination was not the issue on collateral review but the fairness of the corrective process.[4]

It is possible that in the case of *Moore* v. *Dempsey*...(1923), the Court "discredited" or "repudiated" *Frank's* limitation on the *habeas* power of the federal courts and settled the power of those courts to determine a convicted defendant's constitutional claims on the merits, giving to state court judgments weight but not conclusive weight.[5] In any event, *Moore* arose as did *Frank* in a situation in which it was alleged that mob domination of a trial had procured the conviction unfairly; the appellate court in *Moore*, unlike the *Frank* court, conducted no independent inquiry of its own but perfunctorily rejected the claim of mob domination. In an opinion by Justice Holmes, who had dissented from the denial of *habeas* in *Frank*, the Court reversed and held that the federal district court was under a "duty" to examine the facts for itself and determine if the allegations of mob domination were true. The brief, ambiguous Holmes opinion will admit of either the interpretation that all federal constitutional claims are cognizable on *habeas*, regardless of the state's previous consideration of the issues, or the interpretation that, consistent with *Frank*, the consideration by the state courts of the federal constitutional claims was so inadequate that federal court collateral review was appropriate.[6] When read in the context of

---

[4] This standard is, of course, that of the Court with respect to the exclusionary rule question on collateral review in *Stone* v. *Powell*. On *Frank* v. *Mangum*, see Bator, *op. cit.*, 483-487. Compare *Fay* v. *Noia supra*, 420 (Justice Brennan for the Court), with *id.*, 456-457 (Justice Harlan dissenting).

[5] "Discredited" is Professor Hart's term. "Foreword: The Time Chart of the Justices," 73 Harv. L. Rev. 84, 105 (1959), while "repudiated" is Justice Brennan's. *Fay* v. *Noia, supra*, 421. For *contra* views, contending that *Moore* and *Frank* are consistent, see *id.*, 457-458 (Justice Harlan dissenting); Bator, *op. cit.*, 488-489.

[6] "We assume in accordance with [*Frank*] that the corrective process supplied by the state may be so adequate that interference by *habeas corpus*

Holmes' *Frank* dissent, however, the Moore opinion does seem, at the least, to be saying that, regardless of state corrective process, some federal constitutional claims are so fundamental that they are collaterally reviewable on *habeas*. See Hart & Wechsler, op. cit., 1469. That the opinion did not go as far as *Brown* v. *Allen, supra*, did is true, but that it went further than *Frank* appears also to be reasonably clear.

No clear rule of law emerged from the cases between *Moore* and *Brown* v. *Allen* in 1953. On the one hand, the Court expanded the "lack of jurisdiction" basis of *habeas* in several cases, *Mooney* v. *Holohan*...(1935) (use of perjured testimony to procure conviction would deny due process and oust trial court of jurisdiction and is cognizable on *habeas*): *Johnson* v. *Zerbst*...(1938) (denial of effective assistance of counsel in federal court ousts jurisdiction and is cognizable on *habeas*) before holding in *Waley* v. *Johnston*... (1942) that the use of the writ was not restricted to those cases where the judgment of conviction is void for want of jurisdiction of the trial court to render it but extends also to those exceptional cases where the conviction has been in disregard of the constitutional rights of the accused and where the writ is the only effective means of preserving the defendant's rights. Other cases during the period contain expressions broadening and narrowing the interpretations of *Frank* and *Moore* and the scholarly commentary is divided.[7]

In any event, in *Brown* v. *Allen*..., eight of the nine justices either held or assumed that on *habeas corpus* federal district courts must provide review of the merits of constitutional claims fully litigated in

---

ought not to be allowed. It certainly is true that mere mistakes of law in the course of a trial are not to be corrected in that way. But if the case is that the whole proceeding is a mask—that counsel, jury and judge were swept to the fatal end by an irresistible wave of public passion, and that the state courts failed to correct the wrong, neither perfection in the machinery for correction nor the possibility that the trial court and counsel saw no other way of avoiding an immediate outbreak of the mob can prevent this Court from securing to the petitioners their constitutional rights." *Id.*, 91. "We shall not say more concerning the corrective process afforded to the petitioners than that it does not seem to use sufficient to allow a judge of the United States to escape the duty of examining the facts for himself when if true as alleged they make the trial absolutely void." *Id.*, 92.

[7]Compare Bator, *op. cit.* 489-499, who, while recognizing the wavering of the Court, argues that the cases are all basically consistent with *Frank*, with Hart, *op. cit.*, 104-106, who reads the cases as broadening the scope of the writ beyond that in *Frank*.

the state court system.[8] Basis of the decision, in Professor Hart's words, *op. cit.,* 106, is "that due process of law in the case of state prisoners is not primarily concerned with the adequacy of the state's corrective process or of the prisoner's personal opportunity to avail himself of this process... but relates essentially to the avoidance in the end of any underlying constitutional error. ..." In Justice Frankfurter's view, the result in Brown was required by the congressional enactment of the Habeas Corpus Act of 1867 by which Congress had determined not to leave the enforcement of federal constitutional rights governing the administration of criminal justice in the states exclusively to the state courts. While state courts are under the same obligation as federal courts to respect federal constitutional rights, Congress may well have considered, and continued to consider, that the enlargement of federal constitutional rights in the imposition of an expanding due process clause upon the states called for access to the federal courts as another assurance of those guarantees. *Brown* v. *Allen.* ...[9]

Ten years after *Brown* v. *Allen,* the Court in its famous trilogy, *Fay* v. *Noia,* ...*Townsend* v. *Sain* ...(1963) and *Sanders* v. *United States* ...(1963) again considerably expanded the availability of the writ. *Noia* was the principal case, construing the "exhaustion" requirement in *habeas* and developing standards for determining when a prisoner could be said to have forfeited his right to seek the writ by failing to present his constitutional challenge to state consideration. The point of the "exhaustion" doctrine is to avoid the disruption of federal-state comity that would inhere in upsetting state court convictions without first allowing the states an opportunity to correct constitutional defects. *Darr* v. *Buford* ...(1950).[10]

---

[8] Three cases were before the Court and on the merits the Court held, 6-3, that defendants' rights had not been violated. There were in effect two opinions of the Court, one by Justice Reed...and one by Justice Frankfurter... Only Justice Jackson...(concurring in result), disagreed with the view that federal *habeas* courts should ordinarily decide the federal constitional issues for themselves rather than deferring to state court resolution of the issues.

[9] See, favoring *Brown,* Reitz, "Federal *Habeas Corpus*: Postconviction Remedy for State Prisoners," 108 U. Pa L. Rev. 461 (1960); Wright & Sofaer, "Federal *Habeas Corpus* for State Prisoners: The Allocation of Fact-Finding Responsibility," 75 Yale L. J. 895, 897-906 (1966).

[10] "Developments—" *op. cit.,* 1093-1103.

And it is not good enough that a petitioner has been to the state courts; he must have there presented the same claim he seeks to advance in his federal habeas petition. . . . But once having presented the claims to a state court, as on appeal, he is not required to seek state collateral relief. *Brown* v. *Allen.* . . .

Fay v. *Noia* dealt with the conceptually different but related concept of state procedural default by a prisoner; that is, whether a federal collateral attack can be made on a detention based on a state court judgment resting on an "independent and adequate state ground," *i.e.*, on a ruling that, because of noncompliance with a fair and reasonable state procedural rule, the defendant has forfeited his right to a decision on the merits of a federal constitutional claim. *Noia* resolved the issues by holding that the requirement of "exhaustion" refers only to remedies still available when *habeas* is sought and has nothing to do with the effect of a past procedural default in the state courts. Only if it is found that a defendant deliberately by-passed state procedures in the federal courts to hold him to his choice and deny him *habeas* relief.[11]

Townsend v. *Sain*, supra, dealt with the issue of holding evidentiary hearings by *habeas* courts and propounded the rule that where the facts are in dispute, the *habeas* court must hold an evidentiary hearing if the *habeas* applicant did not receive a full and fair evidentiary hearing in a state court, either at the time of the trial or in a collateral proceeding. Sanders dealt with the question of the deference owed to a previous federal habeas proceeding and broadened the possibility of the prisoner obtaining a new hearing.

Basically, then, . . . the rule of the Court limited in *Stone* v. *Powell* was not a recent innovation but rather traces in full flower back to *Brown* v. *Allen* in 1953 and in substantial part back through

---

[11] "If a *habeas* applicant, after consultation with competent counsel or otherwise, understandingly and knowingly forewent the privilege of seeking to vindicate his federal claims in the state courts, whether for strategic, tactical, or any other reasons that can fairly be described as the deliberate bypassing of state procedures, then it is open to the federal court on *habeas* to deny him all relief if the state courts refused to entertain his federal claims on the merits." *Id.*, 439. The Court has this term in two cases limited, without addressing, *Noia*, holding in *Estelle* v. *Williams*. . .(May 3, 1976) that the failure of a defendant to object at trial to his being compelled to stand trial in prison garb, and in *Francis* v. *Henderson*. . .(May 3, 1976) that the failure of a defendant to challenge the composition of the grand jury that indicted him before trial in accordance with state rules precluded both defendants from raising the issues on *habeas*.

consistent broadening of the scope of the writ in the 1930s and 1940s to the *Moore* decision in 1923. . . .

II. CONGRESSIONAL ACTIONS

The Court's decision in *Stone* v. *Powell* must also be evaluated in the context of congressional responses to the judicial interpretations of the scope of the writ of *habeas corpus* over the years. It is important to note that the scope of the writ, insofar as the statutory language is concerned, has not been altered since 1867.[12]

In 1948, title 28 of the U.S. Code was revised and codified. Judge John J. Parker of the Fourth Circuit was chairman of the Judicial Conference Committee that drafted the revisions of the Habeas Corpus Act. According to Judge Parker, the object of the revisions was to "put an end to the abuse that has arisen because, under recent decisions of the Supreme Court, it has been possible for prisoners to use the writ to attack the procedure of the courts under whose judgments they are imprisoned. . . . [The decisions] opened wide the door to review by way of federal *habeas corpus* of every criminal proceeding, state or federal, in which a person convicted of crime was willing to make oath that he had been denied a fair trial." Parker, "limiting the Abuse of *Habeas Corpus*," 8 F.R.D. 171 (1948).[13]

The changes were, however, modest. A new proceeding was instituted for persons convicted in federal courts, 28 U.S.C. § 2255, requiring such persons to move to vacate their sentences. See *United States* v. *Hayman*. . .(1952). So far as state prisoners were concerned, the revision codified the court holdings requiring exhaustion of state remedies and the absence of an adequate remedy available in the state courts. *Brown* v. *Allen*. . . .[14]

Following *Brown* v. *Allen,* the Judicial Conference of the United States, again under the leadership of Judge Parker, sought to restrict the scope of the writ. Reporting that the expansion of *habeas*

---

[12]C. Wright, *Law of Federal Courts* (2d ed. 1970), 209.

[13]Judge Parker's cited cases began with *Moore* v. *Dempsey* and included the major cases of the period before *Brown* v. *Allen.*

[14]Judge Parker construed the new § 2254 considerably more restrictively than the Court proved to do. Compare Parker, *op. cit.*, 175-177, with *Brown* v. *Allen, supra,* 447.

jurisdiction had "greatly interfered with the procedure of the state courts," the Conference recommended that "[w]here adequate procedure is provided by state law for the handling of such matters, it is clear that the remedy should be sought in the state courts with any review. . . only by the Supreme Court. . . . ."[15] The recommended bill received the support of the Conference of State Chief Justices, the Association of Attorneys General, the American Bar Association, and the Department of Justice. Twice it passed the House of Representatives (in 1956 and 1958), but the Senate never approved it.[16]

Finally, in 1966, Congress did amend the Habeas Corpus Act, largely to incorporate therein the standards established by the Court in its *Noia-Townsend-Sanders* trilogy. . . . The amendments principally did three things. (1) They dealt with the problem of repetitious and meritless *habeas* petitions by prescribing, in line with *Sanders*, the circumstances under which district judges should exercise their discretion to decline to entertain such applications. (2) They provided that when a prisoner has had his case before the United States Supreme Court on appeal or *certiorari*, the Court's disposition of the case is conclusive on all legal and factual issues actually adjudicated by the Court; only when a *habeas* court finds a new and controlling fact which could not have been placed in the record by the exercise of reasonable diligence is the rule of conclusiveness inapplicable. (3) They enumerated and restated the Court's *Townsend* principles to guide the federal courts in the exercise of their discretion in determining whether to hold an evidentiary hearing.

Again, in 1968, an effort was made to constrict the availability of *habeas* for state prisoners, as the Senate Judiciary Committee included § 702 in. . . the Omnibus Crime Control & Safe Streets Act,

---

[15]*Hearings on H.R. 5649* before Subcommittee No. 3 of the House Committee on the Judiciary, 84th Cong., 1st sess. (1955), 89-90.

[16]102 *Cong. Rec.* 940 (1966); 104 *id.* 4675 (1958). The bill would have permitted the issuance of the writ "only on a ground which presents a substantial federal constitutional question (1) which was not theretofore raised and determined (2) which there was no fair and adequate opportunity theretofore to raise and have determined and (3) which cannot thereafter be raised and determined in a proceeding in the state court, by an order or judgment subject to review by the Supreme Court of the United States on writ of *certiorari*."

giving to judgments of state courts in criminal cases conclusive effect with respect to all questions of law or fact which were determined or which could have been determined in the action leading to the judgment, except for direct appeals of those judgments. . . . [T]his section was struck from the bill by a vote of 54 to 27 114. . . .

The most recent efforts to curb the use of the writ by state prisoners was initiated by then Assistant Attorney General Rehnquist in testimony on the proposed speedy trial bill.[17] He proposed that *habeas* claims by state prisoners be restricted to claims involving the basic fairness of trial and suggested that petitioners be required to show that a violation of the constitutional right claimed had a substantive effect on the outcome of his trial. These proposals and several others were incorporated into a bill drafted by the Justice Department and introduced. . . in the 93d Congress.[18]

The bill is interesting when read in the light of *Stone* v. *Powell*. First, the bill would have limited the constitutional claims that could be raised on collateral attack in federal court by state prisoners to those (1) which were not theretofore raised and determined in a state court, and (2) which there was not fair and adequate opportunity theretofore to have raised and determined in a state court, and (3) which could not thereafter be raised and determined in a state court. The object of these provisions, Attorney General Kleindienst said, "would be to add a significant degree of finality" to state court judgments and overturn the contrary holdings of *Brown* v. *Allen* and *Fay* v. *Noia*. . . . Once a state court had ruled on the merits of an issue, either on direct appeal or collateral attack, the only possible remedy would have been direct review by the Supreme Court. The second and third provisions would have altered the waiver and exhaustion standards previously set out in such decisions as Noia so as to treat failure to utilize an available state remedy as a deliberate bypass barring federal habeas relief.

---

[17]*Hearings on S. 895* before the Subcommittee on Constitutional rights of the Senate Judiciary Committee, 92d Cong., 1st sess. (1971), 94-121.

[18]An identical bill had been introduced in the Senate and a similar bill into the House near the end of the prior Congress. S. 3833 and H.R. 13722, 92d Cong., 2d sess. (1972). Senator Hruska introduced S. 567 on Jan. 26, 1973. . . .119 *Cong. Rev.* 2220-2226. See Note, "Proposed Modification of Federal *Habeas Corpus* for State Prisoners—Reform or Revocation?" 61 Georgetown L. J. 1221 (1973).

Second, the bill set out another test that a prisoner who had gotten past the first series must meet. That is, the convicted defendant would be limited to raising constitutional claims to violations of any right "which has as its primary purpose the protection of the reliability of either the factfinding process at the trial or the appellate process on appeal from the judgment of conviction.". . . The Attorney General explained that this "reliability" test was derived from the standards employed by the Supreme Court to determine whether to accord retroactive effect to its constitutional decisions. If the constitutional right goes to safeguarding the reliability of the trial and appellate process, it is generally accorded retroactive effect. Those types of claims that would be barred by this provision, said the Attorney General, would be (1) claims objecting to the admissibility of voluntary confessions because of failure to comply with Miranda, (2) claims objecting to the admissibility of evidence obtained through a violation of the search and seizure guarantees, and (3) claims objecting to the admissibility of identifications made in line-ups conducted without consel in violation of *Wade*. . . .

Third, the proposal would have further required a prisoner having gotten past the first two requirements to show "that a different result would probably have obtained if such constitutional violation had not occurred.". . . This provision was designed to require that a *habeas* petitioner show only "a probability of acquittal on the actual charge on which a verdict was returned, or that without the violation he would have been convicted only of a lesser included offense, He would not need to show that he would also have been acquitted of all lesser included offenses or that he was in fact innocent.". . .

III. STONE V. POWELL ANALYZED

In his opinion for the Court, Justice Powell did not reject the expansion of the scope of *habeas corpus* which he thought had been accomplished in *Brown* v. *Allen*; that is, federal constitutional claims are generally open to relitigation in collateral actions in federal courts. He did not believe, however, that during the period of expansion the Court had ever "consider[ed] whether exceptions to full review might exist with respect to particular categories of constitutional claims." *Stone* v. *Powell*. . . . He recognized of course, that the Court had on a number of occasions accepted jurisdiction in state prisoner cases in which collateral claims of Fourth Amendment violations were made, had decided these cases on the merits, and had granted relief in some of them on the basis of Fourth Amendment violations.[19] And in *Kaufman* v. *United States*...(1969), the Court had held that federal prisoners could collaterally litigate search-and-seizure claims under 28 U.S. § 2255, largely on the basis that state prisoners could collaterally litigate search-and-seizure claims on *habeas* and the rights of the two classes should be parallel. But Justice Powell concluded that the Court had never really closely considered the question and reached an informed, principled decision on the issue; the question thus being considered an open one, be then canvassed the rationales of the exclusionary rule and the principles governing the scope of the habeas writ and announced for the Court the holding that *habeas* is not available to state prisoners to challenge the admissibility of evidence allegedly unconstitutionally seized, provided that the state afforded the defendant an opportunity for a full and fair litigation of his claim.

(A) The Purpose of the Exclusionary Rule: According to Justice Powell, the primary justification for the exclusionary rule is the deterrence of police conduct that violated Fourth Amendment rights. The rule is not a personal constitutional right; it is not calculated to redress the injury to the privacy of the victim of the search or seizure. The rule is but a "prophylactic" device by which the Court seeks to ensure compliance with the Fourth Amendment. This almost exclusive focus upon the deterrent purpose of the rule is one already well established in the Court's cases, e.g., *United States* v. *Calandra*...(1974); *United States* v. *Peltier*...(1975), and it furnished the basis for the Court's refusal to give retroactive effect to its search and seizure decisions. E.g. *Linkletter* v. *Walker*... (1965). *Mapp* v. *Ohio*...(1961), extending the exclusionary rule to the states, relied on deterrence but it addressed as well the "imperative of judicial integrity", suggesting that the exclusion of illegally seized evidence prevents contamination of the judicial process. ... Indeed, it is difficult to understand the decision in

---

[19]E.g., *Lefkowitz* v. *Newsome*, 420 U.S. 283 (1975); *Cardwell* v. *Lewis*, 417 U.S. 583 (1974); *Cady* v. *Dombrowski*, 413 U.S. 433 (1973); *Adams* v. *Williams*, 407 U.S. 143 (1972);*Whitley* v. *Warden*, 401 U.S. 560 (1971); *Chambers* v. *Maroney*, 399 U.S. 42 (1970); *Harris* v. *Nelson*, 394 U.S. 286 (1969); *Mancusi* v. *DeForte*, 392 U.S. 364 (1968); *Carafas* v. *Lavallee*, 391 U.S. 234 (1968); *Warden* v. *Hayden*, 387 U.S. 294 (1967).

Elkins v. *United States*...(1960) in any sense out a judicial concern for the integrity of the judicial process.[20]

Therefore, the incremental increase in deterrence, if any, occasioned by the *habeas* courts utilization of the exclusionary rule was greatly outweighed in the balance by the harm done to the judicial process through enforcement of the rule. This conclusion was reached upon consideration of several factors.

(B) The Harmful Effect of the Rule: Application of the rule, Justice Powell wrote, "deflects the truthfinding process and often frees the guilty." *Stone* v. *Powell*. ...

(1) Reliability. The physical evidence seized by police which is sought to be excluded is typically reliable and often the most probative bearing on guilt. However, the evidence is obtained, it in and of itself is not suspect, not tainted, in the same way that a coerced confession is. (2) Search for Truth. Emphasis upon the admissibility of evidence turns the trial away from what should be its primary goal, the ascertainment of the truth. The evidence if excluded may prevent the attainment of this goal. (3) The question of Guilt or Innocence. Excluding reliable and probative evidence will often permit the guilty to go free; in any event, disputes over admissibility does not contribute to effectuating the goal of convicting the guilty and freeing the innocent.

While the exclusionary rule serves the vital function of enforcing respect for Fourth Amendment values, continued Justice Powell, and the Court will adhere to it in the instance of trials and on direct appeal of trial court convictions, it does not serve the interests so well that the detriment of its enforcement through habeas proceedings is justified.

---

[20]*Elkins* overturned the "silver platter" doctrine under which evidence illegally seized by state officials could be turned over to federal officials for use in federal trials even though the evidence would have been inadmissible had federal authorities seized it. At the time, while the Fourth Amendment applied to state searches, the exclusionary rule did not govern admissibility of the evidence so obtained into state trials. *Wolf* v. *Colorado*...(1949). The deterrent effect of excluding the evidence from federal trial was so attenuated that it is hard to believe it would have furnished a basis for decision even if the Court was at the time concerned with deterring state action. Confirmation of these conclusions may be found in *United States* v. *Janis*...(July 6, 1976), refusing to bar from federal civil trials evidence unconstitutionally scized by state officers.

Thus, one can follow many of the parallels between *Stone* v. *Powell* and S. 567. The accomplishment of the aims of the decision and the bill is attempted in somewhat different fashions but the same aims are firmly fixed. In both instances, the federal *habeas* role will be diminished by state provision of the opportunity for a litigation of federal constitutional claims. The bill would have precluded search and seizure claims altogether and the decision leaves the possibility that some such cases may still be brought into federal *habeas* courts upon contentions that the state did not afford a full and fair opportunity for litigating the issue. But what is a full and fair opportunity?

Stone v. *Powell* does not attempt to define the circumstances under which it will be deemed that such an opportunity has been provided. The Court did not, however, remand the two cases before it to the federal courts for evaluation of the fullness and fairness of the opportunity the *habeas* petitioners had in the trial courts, it simply reversed. Whether this constitutes approbation of the California and Nebraska procedures is unclear. In both instances, trial courts had rejected the claims of the defendants; in the California case, the appellate court had not reached the merits but had decided that the error, if any, had been harmless, while the Nebraska appellate court rejected the claims on the merits.[21] It will be remembered that in *Frank* the Supreme Court approved the state court's process as adequate when it undertook an independent inquiry and carefully considered the defendant's claims; in *Moore*, on the other hand, if it be considered consistent with *Frank* and not an extension of it, the state appellate court's rather perfunctory rejection of the defendant's claim on the record did not immunize the conviction from *habeas* attack.

The court's analysis, it may be noted, permits further decisions along the line set out in S. 567. The reliability standard, the irrelevance to the search for truth and the question of innocence, and the purpose to deter are all present with regard to confessions obtained in violation of *Miranda* and to line-up identifications made in violation of *Wade*. ... The Court's analysis in *Michigan* v.

---

[21] It appears on the basis of applicable precedents that both appellate courts were wrong and the federal courts so found. But the requirement is of an opportunity, not that the state courts will correctly decide the claim. Petitioning the Supreme Court for *certiorari* is the only avenue of relief from incorrect decisions.

Tucker...(1974) of the *Miranda* requirements as "prophylactic standards" not themselves rights protected by the Constitution but judicial constructions to protect the right against self-incrimination prepares the way for a *Stone* v *Powell* holding in a *Miranda* case.

Whether there are not also other constitutional decisions so to be treated is a question we need not here deal with. But the analysis would not appear to be narrowly limitable.[22]

IV. CONGRESSIONAL ALTERNATIVES OF STONE V. POWELL

Although the Court's opinion in *Stone* v. *Powell* is silent with regard to the kind of authority it is exercising, constitutional interpretation or statutory interpretation, and while its language with respect to the exclusionary rule is to some extent both types of interpretation, clearly its decision that a *habeas* court's power should not extend to hearing search and seizure claims when the petitioner has had an opportunity to raise them previously has to be based upon its construction of 28 U.S.C. § 2254, the *habeas* statute. True it is that Justice Powell announces that "the Constitution does not require" that state prisoners have the opportunity to present such claims under such circumstances..., but the question here is whether the Constitution permits the exercise of such power by federal courts. A long line of cases previously has required federal courts to litigate such claims, the language of § 2254 is adequately broad, and its constitutionality is so accepted by the Court that when the attorneys general of 41 states joined in an attempt to have the 1867 *habeas* statute declared unconstitutional the Supreme Court refused even to review the Court of Appeals rejection of the contention. *United States ex rel. Elliott* v. *Hendricks*, 213 F. 2d 922 (C.A. 3), cert. den., 348 U.S. 851 (1954) See *Ex parte Royall*, 117 U.S. 241, 249 (1886); *Frank* v. *Mangum*, supra, 331. Thus, Justice Powell must be understood as holding, though he did not even cite the statute nor quote the particular language, that a state prisoner convicted at least in part on the basis of evidence seized in violation of the Fourth Amendment but who has been able to raise that question at trial and on appeal, even though he lost, is not "in

---

[22] Attorney General Kleindienst thought there were several other claims that would be precluded by the reliability standard of S. 567, including jury trial denial claims. 119 *Cong. Rec.* 2225 (1973).

custody in violation of the Constitution or laws of the United States.''...

Indeed, the logic of the Court's opinion with respect to the exclusionary rule is that in no event does the admission at trial of evidence seized unconstitutionally violate a defendant's Fourth Amendment rights. One has a Fourth Amendment right not to have one's privacy invaded by officers not acting in accord with Fourth Amendment requirements. But the violation once accomplished is completed. It does not continue through to the admission of the evidence so obtained. Such admission works no new Fourth Amendment violation. *United States* v. *Calandra,* supra, 354; *United States* v. *Peltier,* supra, 535-539. "The primary meaning of 'judicial integrity' in the context of evidentiary rules is that the courts must not commit or encourage violations of the Constitution. In the Fourth Amendment area, however, the evidence is unquestionably accurate, and the violation is complete by the time the evidence is presented to the court. ... The focus therefore must be on the question whether the admission of the evidence encourages violations of Fourth Amendment rights. As the Court has noted in recent cases, this inquiry is essentially the same as the inquiry into whether exclusion would serve a deterrent purpose." *United States* v. *Janis....* [23]

Mapp v. *Ohio,*...however, held that the exclusionary rule was binding upon the states because it is "an essential part of the right to privacy" protected by the due process clause of the Fourteenth Amendment. Congress, if it should so decide, would not be precluded by *Stone* v. *Powell* in its statutory construction from concluding that the imprisonment of one pursuant to a state conviction based at least in part on evidence seized in violation of the Fourth Amendment does mean that he is "in custody in violation of the Constitution." The Fourth Amendment guarantee is applicable to the States through the due process clause of the Fourteenth Amendment, *Wolf* v. *Colorado*..., and the due process clause independently imposes upon the states a requirement of funda-

---

[23] If the exclusionary rule is not a substantive constitutional right, the serious question is raised about the Court's power to mandate its observance by state courts. If the rule is not a necessary corollary of a constitutional right but simply a judicially created remedial device, the Court's power should be much more limited than otherwise. See Monaghan, "Forward: Constitutional Common Law," 89 Harv. L. Rev. 1, 3-10 (1975).

mental fairness. Under § 5 of the Fourteenth Amendment, Congress has the power to enforce "by appropriate legislation" the guarantees of the due process clause.

As for the deterrence issue, it is primarily a question of judgment whether applying the rule in one situation will constitute a significant deterrence of Fourth Amendment violations while applying it in another would have minimal effect. When the matter turns on such judgments, Congress has a special ability to develop and consider the factual basis of a problem that the Court does not have. *Oregon* v. *Mitchell*...(1970) (Justice Brennan concurring and dissenting).

An example of congressional decisionmaking in this area which extended protection beyond that found by the Court to be required by the Constitution is 18 U. S. C. § 2515, in the electronic surveillance statute, mandating the application of the exclusionary rule with respect to evidence not obtained in compliance with the statute. In *Gelbard* v. *United States*...(1972), the Court held, on the language of § 2515 and its legislative history, that it could be invoked by a grand jury witness as a defense to a contempt charge brought for refusal to answer questions based on information obtained from the witness' communications unlawfully intercepted through wiretapping; in *United States* v. *Calandra*,...the Court held that, under the Fourth Amendment exclusionary rule, a grand jury witness could not refuse to answer questions based on unconstitutionally-seized evidence, noting the statutory basis of Gelbard. ...

Some thought might be given by Congress to the possibility that the Court will soon modify the exclusionary rule itself. One of the arguments raised by the states in *Stone* v. *Powell* was that the Court should permit a "good faith defense" to the exclusionary rule in situations where, for example, police conduct was only in technical violation of constitutional requirements or where police acted in "good faith" in believing they had a right to search. Chief Justice Burger, in a concurring opinion, and Justice White, in dissent, urged adoption of such a modification. And the Court's opinion in *United States* v. *Peltier*...clearly seems to lay the basis for such a holding. ...

...In *Mackey* v. *United States*...(1971), Justice Harlan wrote a lengthy opinion arguing that the Court had gotten itself into a quagmire in its retroactivity rules and that it should instead draw a distinction between cases still open to direct review and cases where the conviction is final in the sense that only collateral relief is available. New constitutional doctrines must be fully retroactive within the former category while on *habeas* cases the courts should generally apply the law prevailing at the time a conviction became final rather than disposing of all such cases on the basis of intervening changes in constitutional interpretation. ...

Cases Abridged or Cited

Index

227